Instructional Methods

in Occupational Education

Instructional Methods in Occupational Education

Dennis C. Nystrom
G. Keith Bayne
L. Dean McClellan

Department of Occupational and Career Education
University of Louisville

A Howard W. Sams Book
PUBLISHED BY BOBBS-MERRILL EDUCATIONAL PUBLISHING
INDIANAPOLIS

To Carl, Mary, Alice, and Sara

The Bobbs-Merrill Company, Inc.
4300 West 62nd Street
Indianapolis, Indiana 46268

First Edition
First Printing 1977
Designed by Anita Duncan

Library of Congress Cataloging in Publication Data

Nystrom, Dennis C
    Instructional methods in occupational education.

    "A Howard W. Sams book."
    1. Vocational education.   I. Bayne, G. Keith,
joint author.   II. McClellan, L. Dean,
joint author.   III. Title.
LC1044.N95   370.11'3   76-43204
ISBN 0-672-97111-9

Contents

Preface

This book is intended as a practical guide to instructional methods for students enrolled in occupational or career development teacher education programs. It should also be of value to both beginning teachers and experienced teachers who are interested in improving instruction through formal or informal in-service professional development activities.

Throughout the book, emphasis has been placed not only on traditional vocational preparation level instruction and learning, but also on programs at the orientation and exploration level. This book should meet the professional development instructional methods needs of practical arts, industrial arts, orientation and exploration level career education, and preparation level vocational education personnel. Examples and cases have been drawn from numerous occupational clusters including business and office, distributive education, agriculture, health occupations, home economics related occupations, public service occupations, and industrial related occupations. It is intended to be a basic text for use in comprehensive occupational education programs whose goals include close cooperation among various service areas. It is not intended to be a detailed treatise on specific instructional methods in any single occupational area or cluster.

Emphasis has been placed on instructional methods, techniques, and procedures that will facilitate learning in an articulated K-adult occupational education program. Consideration has been given to both public and private educational agencies whose primary goals include emphasis on the vocational maturation process and on ultimately providing employment skills for their product.

In many cases, the individual chapters have been designed to stand alone as information sources regarding particular instructional methods. In other chapters, such as *Grading and Record Keeping, Facilitating Learning, Media for Improving Instruction, Cooperative Education as an Instructional Method,* and *Laboratory Management and Planning,* the emphasis has been placed on basics. The reader may wish to further explore these areas in the references cited at the end of each of these chapters.

The writers are deeply indebted to our families, who have learned to live with the tension that goes along with deadlines; our administrators, who have helped establish a work atmosphere conducive to professional publication; and to Becky, Karen, and Debbie, who have endured a rather heavy work load these past months.

Introduction

Occupational education is an unique and exciting component of the total educational system. Its acceptance, as well as rapid growth in enrollment, can only be characterized as phenomenal. This growing educational area has placed increased responsibilities on those individuals—the expanding professional faculty—responsible for the quality of its product—the student.

This chapter is designed to assist the reader in the accomplishment of the following objectives:

- **Identify the primary factors contributing to the growth of occupational education.**
- **Define the various settings in which occupational education programs operate.**
- **Describe the levels at which occupational education programs occur.**
- **Describe the nature of the population served by occupational education.**
- **Differentiate among the various types of occupational education professionals.**

Occupational education programs in public and proprietary institutions have increased dramatically during the past decade. Projections for the future indicate that the availability of occupational education offerings will continue to grow. This unprecedented growth can be attributed to a multitude of factors.

1. With the passage of the *Vocational Education Amendments 1968*, the *Education Amendments 1976*, and subsequent annual appropriations, hundreds of millions of federal dollars have been made available to states for assistance in various kinds of occupational education programs. In excess of $400 million annually has been appropriated for public vocational education. In addition, enactments such as the *Elementary and Secondary Education Act*, the *Education Amendments of 1972*, the *Comprehensive Employment and Training Act*, and the *Education Professions Development Act* have provided financial assistance to occupational education.

2. While federal support has been extensive, local and state financial commitment to occupational education has been even more impressive. Approximately seventy percent of all resources utilized in the development and operation of occupational education programs comes from state revenue sources. While there is considerable variance among states regarding their commitment of revenue to occupational programs, all exceed the federal share for program support.

3. Local governing boards of education have also committed unprecedented resources to occupational education programs in local schools. Each year thousands of local school districts allocate millions of dollars for occupational education facilities, equipment, supplies, and salaries. The local citizenry are becoming keenly aware of the need to provide sound entry-level occupational skills to secondary school and community college youth and adults.

4. Local business and industry, generally through representation on occupational or craft advisory committees, have donated specialized equipment and supplies to occupational education programs. Advisory committees also supply information regarding curriculum, job placement, and evaluation of student performance to insure relevance of program offerings and currency of technical skills taught in these curricula.

5. Perhaps of greatest importance has been a rapid change in parent and student attitudes toward occupational education. No longer "a good program for someone else's kid," parents have begun to see the importance of their high school or

community college graduate's need to possess some salable skills along with basic or general education abilities. The career education movement has done much to change old attitudes and will do much to prepare youngsters to make realistic occupational choices throughout their lives. This is especially true as elementary school career-awareness and career-orientation programs continue to develop and become a significant part of the curriculum. Elementary school instructional units are utilizing occupations as central themes.

6. The teaching profession itself has done much to bring about the rapid growth in occupational education programs. Not only are occupational education professional educators better trained now than ever before, but general education faculty have begun to accept, and in fact, promote quality programs at all levels in occupational education. No longer are vocational and practical arts facilities found in substandard buildings or near the school's boiler room. Many new educational facilities are centered around the various laboratories and shops in which job skills are taught. Much of the general education curriculum is designed to enhance occupational education experiences.

Occupational education has become, or is rapidly becoming, a central or primary component of the curriculum in nearly all school systems. No longer is it being treated as a peripheral function of the school, but is viewed as a viable method of providing educational experiences for the 80 percent of students who could profit from these programs. However, as general support and commitment to occupational education increases, so does the responsibility for the maintenance of quality programs. This responsibility rests to a great extent on the teaching personnel. Quality programs responsive to student and manpower needs begin in the occupational education laboratory and at the cooperative education work station. The professionals responsible for facilitating learning in these settings must possess the highest level of professional skills available.

THE OCCUPATIONAL EDUCATION SETTING

Perhaps more than any other educational area, occupational education has accepted the concept that learning takes place in a variety of settings and at several levels. Occupational education instructional settings may be determined by availability of instructional resources in the school and in the community, student learning objectives, and tradition. Instructional levels are determined by vocational maturity of students, prior occupational experience, and general curriculum design.

The occupational education teacher may be found at work in public elementary, secondary, and post-secondary schools; correctional facilities; mental health agencies; private business and industry; and in other settings. Occupational education programs may be directed toward entry-level instruction for youth and adults, retraining for individuals seeking new careers, and upgrading skills for people desiring this type of education. The diversity of educational settings coupled with the variation in curricula among program levels demands that occupational education teachers be thoroughly familiar and competent in the art and science of teaching.

In a given instructional day, the occupational education teacher may instruct ninth and tenth grade occupational students, eleventh grade students in a job-simulation laboratory, twelfth grade students at cooperative education work stations, and an adult evening class in skill upgrading. In addition, the occupational education faculty member may be called upon to assist elementary and middle school faculty in the design and implementation of occupational orientation programs. This same faculty member may also hold a part-time teaching assignment at the local community college.

There are four generally accepted instructional levels in occupational education (FIGURE 1-1). To some extent, these levels can be related to educational grade levels. A brief description of each of these levels follows. Later chapters will detail various instructional methodologies for each category.

The general nature of curricula at the preparation level is characterized by primary concern for entry-level occupational skill development. Conversely, orientation-level curricula are directed toward basic occupational information and attitude development with little emphasis on specific skill development. (See FIGURE 1-1.)

Awareness (K-4)

Attitudes are best formed in the early childhood years. Work attitudes are no exception. Occupational education at the awareness level is generally concerned with this type of development. In most cases, occupational education at the early elementary level is very basic in nature. Elementary teachers incorporate work attitude and general occupational information units in their curricula. Basic concepts such as the differences between work and play, definitions of productive effort, etc., comprise awareness-level instruction.

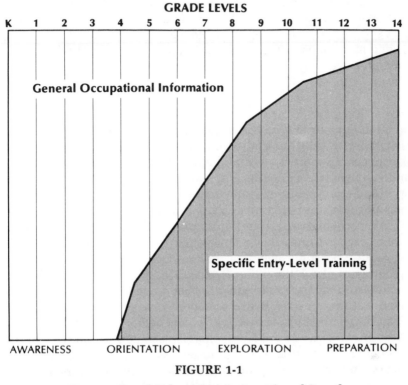

GRADE LEVELS

FIGURE 1-1

Occupational Education Instructional Levels

Orientation (5-8)

The middle school and early junior high school occupational education curriculum is generally directed toward occupational orientation. That is, basic instruction in broad clusters of occupations prevails. As few as three and as many as twenty-five occupational clusters are studied. Basic occupational information and hands-on experiences are stressed. Teachers at this level need a broad background of training or work experience in one or more of the clusters taught. In addition to basic professional preparation, instructional personnel must be familiar with the nature of the pre-adolescent and the early adolescent.

Some examples of the broad occupational clusters that might comprise an orientation program are: transportation, manufacturing, health occupations, public service, personal service, business and marketing, industrial, and economics of work.

Please note that these are representative samples and in no way exhaust the possible occupational clusters that might exist. Likewise, the aforementioned clusters are not intended to be mutually exclusive.

Exploration (9-10)

Slightly more specificity in an occupational cluster characterizes the exploration level of occupational education. Rather than general experiences in agriculture or biological sciences, students at the exploration level will be involved in practical experience in ornamental horticulture or dairy production or range science. The primary objectives of exploration programs will not include entry-level job skills, but may well be prerequisites to occupational preparation programs.

The exploration-level teacher will be involved in close coordination with preparation-level instructors. In fact, they may well be the same individuals. Articulation with regard to content and method is paramount, since the exploration and preparation levels are closely related. For example, the instructor of power mechanics must coordinate with the automotive mechanics instructor, the agriculture mechanics instructor, and the diesel engine instructor so that students in his or her exploration-level program are given the essential skills and information to assure entry into the preparation-level courses. In the area of health occupations, the exploration-level instructor must provide hands-on experiences for students in such occupations as health-care aide, dental assisting, licensed practical nursing, laboratory technician, and dental hygiene to mention a few. This is particularly important if these various preparation programs are available to youngsters in later years.

Instructional methods at the exploration level may vary considerably from those at the preparation level. Classroom and laboratory experiences will in most cases comprise the bulk of exploration-level programs. However, at the preparation level, other alternative instructional methods may be utilized, such as employer-based instruction or clinical experience.

In most occupational areas, the precise role of the exploration-level instructor is at best poorly defined. There is also a lag in instructional methodology and technology at this level, primarily because of a lack of clearly defined curricula for exploration-type programs. Many states are currently studying the relationship between exploration- and preparation-level learning in an effort to more effectively articulate these activities.

Preparation (11-14)

Occupational preparation programs generally occur at the eleventh grade through Associate degree or post-secondary certificate levels. Federal legislation and tradition have done much to assure that formal preparation programs do not begin for most students prior to their fifteenth birthday. In many places, state and local regulations prevent students from enrolling in preparation programs prior to the eleventh grade. However, informally, many youngsters are involved in vocational preparation long before their fifteenth birthday. This is particularly true in agricultural occupations and in family operated businesses.

Occupational preparation and specialization programs must be differentiated between secondary and post-secondary levels. Student maturity, general education prerequisites, and the specific nature of the occupational specialization area demand this differentiation. This point may well be argued by various occupational education professionals, but it is the authors' contention that there is a definite difference between instructional methods at these levels. An inarguable point is that, in all cases, these programs must be carefully articulated to prevent extensive duplication of content and method.

Preparation programs entail occupational education for specific entry-level skills. The primary responsibility of the preparation-level teacher is to provide students with essential skills, knowledges, and attitudes to assure entry into their chosen occupations. It is the occupational educator's responsibility, in cooperation with vocational guidance personnel, to place all program completors in occupations or further training related to their area of specialization.

Occupational-preparation programs have been traditionally classified in several areas. These are: agriculture, business and office, distribution and marketing, industrial, home economics—gainful, health, and public service.

Further information regarding preparation-level occupational teaching—is provided in Chapter 3.

THE OCCUPATIONAL EDUCATION STUDENT

In many localities, occupational education comprises nearly fifty percent of the total school enrollment. Current trends indicate that this percentage will certainly increase over the next ten years. As a result, the occupational education instructor can expect to have a representative sample of the total student population enrolled in his or her classes and programs. To try to categorize or type occupational education students is indeed a mistake. As an individual, each student is different. Each student has specific likes, dislikes, needs, fears, and interests. Because of these differences, the occupational education teacher is faced with the increasingly difficult task of selecting instructional methods and techniques which will effectively meet the needs of most students.

To account for individual differences, many occupational education programs have begun the use of competency-based instruction. This procedure involves the specification of minimum performance levels for identified competencies necessary for entry-level employment in a specific occupation. Each major competency is presented in a unit learning-module format. Students utilize the learning modules in various ways to assist them to achieve the stated performance level for each competency or task. This process is described more thoroughly in Chapter 8.

The occupational education teacher must recognize that while competency-based education procedures are one means to insure that students exit with salable skills, they are not a panacea. Competency-based education is primarily a curriculum matter and not a substitute for sound instructional methods. In the end, it is the teacher's rapport with students and his or her ability to present instructional material in a palatable manner (regardless of the form of the curriculum) that constitutes good teaching. For far too long, educators have tried to substitute innovative instructional technology and curriculum for sound instructional methods. Methods, media, and curriculum are separate, yet interrelated, components of a total program. Improvement in one cannot overcome poor quality in the others.

In short, good teaching must account for the individual differences of students. Instructional methods and techniques must be modified to fit specific student needs and curriculum areas. Alternative methods must be utilized for students who tend not to respond to the regular instructional method. The occupational education teacher must have a repertoire of available methods and techniques from which to draw when special needs arise.

Recently, much criticism has been leveled at education and especially occupational education for not providing specialized services and instruction to students classified as disadvantaged and handicapped. Much of the negative criticism might have been averted if occupational education instructional personnel were able to clearly identify the multitude of special instructional methods and techniques being utilized in their programs.

NATURE OF THE STUDENT

Many factors affect the nature of the student population being served by occupational education teachers. Among these are age, socioeconomic and cultural background, previous educational success, parental influence, and prior experience in occupational or career development programs. Following is a more detailed analysis of these factors.

Age

In most cases, the younger the student the less likely will he or she be able to make realistic career decisions. Likewise, the younger student will be less able to accurately assess personal interests and career priorities than will be the older and more mature student. For this reason, it is extremely important that orientation- and exploration-level programs be as flexible as possible. Students should be permitted to move about through various occupational clusters or areas.

For example, an orientation-level program for eighth grade youngsters in industrial occupations must permit student experiences in several areas such as metals, electronics, construction, etc. Conversely, a preparation-level program in electrical construction and maintenance would not permit such curriculum flexibility. However, the instructional methods utilized for various units in the preparation program should be flexible enough to allow various procedures for youngsters who may be experiencing special problems.

Many occupational education programs are offered exclusively to adults. For most, these programs serve a retraining or skill upgrading function. For this group, occupational education does not serve as an exploration function. They know what they expect of the program, and they expect essential employment skills.

It would be in error, however, to assume that all adults, regardless of age, have made firm career commitments and are in need of only preparation-type programs. Many will enroll in occupational education programs to "try out" various occupational roles. These people may be interested in occupational exploration activities or avocational pursuits.

To assure the effective utilization of appropriate instructional methods, the occupational education teacher should carefully determine the specific goals of adult students.

Prior Experience in Occupational or Career Development Programs

Of course chronological age may not be as significant within various program levels as would vocational maturity. Just as individuals possess varying degrees of physical and emotional maturity, they also possess varying levels of vocational maturity. Vocational maturity may be greatly influenced by previous occupationally related experiences or career development educational programs. As with most maturation levels, chronological age will correlate with vocational maturity. However, students will vary considerably within age groups. This variation mandates orientation and exploration programs sensitive to individual needs. The orientation- and exploration-level instructor must be able to provide instruction that will meet these various needs.

It is imperative that the orientation/exploration teacher place primary emphasis on the developmental nature of the learner and on the educational process, rather than on curricular content and technical subject matter. The traditional occupational analysis approach to curriculum development which finds general acceptance in preparation-level programs must take a back seat in orientation-level programs, because the students will lack the level of vocational maturity so essential to entry-level skill learning.

Parental Influence

Parental attitudes and influence greatly affect the nature of the student enrolled in educational programs. In past decades, this has generally been a negative influence with regard to occupational education programs. Parents have generally been the prime movers of the "go to college" syndrome. As a result, many students enrolled in occupational programs have had little support from home regarding their selected area of studies.

This situation is rapidly changing. New parental attitudes are emerging. These attitudes have developed as a result of a general awareness that skilled occupations and careers are indeed noble, and people possessing less than a baccalaureate degree may indeed have a large earning potential.

Parental problems stemming from economic concerns, marital difficulties, and ill health may be reflected in student performance in the classroom or laboratory. The best instructional methods and techniques will do little to quell student anxieties in the face of such problems. The occupational education teacher must be aware that such concerns do affect students and must be willing to assist through personal understanding and humanistic treatment. Prescribed responses to youngsters facing these problems do not exist.

Socioeconomic and Cultural Background

Occupational education programs serve students with a variety of socioeconomic and cultural backgrounds. Any single laboratory or cooperative education class may be composed of students from all economic levels and cultural backgrounds within the community. It behooves the occupational education instructor to be familiar with the specialized needs of each student and have available a variety of instructional methods and techniques to serve these individual needs.

Thanks to forward-thinking legislators, separate funds are provided through vocational education legislation to support special services to disadvantaged students. The concept of disadvantaged is defined by each state, but in most instances includes those individuals identified as "socioeconomic" and "culturally" disadvantaged. The identification of these students and the development of special services for them is a high-priority concern in occupational education and will be discussed in a later chapter.

The occupational education instructor must also be concerned with socioeconomic and cultural differences that may affect student performance and may not fit the disadvantaged categories. For example, the student from a particularly wealthy family may have special concerns and problems related to occupational programs in which he or she is enrolled. The instructor may need to design specific instruction for this student. In most cases, financial resources will not be available for such specialized concerns. In that event, specific instructional methods or techniques, utilizing internal resources, must be designed.

In all cases, it is extremely important that the occupational education instructor be aware that each student in the program has specific needs stemming from social, economic, or cultural experiences. Specialized instruction may be required to help students meet these specific needs. Meeting these individual needs is what constitutes "good teaching."

Previous Educational Success

In years past, determining the previous educational success of students enrolled in occupational education programs was a simple task. Many students were enrolled in occupational education curricula because they had experienced little or no previous success in nonvocational education programs. To some extent this is even true in contemporary programs. However, this is changing.

Because of a general acceptance of occupational education as programs suited to fit individuals for skilled-level employment, all types of students are entering programs. Students who have been extremely successful in academic pursuits, as well as those less fortunate, are finding their way to exploration- and preparation-level courses. While this is as it should be, it complicates the tasks of instruction required of the occupational education teacher.

The increased diversity of students with respect to prior educational success adds a heavy burden to the occupational education teacher. The variations in educational achievement, past success in academic endeavors, and a variance with regard to general attitudes toward school demands that teachers have at their disposal a wealth and variety of instructional methods to fit given situations. An expanding need for individualized instruction, potential discipline problems (at the secondary level), and curriculum variations puts even the most experienced teachers to the test. It is, therefore, essential that occupational education teachers be aware of the variations in prior educational success of the students enrolled in their classes, laboratories, and cooperative education work stations.

THE OCCUPATIONAL EDUCATION TEACHER

While certification procedures differ among states, there generally exist two primary methods through which occupational education instructional personnel are certified. In the area of health occupations and industrial education, extensive work experience and/or professional association registration serve as the primary concern with regard to teacher certification in vocational education. In areas such as agriculture, business and office, home economics, and distributive education, the primary certification emphasis is on college or university degree programs with less weight placed on formal occupational experience.

While certification procedures do little to affect the specific nature of individual teachers, they do cause general differences among various specializations. Three typical approaches to teacher certification are diagrammed in FIGURE 1-2. The product of each approach tends to subscribe to a particular philosophical trend.

Group A teachers are holders of Bachelor of Science or Bachelor of Arts degrees (see FIGURE 1-2). Their occupational specialization was earned as university credit. Their degree program had a rather extensive general education and professional education component. For the most part, these teachers have no formal work experience in their occupational specialization. Traditionally, teachers in this group have been in the areas of industrial arts, home economics, and business education.

Group B teachers do not hold a Bachelor of Science or Bachelor of Arts degree (see FIGURE 1-2). In most cases, they have completed fewer than fifty college-level credits. This college-level work has been in the professional development area. They possess extensive work experience and/or are registered to practice their occupational specialization. This approach has as its philosophical base the concept that a teacher must first and foremost be a skilled practitioner in the occupational specialization to be taught. Traditionally, teachers in this group have been in the areas of vocational-industrial and health occupations education.

Evolving within the past decade is a new breed of occupational education teacher. Group C represents this pragmatic approach to occupational teacher preparation. The Group C teacher holds a Bachelor of Science or Bachelor of Arts degree (see FIGURE 1-2). The occupational specialization is based on extensive prior work experience or a combination of supervised work experience and post-secondary (usually community college) technical course work. Approximately 48 to 60 credits are granted toward the degree for these experiences. The traditional general education component as found in Group A is included in the preparation of this teacher. A professional development component is also included in this program. This type of program combines the best of both of the earlier approaches. It recognizes the importance of work experience in the specialization to be taught and provides the general education core so essential to good teaching.

The occupational education teacher will come into contact with fellow professionals whose backgrounds stem from these three major teacher preparation approaches. These approaches do tend to cause some variance in the general educational philosophy subscribed to by the products of the programs. However, the basic goal of these professionals, regardless of preparation, will be occupational orientation, exploration, and preparation programs of excellence suited to the needs of students and directed toward employability of program completors or those who exit the curriculum prior to completion.

Generally speaking, the occupational education teacher will enter his/her first teaching assignment as a slightly older, hopefully more mature person possessing more related work experience than counterparts in nonoccupational education programs. The occupational education teacher will have greater responsibility based on the expensive nature of instructional facilities and methods. The instructor will possess both essential technical skills and professional teaching skills with specialized training in the area of services to target populations such as the disadvantaged and handicapped.

SUMMARY

Occupational education has experienced unprecedented growth during the past decade. Increased federal, state, and local financial support as well as a general attitudinal change on the part of professionals and the general public has led to this expansion.

Occupational programs occur in a variety of settings. Various programs may be found in public schools, community colleges, universities, correctional institutions, community agencies, and mental health facilities. Programs are offered at the awareness, orientation, exploration, and preparation levels.

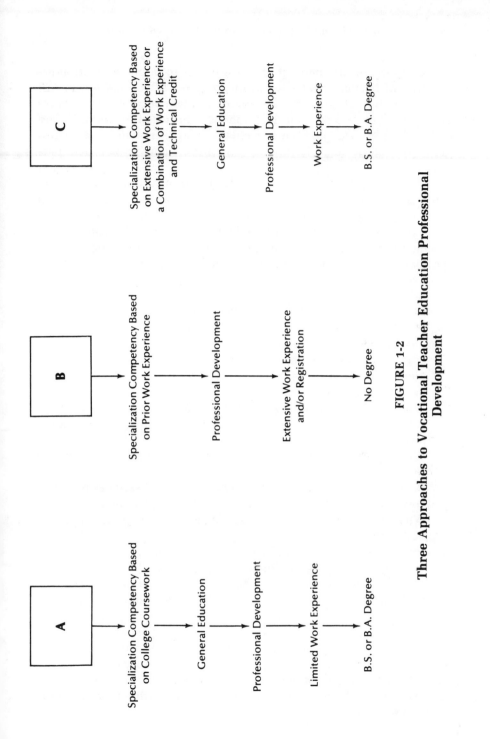

FIGURE 1-2

Three Approaches to Vocational Teacher Education Professional Development

In excess of fifty percent of the students in public education are enrolled in occupational education programs at various levels. All manner of students are served by occupational education professionals. Elementary and early middle school or junior high students may be enrolled in awareness and orientation programs. Secondary students and adults may be taking exploration and preparation programs.

Based on prior experience and formal professional preparation, three general types of professionals are involved in occupational education. Programs may be taught by nondegree professionals who possess extensive work experience in their specialization, degree teachers with extensive technical course work, and degree teachers with work experience and formal technical training.

REVIEW QUESTIONS

1. Identify and describe those factors contributing to the rapid growth of occupational education.
2. Identify and describe those settings in which occupational education teachers may work.
3. What are the four primary levels at which occupational education courses are offered? What is the basic nature of courses at these levels?
4. What are several factors that may serve to define a disadvantaged student? A handicapped student?
5. How does prior educational success affect students enrolled in occupational education?
6. What effect does parental influence have on occupational education students?
7. How does the socioeconomic and cultural background of a student affect teaching methods?
8. What are the primary factors that differentiate the three types of occupational education teachers described in this chapter?

STUDENT ACTIVITIES

1. Develop a listing of agencies in your locality, both public and private, in which occupational education is offered. Describe the types of programs offered in each.

2. Obtain a copy of your state's plan for vocational education. List the criteria specified for the identification of disadvantaged and handicapped students. Can you add additional criteria?
3. Conduct a case study of an occupational education student enrolled in a local program. You may wish to use yourself. Identify and describe such factors as prior educational success, socioeconomic background, cultural background, parental influence, previous formal or informal career development experiences, maturity, etc.
4. Identify in which of the three types of occupational education professional development programs discussed in this chapter you are enrolled. List the strengths of your particular program. List the weaknesses. Develop a professional development plan that will provide experiences to help overcome any deficiencies you have noted.

2

Orientation- and Exploration-Level Teaching

Occupational education programs, as components of the total career education system, provide students with skills essential for the world of work, thus facilitating that part of their personal career development. Career development, on the other hand, is an instructional process through which students systematically explore basic concepts related to the occupational environment and correlate this learning with their individual needs and interests. This process requires that early career education experiences be sufficiently comprehensive to assure that each student has the opportunity to explore many broad categories of occupations. The orientation and exploration levels of occupational learning are the basis of this chapter.

This chapter is designed to assist the reader in the accomplishment of the following objectives:

- **Define the exploration and orientation levels of occupational education.**
- **Describe the basic concepts underlying the curriculum and instructional methods used at the orientation and exploration levels.**
- **Identify and describe the traditional school settings in which instruction and learning at these levels takes place.**
- **Define specific instructional methods and techniques that will facilitate learning at these levels.**

- **Differentiate occupational education experiences at various age/grade levels within the orientation and exploration programs.**

As illustrated in FIGURE 1-1 in Chapter 1, there are four basic levels of learning in occupational education subjects. The awareness, orientation, exploration, and preparation levels of instruction serve as basic models on which to develop curriculum and to design instructional methods and techniques.

The awareness level is primarily a function of elementary school instruction and early work-related experiences in the home environment. As such, it becomes the responsibility of the early childhood teacher to develop instructional procedures that will permit students to systematically define broad concepts such as work, play, occupation, and career. To be effective, these concepts must be related to the home environment and the various occupations and activities that take place there. The alert awareness-level teacher is constantly searching for and planning student-centered school activities that will sensitize youngsters to the world of work activities that impinge on their daily lives. Since this is a function of the elementary school and those professionals working there, it will not be further described in this book.

The preparation level is designed to provide specific occupational entry and/or upgrading skills to older youths and adults. Teaching and learning at this level will be discussed in Chapter 3.

This chapter deals directly with the orientation and exploration levels of career education. These two closely related levels are composed of occupational experiences of a sequential nature that permits students to organize the world of work into a systematic structure, to familiarize themselves with general occupational areas (clusters), and to explore the various occupational clusters through laboratory, simulation, and real occupational experiences.

ORIENTATION-LEVEL INSTRUCTION

Orientation-level instruction begins around the fourth or fifth grade. Orientation learning requires that students have had adequate formal or informal awareness-level development. Prior to the orientation program, most youngsters have confined their occupational education learning to basic concepts. They will be able to differentiate between work and play, define productive effort, describe occupations of community helpers such as fire fighters, police officers, mail carriers, milkmen, etc. They will be able to describe those glamor occupations portrayed by various television and movie stars. The youngsters may or may not be somewhat familiar with the work performed by dad and mom and perhaps several neighbors. Students at the early orientation level will also be prepared to discuss what they want to do upon reaching adulthood. Some will have realistic aspirations, but many will base their future career goals on fantasy choices.

It is at this stage of an individual's career development that occupational orientation is most easily facilitated. Occupational or career aspirations, regardless of how unrealistic they may appear to be, can be used as departure points for specific orientation to broad clusters of occupations. For example, the youngster who aspires to become a commercial airplane pilot can be offered the opportunity of exploring air transportation as one component of a larger unit concerned with all manner of transportation systems and support services. The youngster interested in livestock production can use this as a basis for exploration of all agriculturally related employment.

The orientation-level instruction program design must be flexible, broad-based, and somewhat individualized if it is to be effective. While specific occupational clusters may be defined, they must be presented to students on the basis of individual areas of interest. This becomes the most difficult task for the orientation-level teacher. This task increases in difficulty in direct relation to the diversity of the student population, the number of instructional personnel at the orientation level, and the amount of instructional facilities suitable for orientation-level experiences. In short, it presents a problem of coordination.

For many years, schools equipped with industrial arts and home economics laboratories sought to reduce the problems associated with orientation-level learning by matching the student to the occupational cluster on the basis of sex. Hence, girls enrolled in home economics programs, and boys in industrial arts. After several decades of this, schools began to see the error of their ways and began to permit students at the early junior high school to enroll in these areas regardless of sex. Orientation-level teachers did little, however, to revise programs based on this arrangement. As a result, most program completers had a basic "insight and understanding of industry" and a "general awareness of home economics as it related to general education." These outcomes, while indeed important to youngsters, were rather limited when compared to the evolving goals of orientation-level learning. They did not provide cluster studies in the broad area of occupations. Rather, they were limited to orientation activities associated with home economics and industrial arts.

At the same time the above-mentioned programs were operating at the orientation level, new vocational education programs were developing at the preparation level. Expanded offerings and new programs in agriculture, public service occupations, business and office occupations, and health occupations were under way. Students exiting orientation and exploration programs in the traditional areas seldom had experiences that would assist them in selecting the newer preparation offerings.

Recently, new emphasis has been placed on orientation programs. Comprehensive schools have begun to develop orientation programs that provide experiences in all occupational clusters. These experiences are aimed at all students, regardless of their future educational goals. This approach, while absolutely essential in the career development scheme, greatly increases the complexity of the orientation level. No longer can a single teacher expect, within the limited amount of instructional time available, to adequately cover the various occupations associated with his or her broad cluster area. Many new clusters have been added, additional faculty members with special expertise have been assigned, but the total school curriculum has not increased. In fact, many new and expanded curricular innovations are vying for the same fixed amount of time.

Simply, the orientation level may be defined as a two-year period of time in which all broad clusters of occupations must be introduced to students. Hopefully, three to five hours per week can be devoted to learning activities. Since all students should be involved in orientation-level programs, care must be taken to assure that all occupational clusters and levels are represented. Emphasis must not be placed on preparing orientation-level learners to necessarily enter occupational education preparation programs at the secondary level. Many students will ultimately elect occupations that require college and post-graduate-level entry training.

A scheduling arrangement based on the fifteen occupational clusters proposed by the United States Office of Education is shown in FIGURE 2-1. Simple mathematics will indicate that a maximum of four to five weeks may be spent on each cluster.

Other clustering techniques may be utilized. Many states have developed other clusters that better suit their specific needs. For example, Illinois utilizes five broad clusters; Oregon has developed fourteen. Individual school systems may elect other arrangements. The important consideration is that the world of work must be represented in some organized fashion.

Two basic approaches may be utilized to assure that all clusters are adequately presented to each and every student. A group of teachers may be responsible for the total orientation program, or the clusters can be integrated into ongoing activities by all faculty. Both approaches will work, and the decision as to which will be utilized is largely a matter of teacher interest and commitment to the incorporation of career education into the curriculum of the school.

Assigned Orientation-Level Responsibility

This approach will utilize specific programs at the orientation level. These programs may replace traditional practical arts activities in the public schools. In most cases, industrial arts, home economics, and general agriculture teachers will be charged with the responsibility of operating these programs. Other instructional staff may be utilized to assist in clusters where the aforementioned faculty have little or no expertise. For example, fine arts and humanities instructors may assist with the four- or five-week unit in that area. Business and distributive education faculties may assist in those clusters related to their area of expertise.

This technique will utilize regularly scheduled classes for occupational orientation learning. These classes will emphasize simulation, field trips, instructional games, and guest presentors in each cluster area. While individual teachers may have responsibility for the orientation program, other faculty and community resources will be utilized. Instructional units may be structured as shown in FIGURE 2-1.

Integrated Orientation-Level Learning

This approach will place the primary responsibility for coordinating orientation-level learning on a curriculum coordinator or lead teacher. It will be the responsibility of this professional to see that orientation activities are integrated into appropriate and ongoing instructional programs. For example, occupational orientation cluster studies in the marine sciences may become the responsibility of the general or natural science instructor. The personal and/or public

36 WEEKS

YEAR 1

GRADES 5, 6, or 7

| Agribusiness and Natural Resources | Business and Office | Communications and Media | Construction | Health Occupations | Hospitality and Recreation | Manufacturing |

YEAR 2

GRADES 6, 7, or 8

| Marine Science | Consumer and Homemaking Related Occupations | Environment | Fine Arts and Humanities | Marketing and Distribution | Personal Services | Public Service | Transportation |

FIGURE 2-1

Orientation Level Cluster Scheduling (USOE Clusters)

services clusters may be taught in the social sciences area. In most cases, the manufacturing, construction, and transportation clusters will be taught by the industrial arts faculty while consumer and homemaking and hospitality and recreation will be handled by the home economics staff.

The writers believe that this is the best approach to orientation-level learning. It places cluster studies directly with those members of the school community who are best able to perform the necessary tasks. For this approach to be successful, it demands a formal commitment on the part of all faculty to integrate career and/or occupationally related components into their instructional programs.

The most difficult aspect of this approach is that of coordination among the faculty involved. At the outset, inservice workshops must be designed to provide faculty with information relative to careers in their cluster, suggested instructional techniques and resources, and general approaches to curricular organization. Periodic faculty meetings must be scheduled to review progress, identify areas of weakness, and share information relative to successful and perhaps not so successful approaches.

EXPLORATION-LEVEL INSTRUCTION

Exploration-level learning activities vary from orientation-level programs insofar as specificity of content and process is concerned. Exploration-level programs build on that which is accomplished at the orientation level. At this level, emphasis is placed on specific occupations or groups of occupations within specified clusters. This relationship is diagrammed in FIGURE 2-2.

Exploration-level programs are characterized by more hands-on kinds of experiences for learners. While simulation may continue to be a primary instructional method, more emphasis is placed on "trying out" typical kinds of occupational skills and activities associated with a particular cluster or group of related clusters. The relationship between instructional methods at the orientation and exploration levels is indicated in FIGURE 2-3.

Instruction at the exploration level will be the responsibility of teachers assigned to that level or of preparation-level faculty who spend part of their assignment in the exploration program. The comprehensive high school operating reimbursed vocational preparation

World of Work	AWARENESS
Occupational Clusters	ORIENTATION
Occupational Groups Within Clusters	EXPLORATION
Specific Occupational Skills	PREPARATION

FIGURE 2-2

Relationship Among Awareness, Orientation, Exploration, and Preparation Programs

	ORIENTATION	**EXPLORATION**
GOAL:	General orientation to all occupational clusters	Specific exploration of occupations within a single cluster or related clusters
METHOD:	1. field trips	
	2. guest presenters	1. laboratory activities
	3. simulation	2. simulation
	4. occupationally related games	3. community laboratory
	5. student research papers	4. demonstrations
	6. discussion	

FIGURE 2-3

Instructional Methods at the Orientation and Exploration Levels

programs is perhaps the best setting in which exploration-level programs can be implemented. The expertise of preparation-level instructors can be utilized when designing curriculum, determining instructional methods and techniques, and coordinating community laboratory activities. Preparation-level laboratories may be shared with exploration-level students for instructional purposes.

A typical exploration-level program may be as follows. Within the manufacturing cluster, there exist many occupations in which youngsters have exhibited interest. These might include metal fabrication, machine shop, industrial plastics, and furniture construction. An exploration program in this cluster would include activities in all these areas. Students would be provided opportunities in welding, soldering, producing machined assemblies, vacuum forming plastic, and simple furniture construction. These activities would be carried on in laboratory settings in the school or through cooperative agreement with various business and industrial firms in the area. The primary objective of this program would involve basic familiarity with the various tools and processes used in the occupations found within the manufacturing cluster. Through these exploration activities, learners will be able to assemble information relative to future decisions regarding further educational programs. In effect, students will be trying on various work roles associated with occupations within the cluster of their interest.

Exploration-level program design must be flexible enough to permit student learners to move from one group of occupations to another, if they discover that their initial choice was not exactly what they wanted. From this standpoint, exploration-level programs serve a guidance function. They provide information input to learners regarding specific occupational preferences based on experiences with the technology of the occupation.

Four basic instructional methods that may be utilized at the exploration level are listed in FIGURE 2-3. An analysis of each follows.

Laboratory Activities

Most exploration-level learning will take place in school laboratories or shops. Activities should be designed to permit students to gain experience in several occupations within the specific cluster being studied. For example, students involved in the health cluster should be provided experiences related to dental auxiliaries, health-care aide, veterinary assistant, radiology, respiratory technology, community health planning, and others. An example from the manufacturing cluster was cited earlier in this chapter.

As manager of learning experiences in the exploration laboratory, the instructor must try to provide a rather broad array of experiences in several occupations without going into too much detail in any one. In such situations, the exploration instructor must be extra careful not to overemphasize occupations in which he or she has the most interest or expertise.

Simulation

Simulation activities may be effectively utilized at the exploration level. A slightly different approach from that used at the orientation level is desirable. Simulation experiences must be directed toward specific occupations rather than broad clusters.

For example, an agribusiness simulation activity might center on managing a farm supply store or grain elevator, rather than on broad agribusiness activities. In the construction cluster, a simulation activity might be oriented toward residential construction, rather than toward the general construction trades.

Community Laboratory

For exploration-level instruction, the writers have chosen to use the term "community laboratory," rather than cooperative education. A community laboratory experience would be one where the instructor, with a group of learners, utilizes community resources much as they would an in-school laboratory. The instructor would coordinate with the community agency and be on hand to manage learning activities in the external laboratory.

For example, a local motel may permit the exploration-level instructor and his or her students to utilize specific facilities to provide experience in the area of hotel/motel management. Special guest rooms may be set aside for student experience in cleaning and preparation, the students may be responsible for maintaining the swimming pool on certain days, and they may also be provided front-desk experience under direct supervision of the instructor.

The community laboratory method is essential in schools where a broad array of laboratories, suitable for instruction in all clusters, is unavailable.

Demonstrations

The demonstration method, discussed later in Chapter 9, is a procedure used most often in exploration- and preparation-level programs. It will be utilized in connection with all other methods including simulation, laboratory activities, and community laboratory procedures. The instructor will demonstrate, prior to student trial, various techniques, methods, and procedures associated with various occupational skills. This method will be utilized at the exploration level more than in orientation-level teaching.

SUMMARY

Orientation- and exploration-level programs are evolving instructional activities in occupational education. Increased emphasis on career education in recent years has increased the significance of these programs. Traditional practical arts and general agriculture programs have, in the past, done much to fill the orientation/exploration-level learning in all occupational clusters, the traditional approaches must be revised and expanded.

Orientation-level learning is based on broad clusters of occupations. Students must be provided the opportunity of studying all occupations that comprise the world of work. Through occupational cluster categories, the orientation-level program seeks to provide these learning opportunities.

Exploration-level programs begin to focus on occupations or groups of related occupations within clusters. Instructional methods employed at this level are designed to provide hands-on experiences to learners in the specific methods, techniques, skills, and processes of various related occupations.

Learners exiting exploration-level programs will enter vocational or technical programs at the preparation level, or continue the education necessary to enter highly technical or professional-level preparation programs at the post-secondary, baccalaureate, or postgraduate level.

REVIEW QUESTIONS

1. What is occupational orientation-level learning?

2. Differentiate between occupational orientation and occupational exploration-level programs.
3. How have industrial arts and general home economics programs been traditionally utilized to serve orientation- and exploration-level learning?
4. What are two approaches to organizing orientation-level programs?
5. What are the principal instructional methods utilized at the exploration level?
6. Differentiate between occupational simulation activities at the orientation- and exploration-levels.

STUDENT ACTIVITIES

1. Develop a five-week unit for use at the orientation level in a cluster not closely related to your specialization area. Develop instructional objectives, identify appropriate instructional strategies and methods, and identify possible instructional resources.
2. Develop a chart, similar to that found in FIGURE 2-3, comparing and contrasting programs at the orientation and exploration levels. Identify instructional objectives, teaching methods, responsible faculty, and instructional resources.
3. Identify local community laboratory settings that could be utilized in an exploration-level program within your specialization cluster.
4. Travel to several local schools. Analyze those programs that are being conducted at the orientation- and exploration levels. Develop a list of suggestions that you would make relative to improving these offerings. Discuss these with members of your class.

CHAPTER

3

Preparation-Level Teaching

Preparation-level occupational education programs are designed to provide specific occupational entry-level skills for employment requiring less than the baccalaureate degree. Within the parameters of this definition exist both secondary- and post-secondary-level programs. Therefore, occupational preparation programs are designed to provide entry-level job skills to learners enrolled in high schools, community colleges, private trade or technical schools, and formal employer-based programs.

This chapter is designed to assist the reader to accomplish the following objectives:

- **Define occupational education programs and processes at the preparation level.**
- **Describe the basic concepts underlying the curriculum and instructional methods used at the preparation level.**
- **Identify and describe instructional settings in which learning at this level takes place.**
- **Define specific instructional methods and techniques that will facilitate learning at this level.**

When contrasted to the orientation and exploration levels, preparation-level learning is much more specific. Learning at this level is directed toward specific skills and knowledges that are essential for employment in a particular occupation. As discussed in Chapter 2, orientation- and exploration-level programs are broad based and directed toward learning involving clusters of occupations. The orientation- and exploration-level programs serve a much greater guidance function than do the preparation programs. Where people are being educated for the purpose of initial employment, skill retraining, or upgrading, a preparation-level program must be in full operation.

PREPARATION-LEVEL SETTINGS

Preparation-level programs may be found in numerous settings and serving the needs of a broad age range of learners. Traditionally, these programs have come to mean vocational education of less than college grade. As such, secondary vocational schools, area vocational centers, state vocational technical schools, and community colleges have been considered the primary preparation-level training agencies. However, preparation-level programs may also be found in employer-based facilities, in union halls, on military bases, in municipal government establishments, and at various federal and state installations. Federal vocational education funding is not necessarily prerequisite to a preparation program. Preservice teachers considering employment at the preparation level should not limit their horizons to only those programs. Likewise, consideration of instructional method must also relate to those preparation programs not always found in vocational schools and colleges. Many of the best occupational education teachers have received their occupational skill training through participation in apprenticeship and military-based programs.

Most vocational education teachers exiting university-based professional development programs will be entering employment in public vocational education schools and colleges. Therefore, an analysis of programs in these agencies is in order and of primary importance.

Most learners enrolled in preparation programs at the secondary level will be between the ages of fifteen and nineteen. Unlike many of their counterparts in nonoccupational education programs at the high school level, most will be employed outside of school on a full- or part-time basis. Because of this, they may be somewhat more mature, possess greater independence, and view learning from a slightly different perspective. With few exceptions, these students will view their preparation program as a means to financial independence, and perhaps as a terminal educational goal. If they have been involved in effective orientation- and exploration-level programs, they will be ready to learn the skills necessary for initial employment in the occupational area. At this point in time, however, this assumption is probably in error. Hence, the instructor can expect some turnover in the students enrolled in his or her class beyond that which could be expected as a result of illness or mobility.

Post-secondary occupational preparation-level students may tend to be somewhat different from the secondary-level student. They may range in age from eighteen through senior adult. They tend to be somewhat more committed to learning specific occupational entry skills and less committed to learning related or general education material. Many will be enrolled out of economic necessity, having discovered that without a salable skill their employment potential is quite limited. Many post-secondary students will be enrolled in evening programs while being employed full time during the day. Most will have family responsibilities that will demand much of their time and attention. Generally speaking, post-secondary learners will prefer and require less formally structured programs than secondary-level students. Many of the post-secondary adult learners will have been out of formal school for a long time and will not as readily fit back into that structure as will the secondary students who have been in school for several years.

Regardless of level, occupational preparation students will want activity. They will want to be actively involved in learning experiences rather than be passive observers. Therefore, the lecture method of instruction is probably the least advisable. Demonstrations should be kept short and to the point. Emphasis should be placed on laboratory and simulation activities and individualized instruction that is self-paced. This holds true for public vocational education as well as other types of preparation programs, regardless of the type of occupation.

This section has dealt with generalities. It is presented to provide the reader with information relative to the general nature of preparation-level learners and programs. However, the occupational education teacher must keep foremost in mind that students are individuals, and as such, their specific learning styles and patterns should be handled on an individual basis.

INSTRUCTIONAL PROCESS AND
THE PREPARATION-LEVEL LEARNER

Secondary and post-secondary occupational preparation pro-grams may be characterized by specific instructional processes that demand certain kinds of competencies on the part of the instructor. Skills in the use of specific instructional methods, coordination with external learning sites, and an ability to place program completors and noncompletors are among the competencies required of the preparation-level instructor. With the exception of the first category (specific skills in instructional methods), these competencies may be peculiar to the preparation-level teacher.

Preparation-Level Instructional Method

Several chapters throughout this book deal with various kinds of instructional methods that can be utilized at the preparation level. When determining the instructional methods that will best fit a par-ticular learning unit, the instructor must keep foremost in mind the nature of the students being served. For example, if secondary-level students are studying basic industrial processes related to a particular occupation, consideration should be given to their previous back-ground at the exploration level. If they have not had the opportunity of witnessing specific processes in operation in a real work situation, a field trip may be in order. However, if this same process is being taught as a skill upgrading activity to employed adults at the post-secondary level, use their experiences as the basis for a discussion and perhaps demonstration of the process being studied.

The determination of appropriate instructional method is not an easy task, and it requires experience in working with various groups at the preparation level. Be sure to utilize student feedback regarding the effectiveness of a particular method. Above all, do not hesitate to change methods when one does not appear to be working. Spend a few minutes at the end of the instructional day reviewing your own perceptions as to the effectiveness of a particular teaching approach. Adult learners will not be as hesitant to discuss particular teaching /learning strategies with the instructor as will secondary-level learn-ers.

When determining instructional methods, consideration must also be given to the availability of instructional resources within and external to the learning facility. If business and office students are interested in learning about the operation of a magnetic tape selectric typewriter (MTST), and one is not available within the school, go to outside agencies with the class for a demonstration. This approach would be far more effective than trying to explain this operation in a lecture.

The selection of instructional method at the preparation level is based on several primary considerations. These are:

1. occupational specialty being taught
2. nature of the learners (secondary/post-secondary, experienced/inexperienced, special learning handicaps, etc.
3. availability of school and community resources
4. instructor competence in specific methods
5. specificity of objectives being taught

Coordinating External Learning Sites

Chapter 13 is concentrated on cooperative education as an instructional method. The cooperative education work station is an external learning site. That is, it is not located within the confines of the school building. In addition to cooperative education, there are many other types of external learning that take place at the preparation level. Some of this may be formally structured and some may be very informal and not directly linked to the instructional program. The preparation-level teacher capable of coordinating many of these external activities on an individual student basis will be able to enhance the preparation-level learning that takes place.

This instructional coordination function involves three primary components. These include coordination with the external learning site, open communications with the learner, and integrating skills and information learned at the external site into classroom and laboratory activities. In short, the good preparation-level teacher knows his or her students, is aware of learning related work activities in which students are involved, and is able to draw upon these individual student experiences within the formal teaching/learning setting.

This concept is not new. It is the basis on which cooperative education is founded. However, cooperative education programs represent a formal approach to this coordinative function and there are informal techniques which may also be utilized. For example, a student enrolled in a post-secondary auto mechanics program may be employed during the day as a parts man for a local automobile distributor. The experience gained by this student on the job is closely related to the program in which he is enrolled. This student will have information readily available regarding costs of various parts and assemblies, those components which tend to need replacing more than others, and availability of specific repair or replacement parts. Information may be drawn from this student at opportune times to aid in the instructional process. His or her relationship with the operator of the automotive sales and repair business may serve as a good communications link between the school and the employer. It may well serve as the basis for the establishment of a cooperative education work station in that business.

Student hobbies may also be used as coordinative links with the formal instruction program. In many cases, hobbies are the reason why many students enroll in occupational preparation programs. For example, a student's interest in outdoor recreation activities may be the reason why the learner is enrolled in a distributive education program to learn the retail merchandising of sporting goods equipment. These hobby experiences may be the best form of input regarding the design of a specific outdoor advertising display by that student or other students charged with this responsibility.

It behooves the preparation-level instructor to know his or her students, where they work, the nature of their hobbies, and other related interests. Information such as this can improve the quality and relevance of a preparation-level program for the individual learner as well as the rest of the students enrolled.

The Occupational Placement Function

All teachers, be they involved in occupational education or not, are concerned with determining appropriate instructional method. As cooperative education and service learning activities become components of instructional programs, many teachers outside of occupational education are becoming interested in the utilization and coordination of external learning sites. However, at the less-than-baccalaureate level, the occupational placement function is primarily a responsibility of the occupational education teacher or guidance professional and is not a function commonly performed by nonoccupational education professionals.

The ultimate goal of preparation-level programs in occupational education is entry-level skill for the program completor. In many places, the concerned occupational educator is also trying to find employment for learners who exit his or her program prior to completion. This placement function is one of the most important activities in which occupational education professionals at the preparation level are involved. Depending on geographic location and manpower need, it can also be one of the most difficult professional tasks.

Occupational education utilizes three approaches which are very beneficial to the placement function. These include employing teachers with extensive work experience in the occupations to be taught; utilizing occupational or craft advisory committees composed of local business, industry, or health-care employers; and utilizing cooperative education work stations as both a learning and occupational placement activity.

Work experience. In most states, occupational preparation teachers are required to have extensive work experience in the area to be taught. The rationale underlying this requirement is based on the concept that these professionals, having experience in their occupational area, will be better able to determine relevant instructional content as it relates to real requirements on the job.

A secondary rationale for the work experience requirement relates to the placement function. Occupational education teachers who have related work experience will have developed important contacts with employers in that occupational area. Provided these teachers were valued by their previous employers, they may be able to place students completing their programs with these individuals. An employer, discussing a local occupational preparation teacher, once said, "John was the best welder we had, and it grieved me to see him go into teaching. But as I thought about it, I realized that while we were losing John, we would be gaining many more people like him as he began to turn out graduates." This was a spectacular commentary on the value of work experience for occupational education teachers.

Advisory committees. Occupational or craft advisory committees play an important part in the placement function. When local employers have an important advisory role in determining the nature of occupational preparation programs, they are much more willing to hire the students who exit those programs. Therefore, the active advisory committee not only provides guidance with respect to curriculum decisions but also functions as an employment pool.

Cooperative education. The cooperative education approach has received strong endorsements by all manner of state and national organizations. In states where manpower priorities are utilized to determine funding levels for various occupational programs, cooperative education work stations provide a natural entry into employment in the occupational area. Work station supervisors can use the cooperative education approach to groom potential employees. The occupational education teacher-coordinator should expect each new work station opened up at the beginning of the year to be filled by the student who receives cooperative education experiences with that employer. All too often, teacher-coordinators bemoan the fact that a work station is no longer available because a student has been kept on after graduating from the program. This is one of the important roles of the cooperative education approach. The experienced teacher-coordinator knows that if an employer is pleased with a cooperative education student enough to keep him or her on the job, that this employer can probably be counted on to make available two work stations the next year.

SUMMARY

Occupational education preparation-level programs are designed to provide learners with specific job skills needed for initial employment, skill upgrading, or advancement in an occupational area. These programs are offered at both the secondary and post-secondary level to youth and adults, fifteen years of age or older.

Preparation-level programs may be found in a variety of settings, including secondary schools; area vocational centers; state-operated vocational technical schools; community colleges; private technical institutes; union halls; and in business, industry, and health-care facilities. Since preparation programs are offered to such a broad age range of learners, the occupational education teacher must be able to deal with youth and adult populations.

Occupational preparation-level instruction involves three primary functions. These include the determination of method, coordination of external learning sites, and occupational placement. The placement function is the most unique to occupational education. This instructor responsibility is accomplished through using faculty with extensive work experience in the occupational area, establishing occupational or craft advisory committees, and developing cooperative education work stations.

REVIEW QUESTIONS

1. Define occupational preparation-level learning.
2. What is the relationship between exploration- and preparation-level programs?
3. Where may occupational preparation-level programs be found?
4. What is the nature of learners at the preparation level?
5. What is the role of the preparation-level teacher in determining instructional method? Coordinating external learning activities? Assuring occupational placement?
6. How does the work experience requirement placed on preparation-level teachers assist in the placement function?
7. What is the role of the occupational or craft advisory committee in assisting with placement?
8. What is the relationship between cooperative education and placement?

STUDENT ACTIVITIES

1. Develop a detailed listing of occupational preparation-level programs that are available in your community. In small groups, or individually, visit some of these programs. Discuss what you have seen with other members of the class. Identify commonalities and differences among the various programs. In which setting would you be most comfortable as an instructor?
2. Develop a list of procedures that could be utilized by preparation-level teachers in assuring placement of program completors. What can you do to assure placement of learners who enter but do not complete your preparation-level program?
3. Obtain a copy of the cooperative education guidelines from your state. Review and discuss these.
4. Review the literature in adult education particularly as it relates to adult learning theory. Discuss how adults learn differently from children and adolescents. What implication does this have on adult vocational preparation programs?

Students With Special Needs

All students are individuals, and as such, have special needs. In many cases, these needs may be easily identified by the occupational education teacher. However, these needs are often quite subtle and not readily identifiable. Every occupational instructor must learn to deal with the individuality of learners. The individual nature of all students is the primary concern of this chapter, and emphasis is placed on students who, because of socioeconomic background, cultural differences, birth defects, disease, or accident, find it difficult to meet the objectives of various occupational education programs when typical instructional methods are employed. In vocational education terminology, these students are defined as *disadvantaged* and/or *handicapped.*

This chapter is designed to assist the reader in the accomplishment of the following objectives:

- **Identify special-needs learners as they relate to the disadvantaged and handicapped categories included in federal occupational education legislation.**
- **Analyze various categories of special-needs learners, including the gifted.**
- **Develop a model for systematically organizing instructional content and method for special-needs learners.**

- Define primary approaches to curriculum organization and instructional methodology for the special-needs learner.
- Identify several general instructional methods and techniques that may be effectively utilized for the disadvantaged, handicapped, and gifted student.

Special-needs students may be classified into three primary categories. These categories include the disadvantaged, handicapped, and gifted. To many professionals, the process of categorization of students is improper; yet, it is essential if systematic instructional procedures are to be implemented to meet specific student needs. Of greater importance is the utilization of these categories for improving services, rather than affixing labels and assigning levels of expectation to youngsters classified therein. The identification of learners with respect to special-needs categories must be a systematic process conducted by qualified individuals both from within and external to the school environment. Individual learner development and the categorizational criteria must be periodically reviewed to assure that when needs are met the student need no longer be classified in a particular category.

THE DISADVANTAGED LEARNER

The *disadvantaged* student is perhaps the most difficult to identify and serve. A disadvantaging condition in one area of the educational system may not exist in another. Therefore, for the purpose of instructional organization, each student must be evaluated in light of the effects of the condition on learning rather than the cause. For example, an inner-city youngster may not necessarily be considered disadvantaged because of place of residence. If the environment where this individual resides affects his or her performance in specific curriculum areas, then this youngster would be considered disadvantaged. This is a key concept for the occupational education teacher to consider, since the special services must treat the effect and not necessarily the cause.

To further explain, consider the youngster who possesses reading disabilities that prevent him or her from successfully meeting the objectives of an exploration-level occupational education program. The disadvantaging condition might be caused by the social, cultural, or academic setting. The effect of that condition is a low reading ability. Special services must be provided to meet the reading needs of the student. The educational system does not endeavor to treat the cause. It must be remembered that specific services, to all manner of students possessing special needs, must be designed to assure that the student will be able to succeed in the program. Without these services, the learner would not be successful.

Disadvantaged learners have been classified into several different sub-categories. Like the disadvantaged category itself, these sub-categories are seldom universally accepted. The terminology and specific definitions are not nearly as important to the occupational education teacher as are the effects that these conditions have on the individual learner. However, to provide some insight into the various subclassifications, the following analysis is presented. The occupational education teacher should refer to his or her specific state plan for vocational education for statewide definitions and categories.

Culturally Disadvantaged

This category includes those individuals who, because of cultural background, are unable to succeed in vocational education programs. The effects of this disadvantaging condition must be visible to those individuals responsible for the operation of the occupational education program. Where a systematic K-14 career education program is in operation, the effects of this condition will be more apparent at the awareness, orientation, and exploration levels.

Student cultural and ethnic origins and bias will be most apparent to teachers whose background is different from that of the students. These differences, however, must affect the learner's ability to perform in the program and must prevent that youngster from meeting educational objectives before this categorizational title can be applied. In many cases, the differing cultural background and resultant values are "feelings" by both the student and the teacher rather than real hindrances to the ability of the student to meet program goals. In cases such as this, sound human relations activities for both students and teachers are more productive than an assortment of learning laboratories and remedial clinics.

Socioeconomically Disadvantaged

The sub-categories assigned to disadvantaged learners are not mutually exclusive. Nowhere is this more evident than between the culturally and the socioeconomically disadvantaged. Perhaps the best method of discriminating between the two classifications is by placing emphasis on the economic aspects of this grouping.

Economic hardship is perhaps one of the most detrimental components of the disadvantaged category. In both the urban and the rural schools, this problem affects many students. In many cases it will be most evident to the occupational education teacher working at the exploration and preparation levels.

Nonschool agencies and several in-school programs endeavor to help the economically disadvantaged family meet the basic physiological needs. Food, clothing, and shelter can normally be provided through various social agencies. Youngsters from these families must often work full-time evening jobs in order to supplement the family budget and provide some discretionary income for extracurricular activities. Because of these full-time jobs and their resultant effect on student alertness and because of inadequate diet or concern over family financial conditions, many students may not be able to meet the objectives of occupational education programs.

There is little that the occupational education teacher can do to assist the economically disadvantaged student, other than to provide an empathetic attitude and to assist the student in class as much as possible. There are several approaches that can be utilized to assist students, but these are programmatic in nature. For example, cooperative education can be an effective tool. Students can earn money while meeting specific instructional objectives of the occupational program. Work-study programs can be implemented to permit students to work and earn while in school, even though the work activities may not meet specific occupational education program objectives. School administrators may permit flexible course scheduling to allow students to work during hours that might normally be used in school activities. The individual teacher can organize instructional content and assignments to meet the needs of the economically disadvantaged student.

The socially disadvantaged student may exhibit quite different characteristics from his or her economically disadvantaged counterpart. The socially disadvantaged youngster, because of social background, may not be able to succeed in regular occupational education programs without some special help. Social values, mores, and ethics may be different from those generally accepted by the school. In many cases, the socially disadvantaged youngster will be the one suffering from behavior problems. These students, unless they are suffering from severe emotional problems (a handicapping condition), must learn the socially accepted behaviors necessary for success in school and on the job. Such students demand individual attention by the instructor and special related instruction regarding attitudes, behavior, etc. They must be provided with consistent expectations by the instructor and other school personnel. The real difficulty in working with these students is that when they leave the school or work station environment, they generally return to the social structure responsible for their disadvantagement.

Academically Disadvantaged

Some learners suffer from minor academic handicapping conditions that do not meet the traditional classifications of *educably mentally handicapped* or *trainably mentally handicapped*. Many of these students have minor perceptual or motor difficulties that hinder their ability to perform up to expectations in the occupational education program. Many students suffer from a lack of effective early education. As a result, they lack the essential verbal and quantitative skills necessary to meet the requirements of a particular occupational education program or course. These students may be classified as academically disadvantaged.

Several procedures can be utilized to meet the individual needs of these students. The occupational education instructor can modify course handouts, visuals, and reading materials so that students suffering from reading difficulties can understand the information presented. Written, teacher-made examinations can be given orally to youngsters who have difficulty reading (they might also be placed on cassette audio tapes). Special reading and math packages can be designed and placed in the learning lab by the occupational education teacher to assist those students that can avail themselves of that facility. Of greatest importance is close coordination with remedial instructors charged with the responsibility of improving the various academic skills of these youngsters. Many state post-secondary schools now require students enrolled in occupational education programs to be concurrently pursuing the G.E.D. certificate.

THE HANDICAPPED LEARNER

Occupational education for the handicapped is an evolving and exciting area. Recent years have witnessed the increasing concern by occupational education professionals to meet the vocational needs of the handicapped learner. As in the case of the disadvantaged student, federal legislation has demanded that vocational education programs be made available to the handicapped. Before analyzing these special programs, activities, and methods, a brief description of the handicapped category is in order.

Mentally Retarded

The mentally retarded student generally suffers from more severe academic handicaps than does the academically disadvantaged student. This classification is generally subdivided into two groups based on the severity of the condition.

The educably mentally handicapped student is the least severe. These students can be expected to meet entry-level occupational skill requirements in many occupational areas. Students in this group generally develop some writing, reading, and quantitative skills. In most cases, these skills will permit effective communication in a technical society. The educably handicapped student can meet the objectives of nearly all but the most technical areas commonly found in occupational education programs. Exceptions *might* include electronics, higher-level health occupations, some of the business and marketing areas, nutrition, and perhaps a few others. Please note, however, that the term *might* was utilized. Some students may perform exceedingly well in these areas.

While the educable handicapped students can meet the objectives and expectations of many occupational education programs, their learning rates will no doubt be slower than that of most of the students. Therefore, time becomes the important variable in the instructional method. Individualized performance-based curricula will be of the greatest benefit to this group of students. Instruction must be at a slower rate with plenty of opportunity for reinforcement both through curricular materials and teacher/student interaction. These students can be effectively mainstreamed into regular classroom and laboratory activities, provided individualized instructional activities are planned.

The trainable handicapped student is the more severe of the mentally retarded category. As with the educable grouping, there is a wide range of ability represented in this sub-category. Many of these students can profit from occupational education programs; but, based on traditional organization and skill requirements, many cannot.

Therefore, special vocational education programs must be developed for the more severe of the trainably handicapped students.

Because of a general lack of formal educational experiences and little or no experience working with this group of students, occupational education professionals tend to prefer not to be involved with the trainable mentally handicapped youngster and adult. This is particularly true where it is requested that these students be mainstreamed into the regular curriculum in the occupational area. In some cases, the fears and concerns expressed by teachers are well founded. In some industrial, agriculture, and health occupations areas where dangerous equipment or health related hazards are part of the training program, many potentially serious situations could occur when students do not possess the essential technical skills for safe operation. But, in many areas of occupational education, these kinds of situations do not exist, and trainable youngsters could profit from instruction and interaction with other students. In the end, the decision to "mainstream" these youngsters into regular programs should rest with the instructor who has taken the time to determine the individual student's needs and abilities.

Trainable youngsters can definitely develop lower-level skills in many occupational areas, and with commitment from the instructor, can be successfully placed in the employment sector. This responsibility must rest with trained occupational education personnel and not solely on the shoulders of the special education faculty who, in most cases, possess neither the technical skills nor the employment contacts that will profit the student who can be involved in meaningful wage earning activities.

Orthopedically Handicapped

Designing new or modifying existing occupational education methods to meet the needs of the orthopedically handicapped student is one of the easier tasks that befall the occupational educator set on meeting the needs of special populations. In many cases, orthopedically handicapped learners can be provided prosthetic devices that help overcome their handicap. In others, work station redesign, equipment modification, demonstration techniques, and learning activities and projects can be revised to meet individual needs.

The orthopedically handicapped individual may be so because of several reasons; one or more limbs may be missing or underdeveloped, neuro motor coordination may be affected, or a crippling disease may have been the cause. In most cases, unless this handicapping condition is accompanied by others, the student is aware of the handicap and somewhat experienced in dealing with it. For this reason, the instructor should work closely with the student to design the necessary methods and procedures that will permit the student to perform the essential learning tasks.

Of great importance is the need for the instructor to be patient with the student. The student will need to experiment with various procedures and techniques that will work best in particular situations. The teacher must provide constant encouragement to the learner and should encourage this experimentation as long as personal safety of the learner and others in the laboratory or learning station is not affected.

Often, occupational education teachers are involved in the design of new or in the renovation of existing facilities. In such situations, consideration of the needs of the orthopedically handicapped is essential. The wheelchair student not only must be able to get to the learning facility but also must be able to move about in it. Work stations should be flexible enough to meet the requirements of a seated, as well as standing, student. Equipment and supply storage should be available to the orthopedically handicapped youngster as well.

Visually Handicapped

Special concern must be given the visually handicapped student when his or her impairment makes achievement of program objectives through traditional methods an impossibility. Generally speaking, the visually handicapped are divided into two groups: (1) the partially sighted, and (2) the blind. Individuals from both categories can meet with a tremendous amount of success in occupational education programs, provided some individualized attention is provided by the instructor.

The partially sighted learner may utilize special corrective devices to improve his or her sight. However, to be so classified, their corrected vision will not reach normalcy. In most cases, special audio instruction and specially designed large visual materials can be utilized to assist these learners in meeting the objectives of the occupational education program. Many of the materials and much of the specialized equipment necessary for these individuals is available from the various State Associations for the Blind at very reasonable rental rates or perhaps at no cost to the student or school.

The blind students may also wear corrective devices to improve vision; but, because their sight is severely impaired, they will be blind for all practical purposes. There are techniques for both blind and partially sighted learners that can be employed by the teacher to help them in the learning process.

Recognize the condition. As with all handicaps, the instructor must fully recognize the condition and discuss special problems with the student. Do not be hesitant in using the word *blind* with these students. They are aware of their handicap and will discuss it freely with the teacher. Only through working cooperatively with the student can successful procedures be developed that will assist them to achieve the learning objectives.

Emphasize the use of other senses. Contrary to popular belief, the absence of one sense does not make the other senses more acute. Rather, the blind or partially sighted student will learn to make more effective use of the senses of feel, sound, touch, and taste. Likewise, the occupational education instructor must effect learning through senses other than sight.

Encourage participation in learning activities with sighted students. Do not hesitate to utilize films, overhead transparencies, or other audiovisual devices when visually handicapped students are in occupational education classes. There is much to be gained from these media by the visually handicapped. Have sighted students explain visual components to the blind.

Keep a clean house. Good housekeeping makes sense whether handicapped students are involved in the occupational program or not. However, when blind or partially sighted learners are mainstreamed into regular programs, neat and orderly laboratories and classrooms are essential. Visually impaired learners will be able to move freely about the laboratory, classroom, or cooperative work station after a few days of orientation. However, extra supplies and equipment must be kept in appropriate storage areas so that students will not trip and fall over such objects. Floors must be kept clean to prevent accidents.

Hearing Impaired

Students who because of hearing defects cannot meet the program requirements of regular occupational education curricula are classified as hearing impaired. Two classifications within this category are generally accepted.

The hard-of-hearing student may not be totally deaf, but will not be able to discriminate at normal sound levels. These students may wear corrective devices to improve their hearing. The deaf student will not be able to perceive sound, except as vibrations through touch. Both of these handicaps are critical, but can be overcome in nearly all occupational education areas.

With the exception of vision, most of what is learned comes through the sense of hearing. At first, this handicap does not appear significant, but it is. The sound of a motor under stress, an electrical short, improper cutting procedures, and an engine improperly tuned are examples of the ways hearing is used in the learning process. Without this ability, much of the learning that appears to take place automatically does not occur. Students suffering hearing impairment must compensate through the use of other senses.

When working with hearing impaired students, emphasis must be placed on visual learning activities. Lecture/discussion materials must be in readable form and made available to the students. Extensive use of visual aids and written instructional modules will help the hearing impaired student meet the instructional objectives. Given appropriate consideration by the teacher, most hearing impaired students can be successful in nearly all occupational education specializations.

Health Impaired

Students who are suffering from ill health and as a result find it difficult to succeed in regular occupational education programs fall into this classification. Chronic heart disease, respiratory ailments, and kidney and liver diseases are perhaps the most common. Special services to the health-impaired youngster must be different in each case, and must be specifically designed for the individual student. Common sense is perhaps the single most important attribute that the teacher of these students can possess.

For example, in the industrial area, students suffering from respiratory ailments must be provided the necessary protective devices so that dust, fumes, and other such irritants are minimized. In some cases, students cannot participate in programs where excessive dust and fumes are present. The standard dust collecting systems utilized in woodworking laboratories will not be sufficient. Likewise, the fumes associated with lacquers and enamels used in auto body repair can be very harmful to these youngsters.

Many youngsters suffering from heart disease cannot be involved in occupational education areas where physical exertion is common. Such areas might include agriculture production, foundry, welding, etc.

Some health-impaired students might be subject to seizure. In many cases, these seizures may be controlled medically and of no hindrance; in others, they might occur quite often. Instructors must be made aware of the condition, and when students are working with potentially dangerous equipment, close supervision is essential.

Sound orientation- and exploration-level programs are quite important in helping the health-impaired learner select appropriate, yet personally fulfilling, occupations. Information and experience regarding the nature of specific occupations is essential to the health-impaired learner, if he or she is to be aware of the physical requirements and potentially dangerous situations that may occur on the job.

Physical facilities play an important part in determining the type of occupational education programs that might best meet the needs of the health-impaired individual. Emphasis should be placed on facility design, regarding the availability of various programs to these learners. For example, if the business and office education laboratories and simulation facilities are placed on the second floor of the occupational education building, elevators must be made available to the student who, because of health or orthopedic impairment, cannot climb stairs. Emergency health facilities should be placed near the industrial, food service, and agriculture laboratories. Special guards and other such devices can be designed by the occupational education instructor to prevent injury in the event a student suffering from a health impairment is using a particular piece of equipment.

The health-impaired student is often the most overlooked learner in the school. They too deserve the individual attention necessary to assure their success in the occupational program.

THE GIFTED LEARNER

The nature of the economic times, evolving manpower needs, and a general enlightenment on the part of the general public regarding occupations is having a great effect on enrollments in occupational education. As enrollments increase, so does the variety of abilities of learners. Today, more and more gifted students are finding their way into occupational education programs at all levels from awareness through preparation.

The gifted learner, while not categorized as a special-needs student under existing legislation, has distinct individual needs that will provide a great challenge to the occupational education teacher. This student must be provided the opportunity of moving ahead at his or her own learning rate. However, the learning experiences must be somewhat structured to assure the learner's effective utilization of available time and resources. The guidance necessary for this category of student is as important as that necessary for any other special-needs learner.

All too often, once the gifted student has met the requirements and objectives of a particular occupational education program, he or she was told to "do whatever you want to do for the remainder of the term or year." In some instances, this approach is beneficial to the student; in others, it represents an excessive waste of time.

In developing special curricula and methods for the gifted student, the occupational education instructor must work with the individual to determine specific interests and objectives. This will involve individual conferences and some exploration on the part of the learner. Out of these should develop special learning objectives and goals for that learner. These objectives and their enabling activities must not be limited to the internal resources available within the confines of a particular occupational education laboratory. Emphasis should be placed on utilizing the expertise and facilities of the school and the community.

Many businesses and industries will welcome students (especially on an individual basis) interested in observation of ongoing activities. Some will even consent to employ these students much as a cooperative education activity. Other faculty may have taken a special interest in these youngsters and will be willing to plan cooperative learning activities for them. For example, a very successful electronics technology student may wish to work with the physics faculty in further study of electron theory, or the machine technology student may wish to explore the theory of metallurgy and materials behavior. A student in distributive education may be interested in further study in the areas of economics, sociology, or psychology.

Whatever the individual needs, the occupational education instructor must work with the gifted student in planning and designing a viable learning experience.

ORGANIZING INSTRUCTIONAL METHODS
FOR SPECIAL-NEEDS LEARNERS

The design of instruction for special-needs students must account for the interrelated nature of curriculum, methods, and media. Likewise, instructional design must include consideration of the level at which learning is designed to take place and the specific nature of the related learning that has gone on before. Therefore, the determination of instructional method is a very complex process that must be based on the individual learner. The design of a conceptual model that will assure the consideration of all the foregoing aspects is essential.

An instructional design model that should prove extremely effective in designing instruction for special-needs youth and adults in occupational education is diagrammed in FIGURE 4-1. To fully understand how the special-needs instructional matrix can be utilized by the teacher in instructional design, an analysis of its components is in order.

General Program Approaches

The model incorporates three general approaches to instructional program development for special-needs learners. These three approaches are identified along the receding axis as (1) mainstreaming, (2) modified regular programs, and (3) special programs (see FIGURE 4-1). Each approach may best be suited for a particular category of student, the individual nature of a specific school and its philosophy, or the instructor's strengths and weaknesses. In any event, consideration must be given all three approaches when designing instruction.

Mainstreaming. The mainstreaming concept has received considerable attention in both special education and special occupational education programs. Special-needs students are provided the necessary support services to help them succeed when enrolled in regular occupational education programs with all students, regardless of abilities or backgrounds. This approach is based on the idea that special-needs learners must be provided normalizing kinds of activities and these activities must take place in normal facilities with "normal" students. The mainstreaming approach is quite successful for all but the most severely handicapped learners. However, this technique requires instructional personnel capable of dealing with all manner of handicapping conditions. Since no individual teacher can be thoroughly familiar with the needs of all manner of handicapped learners, this approach requires considerable cooperation among all teachers (including special education personnel), guidance counselors, and administrators. External agencies such as rehabilitation, mental health, associations for the blind, and many others must also be involved in program planning and support services for the handicapped student who is mainstreamed into the regular occupational education program.

Perhaps more than the following two program approaches, mainstreaming requires greater individualization with regard to specific student needs. For this approach to be successful, a formal program plan must be developed for each individual special-needs learner. The learning plan must include a detailed description of the student, including an analysis of all those factors that affect his or her learning. Primary and secondary handicaps must be identified and general instructional approaches defined. An analysis of program objectives and special techniques to be utilized to assist the learner to meet these objectives must be included. Finally, evaluation procedures and techniques must be described.

A detailed outline of special-needs learner instructional plan follows:

Individualized Teaching/Learning Plan

I.   Description of the Learner

This section details information such as name, address, age, mental ability, motor ability, nature of specific handicapping condition, areas of strength and weakness, and personal characteristics.

II.   Instructional Objectives and Special Techniques

This section provides a description of the general instructional objectives and analyzes specific techniques, media, and support services that will be utilized in assisting the learner to meet the objectives.

III.   Evaluative Criteria and Procedures

This part of the plan will describe the specific evaluative criteria to be utilized for each objective and the methods of

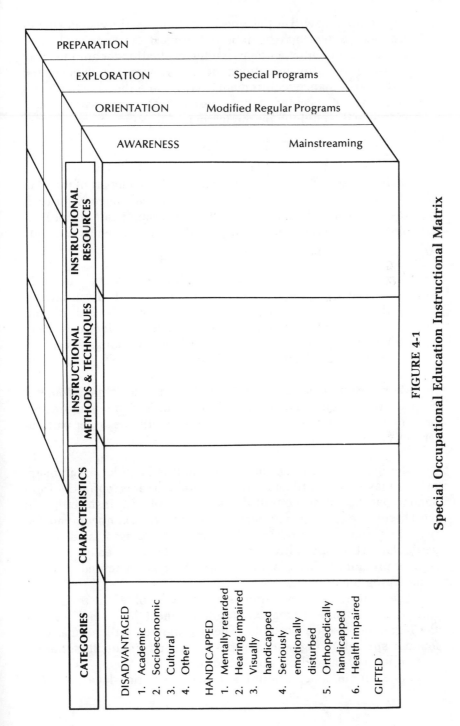

FIGURE 4-1

Special Occupational Education Instructional Matrix

evaluation that will be designed. For example, the visually hand-icapped student may be expected to meet the same evaluative criteria as any other student, but the evaluation techniques may be based on oral examinations and interviews rather than written tests. Performance requirements may remain the same with less emphasis on accepted technique and greater emphasis on indi-vidualized technique by the learner.

IV.   Special Materials and Equipment

Various handicapping conditions require the use of spe-cialized support materials and equipment. This part of the plan should detail all the equipment and materials needed for each instructional unit or objective, where these materials are located, and any special procurement procedures that must be utilized.

V.   Instructional Procedures Evaluation Log

This section of the plan may be utilized by the teacher in assessing the effectiveness of the various individualized methods and evaluation techniques developed for this student. A daily or weekly account of these procedures will be extremely valuable in future instructional planning for youngsters suffer-ing similar handicapping conditions.

Mainstreaming demands individualization and cooperation. It is essential that this plan be developed cooperatively among those pro-fessionals most familiar with the student and with his or her particu-lar individual needs.

Modified regular programs.   The modified regular program ap-proach may be best utilized where several students, suffering from similar handicapping conditions, are available for instruction. In most cases, the severely handicapped learner who cannot operate the typical equipment nor achieve the competencies associated with a particular level or specialization area will not be included in modified regular programs. These students may best be benefited through special programs.

The modified program approach simply involves the revision of various components of a regular program to meet the special needs of the target population enrolled. These programs will normally be found in special settings and facilities designed for students suffering from a particular handicapping condition.

For example, special modifications to orientation-level programs may be designed for learners suffering from hearing impairments. In schools for the deaf, an orientation-level program may be specifically modified to meet the needs of these students.

Somewhat similar to the mainstreaming plan, a modified regular program plan must be designed and utilized. However, the modified program plan will be a total programmatic plan rather than an individualized learner plan. The same components should be included in the modified program plan, but these will relate to total program modification rather than to specific learners as in the mainstreaming approach.

Program objectives may be altered to meet the specific needs and abilities of the learners. However, general program goals will remain essentially the same. All equipment, instructional media, and teaching methods will be revised to meet the needs of the total target group. Any individualized planning that takes place will be based on specific learner needs other than the handicapping condition.

Special programs. Like modified regular programs, special programs will normally be designed for particular target groups. Unlike the modified regular programs, however, general program goals and objectives may be significantly altered. Special programs are designed for learners suffering common and severely handicapping conditions. These conditions will be of such a severe nature as to make the accomplishment of traditional program objectives an impossibility.

For example, severe and profound mentally handicapped learners may never meet preparation-level abilities generally associated with students completing regular or modified regular programs. Since these individuals do have occupationally related potential, special programs must be designed to assure that they can reach their greatest potential. For many, this will be employment in sheltered workshops or at sheltered employment stations where repetitive tasks may be performed at less than generally acceptable production standards. However, basic skills and work habits are important to the relative level of success that these learners will experience. Hence, training programs are essential to their well-being and happiness.

In many instances, the occupational education teacher involved in special programs must be willing to accept what appear to be small gains to him or her as miraculous accomplishments for the learner. However small these accomplishments may appear to be, they represent important steps on the part of the learner toward self-respect and personal accomplishment that are important both to the well-being of the individual and of society. At perhaps no other place in the educational enterprise are occupational and general education goals so closely related.

SPECIAL NEEDS INSTRUCTIONAL MATRIX

Note the components of the instructional model in relation to the foregoing discussion (see FIGURE 4-1). The design of instruction, including the determination of method, involves an active consideration of all aspects of the teaching/learning process. Each program must be based on the level at which it is designed to occur, the nature of the individual learner, the type of delivery system to be utilized, and the availability of essential supporting services and materials. When designing instructional methods for special-needs learners, carefully consider the material presented in this chapter as it relates to the program levels, the nature of instructional media, and specific instructional techniques described in other sections of this book. In all cases, keep in mind that special-needs learners possess individual characteristics as do normal learners, and these characteristics must be considered when designing instruction.

SUMMARY

Special-needs learners may be categorized into three primary categories including the disadvantaged, handicapped, and gifted. Much of the research and commentary in the literature of occupational education is directed toward the handicapped and disadvantaged learner. However, the gifted student must also be considered when designing special instruction in occupational education.

The disadvantaged learner may be so classified because social, economic, cultural, or academic disadvantagements that prevent them from succeeding in regular occupational education programs.

The handicapped learner may suffer from many handicapping conditions, including mental retardation, orthopedic handicaps, visual and hearing defects, health impairments, or a combination of several of these conditions.

Effective instructional organization to meet the needs of special populations requires that the instructor be able to deal with several factors simultaneously. These factors include program level, nature of the learner, type of special instructional organization, and the availability of special resources. Sound occupational programs require cooperative planning among all professionals familiar with the individual nature of the learner.

REVIEW QUESTIONS

1. What is a disadvantaged student?
2. What are the primary factors that cause a learner to be considered disadvantaged?
3. Define the term *handicapped learner*.
4. What are some of the categories associated with the handicapped student?
5. What types of special instructional considerations must be given to the mentally handicapped, orthopedically handicapped, visually handicapped, hearing-impaired, and health-impaired student?
6. What are some other handicapping conditions that were not discussed in this chapter?
7. Has the gifted student been overlooked in occupational education? If so, why?
8. Identify several special considerations that an occupational education teacher should give to teaching the gifted learner.
9. What are the three general program approaches used to meet the needs of handicapped and gifted students?
10. Define mainstreaming. What are some special problems associated with this approach?

STUDENT ACTIVITIES

1. Review your State Plan for Vocational Education. Develop a listing of the categories used in defining disadvantaged and handicapped learners. Determine whether or not special emphasis is placed on gifted students.
2. Consult your state teacher certification guidelines. Determine the special requirements for teachers of the disadvantaged or handicapped in occupational education. If there are no special requirements, list those that should be included in a teacher education program.

3. Visit a special education program or a sheltered workshop. Consult with the instructional coordinator regarding specific activities that are happening. Prepare a short paper describing the nature of the people involved, their handicapping condition, and the training activities in which they are involved.
4. Invite guest speakers from your local vocational rehabilitation office, council on exceptional children, and other service agencies. Ask them to direct their discussions to the individual needs and abilities of various special populations.
5. Develop an individualized Teaching/Learning Plan for a hypothetical special-needs student enrolled in your program.
6. Design a special services matrix. Identify several handicapping conditions and describe special considerations that must be included in instructional design at the awareness, orientation, exploration, and preparation levels. You may delimit your responses at the exploration and preparation levels on the basis of your area of technical specialization.

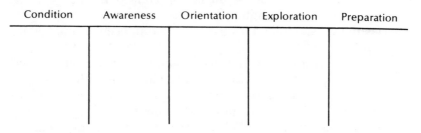

SPECIAL CONSIDERATIONS

Condition	Awareness	Orientation	Exploration	Preparation

REFERENCES

Chinn, P.C.; Drew, C.J.; and Logan, D.R. *Mental Retardation.* St. Louis: Mosby, 1975.

Gearhart, B.R. *Learning Disabilities.* St. Louis: Mosby, 1973.

———. and Litton, F.W. *The Trainable Mentally Retarded.* St. Louis: Mosby, 1975.

Hammill, D.D. and Bartel, N.R. *Teaching Children with Learning and Behavior Problems.* Boston: Allyn and Bacon, 1975.

Haring, N.G. *Behavior of Exceptional Children.* Columbus, Ohio: Merrill, 1974.

Hewitt, F.M. *Education of Exceptional Learners.* Boston: Allyn and Bacon, 1974.

Kirk, S.A. *Educating Exceptional Learners (2nd Ed.).* Boston: Houghton Mifflin, 1972.

————. and Lord, F.R. *Exceptional Children: Educational Resources and Perspectives.* Boston: Houghton Mifflin, 1974.

L'Abate, L. and Curtis, L.T. *Teaching the Exceptional Child.* Philadelphia: Saunders, 1975.

Long, N.J.; Morse, W.C.; and Newman, R.G. *Conflict in the Classroom (2nd Ed.).* Belmont, Calif.: Wadsworth, 1971.

Wallace, G. and Kauffman, J. *Teaching Children with Learning Problems.* Columbus, Ohio: Merrill, 1973.

Schwartz. *The Exceptional Child: A Primer.* Belmont, Calif.: Wadsworth, 1975.

5

The Teaching/Learning Plan

In the teaching profession, as in other enterprises, a plan of action is essential for efficient and effective learning. When appropriate planning and preparation have been completed prior to beginning the teaching/learning process, the opportunity for learning is greatly enhanced. This chapter is designed to assist the reader in accomplishing the following objectives:

- **Define the teacher's role in the teaching/learning process.**
- **Define the students' role in the teaching/learning interaction.**
- **Describe short- and long-range planning for instruction.**
- **Develop specific daily lesson plans.**

Planning is a major prerequisite for successful teaching. This fact may not be immediately evident to many who observe an experienced and skillful teacher in action. A lesson may seem to develop so extemporaneously, often without visible evidence of lesson plans or unit plans, that the observer at first thinks no special planning was involved. However, as the lesson progresses, the observer gradually becomes aware that learning is taking place in a logical, well-defined way. The problems being raised are systematically solved, the materials necessary for exercises or demonstrations are readily at hand or are available in the right place at the right time. When references are needed for further information or to check conclusions, the books are ready. The observer now realizes that this kind of teaching and learning occurs as a result of intensive planning and preparation.

It is evident from the situation described above that the teacher's role is critical to the teaching/learning interaction. Therefore, it is essential that each teacher, whether a beginning teacher or one with considerable experience, examines his/her role in the teaching/learning process. Further, a sound understanding of how students learn and the role of the student in the educational process is essential for successful teaching at all levels of instruction.

It is often taken for granted that a person who has reached a high level of skill and knowledge in an occupational specialty is at once prepared to teach that specialization to others. An extremely competent toolmaker and diemaker, for example, may feel that he can readily instruct others in the skills and knowledges required of that occupational specialty. Instruction appears to be a simple process of explaining and demonstrating the principles and processes which comprise the toolmaking and diemaking trade. It is only after teaching in this manner and discovering how little students have learned that the instructor realizes the need for a better understanding of the instructional/learning process. In order to have students learn, the teacher soon finds that there are certain things that the instructor must do and there are other things which the learner must do. The teacher must thoroughly plan all activities related to the learning environment.

Faced with the necessity of deciding what will take place in the classroom, a beginning teacher will usually focus attention upon personal actions, when in fact the question should be asked, "What must the students learn?" or, to put it in another way, "What behavioral changes should students exhibit at the end of the instructional period?" When considering the activities which might be carried out in the job-simulation laboratory or classroom, the neophyte teacher must of necessity draw from his/her own background of experiences. Many times the new teacher will try to duplicate some of the procedures employed by previous teachers. Events such as class discussions, lectures, demonstrations, use of motion-picture films, and guest speakers may be recalled. Other activities such as field trips and student reports may be considered. In each of these activities, the teacher is focusing on procedures that he/she might use in the classroom or laboratory setting. Attention is given to the instructional activities that will be used, rather than to the student outcomes these means are supposed to produce. Teaching in the traditional sense has been defined as an activity in which the teacher dispenses information while the students receive the information. Today's students and teachers, however, are faced with an entirely different situation; new sources of information are available, and educational technology has provided many alternative methods of learning the skills and knowledges essential to become a competent and productive worker. The teacher is no longer the only, or one of a few, source of information available to the student.

Therefore, the role of the teacher has changed from that of an information dispenser to that of a learning manager whose primary responsibility is that of facilitating learning and also that of developing skills and techniques of learning. Classroom activity has changed from a unidirectional process (teacher → student) to a dynamic interaction in which both students and teacher (teacher ⇌ students) are active participants.

Further, the teacher must manage the learning environment in such a manner as to create freedom of interaction between students (student ⇌ student), as well as between teacher and students.

The basis of occupational education is an analysis of the training needs of adults and young people in the essential skills and knowledges for a particular occupation. Therefore, it is important that the teacher always keep in mind the group of students for which the program is designed and the job tasks which these students must understand and be able to perform in order to become competent productive workers. Because of the diverse nature of the students enrolled in the many occupational programs, occupational teachers will be required to use a variety of methods, techniques, instructional media, materials, and equipment. It will also be necessary for each teacher to be prepared to adapt procedures to meet changing laboratory situations. Each teacher must be aware of the possibilities, advantages, and limitations of each learning activity which could be adapted and used in the classroom or job-simulation laboratory, and be prepared to use that method which most effectively meets the situation at hand.

The student's role in the teaching/learning interaction has also changed. In contrast to predecessors, today's students bring to each class session more information, and in many cases a broader experiential background, than ever before. Because of this broad spectrum of experiences, today's students, more than ever, need programs which will help them learn the techniques of learning.

The demand for "accountability" has caused educators to focus upon the learner. Goals and objectives which specify what the student is to know or the skills that are to be possessed at the end of the instructional period have become the focus of attention when planning and developing educational activities. As a result of this changing role, students have become active participants in the teaching /learning interaction. *Performance* objectives specify the kinds of things a student should be able to do at the end of the course or unit of instruction. Therefore, the learner knows what is expected at the outset of instruction.

There has been a significant change in the role of students and teachers. Teachers now have a charge to fulfill the role of "manager learning." They must utilize a multitude of methods and techniques which will enhance the learning of their students if competent workers are to be trained for the ever-changing manpower needs. Students, on the other hand, bring to each learning situation many skills and experiences which are appropriate for the occupational specialty they are entering. These skills and knowledges must be verified and, if found to be at the mastery level, used to determine the point at which the student must begin to develop new competencies. Verification of previously learned competencies and appropriate placement will tend to provide the motivation necessary to ensure that each student will become an active participant in the educational setting for producing a competent worker.

The performance objectives of an occupational program, whether it be secondary or post-secondary education, are determined by a careful analysis of the occupation to be taught. This listing of tasks provides a detailed description of a vocation or job as it is performed by a highly skilled person. The skills and information specified in the analysis are examined to determine which tasks are best taught in a school setting and which tasks are best learned on the job. The resultant listing of tasks would then be organized into courses which would comprise the total curriculum for that occupation. In most occupations, approximately two to four years are required to prepare students for productive employment. This means that the curriculum is organized on a yearly basis with individual courses being taught as subdivisions of the curriculum. The course of study or course outline represents the first phase of planning which is conducted by many occupational teachers and in most cases will be the starting point in planning a unit or individual lesson based upon the performance objectives of the occupational program.

UNITS DEFINED

The unit of instruction may be defined as a means of organizing instructional objectives which are similar and related in order to achieve significant educational goals. In occupational teaching units, information and activities are organized to focus upon the development of some significant understanding, skill, ability, or attitude that will confirm or modify behavior. Further, a unit of instruction focuses upon one major topic over a period of time, rather than a day-to-day approach to learning. Simply put, a unit plan is one in which the teacher and the student analyze the entire system rather than the parts. An analogy to unit planning would be that of a person desiring to make a trip by automobile. First, the destination would be determined, a road map would be secured, a route planned, and, if a long trip, overnight stops would be anticipated. By contrast, daily planning without an overall guide would be similar to the person who may know the destination but takes a trip without a map, and must rely upon the directions, or situations faced at each fork in the road to determine which direction will be taken.

The Value of Unit Planning

The unit is a plan of instruction which centers upon a significant area of learning. Instead of disconnected lessons, assignments or tasks, details to be done, all students prior to beginning a unit of instruction should have an understanding of the completed job or learning unit. A great variety of learning activities will be incorporated into unit plans, such as reading, writing, speaking, listening, experimenting, researching, and reporting. Unit planning makes use of many kinds of learning aids, such as audiovisual materials, electronic devices, laboratory equipment, and community resources.

Unit planning also makes possible more adequate provisions for individual differences within the classroom or job-simulation laboratory. Because of the varied materials and activities, a well-developed unit has to offer more opportunities for student choices, greater appeal to diversified interests, and better use of a variety of talents are assumed.

There is also a greater likelihood that each will achieve some measure of success when activities are not limited to those of a verbal nature, as is often true of many courses in the total school curriculum. Also, learning activities are less likely to be dominated by the teacher and more student-centered than under a fragmented day-by-day planning process. The student knows the scope of the instructional plan and does not need to rely entirely upon the teacher for all knowledges.

Unit planning is based upon sound psychological principles of learning. The unit emphasizes learning by wholes, the continuity of learning, and the integration of student learning experiences. Unit learning also seeks to achieve greater breadth of understanding in terms of the interrelationship of all learning activities, whether they be skill oriented or theoretical in nature.

A teaching unit is not preplanned for the purpose of prescribing all aspects of the learning experience, rather it is designed as a basis for further planning. Unit planning serves the function of relating the scope of work planned to the amount of time available to learn. The rate of progress by each student will, of course, depend upon the individual student's ability and motivation. Therefore, rather than a fixed schedule which must be rigidly followed, a unit plan should be viewed as an educated estimate of the time necessary for learning. A time frame, once established and known by both teacher and students, will generally result in efficient use of time and learning resources.

Elements of the Unit

The unit or any other complete instructional plan consists of several basic elements: broad goals, learning outcomes or specific objectives, learning activities or learning experiences, materials, and evaluation. A sample unit is provided for examination with each of the elements illustrated (TABLE 5-1).

The essential elements of a unit plan are described briefly in the following paragraphs in order to provide clarification of each of the components included in the unit plan.

Title

The title and heading of the unit includes title of the programs, course title, grade level, and, of course, the title of the unit itself. The heading of the unit should include the estimated amount of time necessary to satisfactorily complete the unit. The unit title should be concise, but at the same time provide a clear indication of the intended purpose of the unit. It should also suggest the unifying principle around which the unit is organized. Or to put it another way, the

TABLE 5-1

PROGRAM TITLE: ELECTRICITY/ELECTRONICS

Course Title: AC/DC Fundamentals and Principles
Grade Level: 11 and 12

Unit Title: Safety and Housekeeping in the Electricity/Electronics Industry

Approximate Teaching Time: 6 clock hours

Program Goals: Safety of the individual and his peers is essential, and a positive attitude toward safety developed in each person

Competencies (Course Goals)	Performance Objectives	Course Content	Learning Activities	Evaluation
(The student can)	(Give a description of a work setting)	Accident Prevention:		
1.0 Demonstrate a knowledge of general safety practices	1.1 The student will: (1) explain reasons for good housekeeping practices (2) identify clothing and dress practices which could be a hazard	1. Good house-keeping 2. Clothing 3. Safe use of tools and equipment a. grounding devices b. overload preventor c. general safety rules	1.1 L.G.P. Co. Safety Demonstration (2) Film	1.1 Written report (1) Objective test

Objective	Content	Activities	Evaluation
1.2 Demonstrate safe use of electrical tools: (1) explain the purpose of acceptable grounding devices (2) identify electrical tools without proper grounding	4. Toxic fumes 5. Lifting and moving heavy objects	1.2 Film — A.B.Chance Co. film — Grounding High Voltage (2) Check grounding of all electrical tools and equipment at home or shop	1.2 Observation
1.3 Given a heavy object to move, the student will: (1) obtain assistance (2) use mechanical devices available such as handtruck		1.3 Class or small group demonstration by teacher and students	1.3 Observation
2.0 Demonstrate safe electrical practices and procedures			
2.1 Given a description of conditions encountered in a case of electrical shock, the student will: (1) list effects visible to the trained observer (2) list treatment procedures (3) describe cautions to be taken prior to treatment (4) explain correct procedure to give mouth-to-mouth resuscitation	Electrical Shock: 1. Physiological effects of electrical shock 2. Methods of preventing electrical shock Fire Prevention: 1. Care and use of extinguisher 2. Prevention of fire hazards	2.1 Written report (4) Demonstration	2.1 Report (3) Objective test (4) Performance test

unit title should provide the reader with a broad overview of the purpose and content of the unit, when presented with the other elements of the unit heading, i.e., Program Title, Course, Title, Time Frame, and Grade Level. The reader should have an idea of how the unit relates to the course as a whole.

Program Goals, Course Goals, and Performance Objectives

Program goals are broadly stated objectives which cause the learner to focus upon the general direction of the unit of study. While course goals or competencies indicate more specific learner outcomes, performance objectives provide more detailed information regarding the student which would be used to determine performance standards as specified in the performance indicators. These statements represent the acceptable indication of competent behavior.

Course Content

This element of the unit plan provides a scope and sequence to the related instructional topics included in the unit. It also structures the teaching/learning interaction in that specific topics are directly related to the learner outcomes. The topical outline is also helpful in selecting the most appropriate learning activities and materials.

Learning Activities

Learning activities serve several purposes; they may be used to determine what the student already knows, to motivate the students, or to develop the necessary competencies stated in the unit. Alternate learning methods may be used for the development of the same competencies, i.e., audio tapes instead of relying upon the reading of textbooks, or a slide-tape series which would be used in place of a live demonstration by the teacher. Learning activities need to be extensive and varied in order to meet the students' interests, backgrounds, abilities, and learning style.

Evaluation

The unit plan is completed with the evaluation method specified for each performance indicator. The evaluation process will involve many methods of determining the level of performance of the learner.

The unit plan should indicate in each case the performance evaluation method. This can be done with an objective-type test, through observation of the individual as he performs the specified task, or through written reports which are submitted to the teacher for evaluation. Oral reports and group reports can be utilized in the evaluation phase. The important concept is that the evaluation method is determined at the same time the performance indicators are specified and learning activities are selected.

THE LESSON PLAN

A lesson plan is an expanded portion of a unit plan. It is a more detailed analysis of a particular activity described in the unit plan. While the unit plan is viewed as a budget of time over a long duration, the lesson plan represents the events and sequence of events of a smaller segment of the learning unit.

Written lesson plans are, in most cases, utilized by the successful occupational teacher, as well as by teachers of related classes. However, this does not mean that each plan must be written in great detail. It is important, and represents the teacher's anticipation of the events which are likely to occur. Lesson plans can serve as a guide to the teacher, and should be written in such a manner as to cause the individual teacher to feel confident about the planning which has taken place. Such a lesson plan should be written at a level of generality upon which the teacher can function, but not in such detail that the person feels more energy has gone into the plan than the teaching of the lesson. Ideally, the lesson plan should be a quickly, yet thoroughly, prepared outline from which the teacher can work.

The lesson plan has elements which are similar to those found in the unit plan: objectives, materials, activities (teacher and student), and method of evaluating results. Various formats for lesson plans are found in FIGURES 5-1 through 5-4.

A lesson plan provides sufficient guidance for a teacher of electrical occupations (see FIGURE 5-2). The organizational nature of the plan provides some useful cues to the teacher. First, the objectives of the lesson are written in performance terms, thus specifying the student learning outcome. Second, special materials and/or equipment are listed. Third, the activities of the teacher and student are specified with an estimated time frame for each activity. The teacher knows approximately how long each event will take. Use of real time

Lesson Plan Title:

Course:

_____

Objectives: (List performance desired of the student.
                  Should be concise.)

Materials: (Any materials and equipment necessary for the
                  completion of the lesson should be listed here.)

Activities:

TEACHER   STUDENT   TIME
                  (A description of what the teacher is going to do
                  and appropriate student activities are to be listed
                  here.)

Evaluation: (Means of evaluating student performance,
                  product development, or questions to be asked
                  to check student learning should be listed here.)

FIGURE 5-1

Lesson Plan Format

Lesson Plan Title: Accident Prevention: Grounding of Electrical
Tools and Equipment

Course: AC/DC Fundamentals and Principles

Objectives: The Student will be able to:

1. Explain the purpose of acceptable grounding
    devices for electrical handtools and equipment.
2. Identify electrical tools without proper grounding
    devices.

Materials: Samples of grounded electrical outlets
Three-prong male plugs
Adapters

Activities:

TEACHER	STUDENT	TIME
1. Roll, etc.		8:05-8:10
2. Introduction — Objective of film and expected student outcomes — grounding of high voltage		8:10-8:15
3. Show film		8:15-8:25
4. Discussion of film and show example of grounded and ungrounded tools	Compare: grounded and ungrounded electrical devices	8:25-8:40
		8:40-8:50

Homework Assignment:

Inspect home and garage for unsafe electrical equipment	Make list of items found in home which are unsafe	8:50-8:55

Evaluation:
(Student will submit a list of 10 or more items found in the home
which are not grounded properly and a suggested remedy to
correct each unsafe item.)

FIGURE 5-2

Typical Lesson Plan for a Teacher of Electrical Occupations

Title of Course

Unit: Date:

Topic: Level:

Objectives: (List performances desired of the students)

Time	Teacher Activities and Procedures	Student Activities and Evaluation

Assignment or
Practice:

Materials and Equipment	Advance Preparation and References

NOTE: While the format for this lesson plan is somewhat different, the same basic elements are present, i.e., performance objectives, materials and supplies, activities (student and teacher), and evaluation.

FIGURE 5-3

Sample Lesson Plan Format

Lesson Plan Title

Grade level:

Unit:

Specific Objectives	*Proposed Evaluation*
1.	1.
2.	2.
	3.

Time	*Activities*	*Materials and Equipment*

Assignment:

NOTE: While the format for this lesson plan is somewhat different, the same basic elements are present, i.e., performance objectives, materials and supplies, activities (teacher and student), and evaluation.

FIGURE 5-4

Another Type of Lesson Plan Format

referents makes it easier for the teacher to keep track of the elapsed time. However, if the same lesson plan is used for more than one class period, time segments might be used to better advantage. Thus each time segment would be listed in minutes—for example, 5, 10-25 blocks of time. Fourth, the process or product which will be used to evaluate the student performance or to check the effectiveness of the lesson will be determined and specified. In the above example, the students would compile a list of electrical hazards which exist in the home due to improper grounding of tools and equipment.

Lesson plans should be written in a manner that the teacher will feel comfortable and yet specific enough to provide a guide for the day's activities. In addition to stating objectives, materials, activities with a time frame, and evaluating the method, the following are suggested as considerations when preparing lesson plans:

1. Provide a variety of activities in order to keep interest alive and to allow students to respond in more than one manner (report writing, oral response, performance).

2. Consider possible ways of arousing interest and motivating students.

3. Provide some linking mechanism with either the previous lesson or with future lessons.

4. If "discussion" is the activity for the teacher and students, specific questions which should be considered might be listed to ensure these topics will be discussed.

5. Provide sufficient and appropriate practice immediately following a skill demonstration. If a longer laboratory or clinical experience is provided, demonstration might be scheduled at the beginning in order to provide the necessary practice time.

6. Note the names of any particular student you wish to respond. Often there are some individuals who are overlooked, but who need to be brought into a discussion.

7. A lesson plan can have one or more objectives, and one objective might also be used for several daily lessons.

8. Evaluation of student performance can take many forms. The most suitable method should be determined. Paper-pencil test, performance tests, observation, and supervised laboratory activities can be utilized with the emphasis being placed on reinforcing correct learning responses.

9. Materials, equipment, or supplies which will be needed by the learner should also be noted.
10. An outline of the events is often more effective than a complete script, except when specific technical statements are to be given and the precise language is essential.

SUMMARY

The role of the teacher and student in today's occupational education programs has been discussed. This chapter has answered the following questions:

1. What is the role of the teacher in today's occupational program? Teachers have become learning managers and facilitators of learning rather than dispensers of knowledge. However, planning has been and will continue to be necessary prerequisites for successful teaching.
2. What is the student's role in the teaching/learning interaction? The student has become a more active participant in the teaching/learning environment. Goals, objectives, and performance indicators more clearly define for the student what he is expected to be able to do as a result of instruction; and, as a result, he must share the responsibility for learning.

Short- and long-range planning procedures for instruction have been presented. The unit planning process has a primary purpose of providing the whole picture for the student, as well as to assist the teacher in estimating the time necessary for students to meet desired competencies to a mastery level suitable for employment. Additionally, long-range planning assists the occupational teacher in the management of resources; materials and supplies can be ordered in advance and then be available when needed by the students.

Lesson plans are an expansion of the activities listed in a unit plan. They include specific measurable objectives, materials needed for the lesson, activities of the teacher as well as the student, and the evaluation method to be used in determining whether the students can perform as stated.

REVIEW QUESTIONS

1. What is the purpose of a unit plan, and how does this type planning benefit the teacher and the student?
2. What are some of the factors that should be considered when selecting student activities for a unit plan and lesson plan?
3. How has the role of the teacher of occupational programs changed in the past 10-15 years?
4. Most methods of instruction have positive and negative aspects. What are they for a competency-based instructional program?
5. What is the purpose of an occupational analysis and what effect should it have upon a unit plan?
6. What are the advantages and disadvantages of using lesson plans?
7. How will an individualized instruction program affect daily planning?
8. What internal and external factors influence the instructor's choice of learning activities?

STUDENT ACTIVITIES

1. Visit two occupational education teachers and ask them to define their role in the teaching/learning interaction.
2. Visit two competency-based occupational programs and ask those teachers to define their roles in the educational process.
3. Compare/contrast the responses of both groups.
4. Observe several occupational education teachers and list the different student activities used to facilitate the learning of the students (projects, experiments, reports, simulation-clinical experience, work experience).
5. Observe teaching methods used by one or two teachers over a period of one week to determine whether a variety of methods are used.
6. Secure sample lesson plans from several teachers of occupational education programs. Compare the elements of each plan and list the major headings and organization used.
7. Using catalogs, select appropriate audiovisual media for a teaching unit. Utilize at least three or more types of media, i.e., film, filmstrips, models, transparencies, or mockups.
8. Prepare and present a short demonstration unit to your classmates.

REFERENCES

Alcorn, Marvin D.; Kinder, James S.; and Schunert, Jim R. *Better Teaching in Secondary Schools*. New York: Holt, Rinehart & Winston, 1970.

Ashton-Warner, Sylvia. *Teacher*. New York: Simon & Schuster, 1963.

Coppen, Helen E. *Aids to Teaching and Learning*. Elmsford, New York: Pergamon Press, 1969.

Gerlach, Vernon S. and Ely, Donald P. *Teaching and Media: A Systematic Approach*. Englewood Cliffs, N. J.: Prentice-Hall, 1971.

Gold, Milton J. *Working to Learn: General Education Through Occupational Experiences*. Columbia University, 1951.

Hammonds, Carsie and Lamar, Carl F. *Teaching Vocations*. Danville, Ill.: Interstate, 1968.

Hyman, Ronald T. *Ways of Teaching*. 2d. ed. Philadelphia: Lippincott, 1974.

Kenneke, L.J.; Nystrom, D.C.; and Stadt, R.W. *Planning and Organizing Career Curricula: Articulated Education*. Indianapolis: Sams, 1973.

McKeachie, Wilbert J. *Teaching Tips*. Ann Arbor, Mich.: Wahr, 1960.

Mager, R. F. *Goal Analysis*. Belmont, Calif.: Fearson, 1972.

Silvius, G. Harold and Curry, Estell H. *Teaching Successfully in Industrial Education*. Bloomington, Ill.: McKnight and McKnight, 1967.

6

Facilitating Learning

The design of an instructional program for occupational education demands that the principles of learning be selectively applied. Occupational teachers must be aware of the relationship between desired performance and the selected learning activities designed to bring about this performance. This chapter is designed to assist the reader in:

- **Defining the types of performance associated with principles of learning.**
- **Specifying the type of performance required for various steps in performing a task.**
- **Designing appropriate activities for a lesson which will cause students to achieve various levels of thinking.**

In planning an effective instructional program, the occupational teacher must have two things: (1) a list of well-defined performance objectives, and (2) a time frame that needs to be filled. Traditionally, the performance objectives for occupational programs, whether at the orientation, exploration, or preparation level, have been determined through an analysis of the various elements of an occupation, content, instructional methods, and processes. The resulting list of tasks and subtasks provides the information necessary to write performance objectives. Once the list of performance objectives is complete, the occupational teacher must place these objectives in some sequential order and also into an appropriate time frame.

Sequencing of instructional units, tasks, and subtasks and also selecting the best teaching method has presented problems for the teacher and the learner for years. Traditionally, the focus for instructional events has been upon the course content, primarily because educational programs were teacher-oriented rather than student-centered.

The subject matter organization, certainly, cannot be totally ignored. Certain tasks or subtasks are prerequisite to the learning of new concepts. However, the primary concern in determining the sequence, events, and learning activities should be based on student needs and every attempt should be made to make the instruction meaningful. Educational planners must also take into account those tasks which must be learned before the student can proceed to the next task. Selection of teaching/learning activities must of necessity involve both course content and the performance of the individual.

In carefully formulated plans designed to bring about particular behavioral changes in students, the application of known principles of learning must be understood. Different types of learning require different sets of conditions. Factors that influence learning must also be recognized and learning experiences developed which will enhance and meet the special needs of different kinds of learning. Motivation, participation, application, repetition, confirmation, and organization are factors which do, in fact, influence the learning process.

Identification of the varieties of learning and the conditions under which the learning is to take place obviously has some definite implications for occupational educators. In some instances, primary emphasis will need to be placed on two or three types of learning while de-emphasizing others. For instance, repetition is important for establishing the motor chains involved in chasing threads on an engine lathe. But, problem-solving learning may need only to be accomplished one time. A learner who has discovered a new rule or principle can usually remember it later without having to practice its discovery.

Gagne has described eight types of learning.[1] These types of learning appear to be especially appropriate for occupational educa-

---

[1]From *The Conditions of Learning*, Second Edition, by Robert M. Gagne. Copyright © 1965, 1970 by Holt, Rinehart and Winston, Inc. Adapted by permission of Holt, Rinehart and Winston.

tors. A brief review of the eight learning types is found in the next section of this chapter.

SIGNAL LEARNING

This type of learning involves making a precise response to a precise stimulus. The conditions for establishment of this form of learning seem fairly clear. There must be nearly simultaneous presentation of two forms of stimulation: (1) the stimulus producing a generalized reaction of the sort one is interested in establishing, and (2) the stimulus providing the signal.

Three factors play an important role in learning simple responses. These are participation, confirmation, and repetition. The number of times this pairing of stimuli must occur is a question that has no single answer. However, associations and connections are made by repeated exposure to the response-provoking stimuli with immediate confirmation of the active response.

This type of learning generally produces an involuntary reaction. For example, a young child soon learns that "hot" will probably produce pain if the youngster persists in his action. Similarly, military training is often directed toward eliciting involuntary responses upon command.

STIMULUS-RESPONSE LEARNING

This kind of learning involves making very precise movements of the skeletal muscles in response to very specific stimuli or combinations of stimuli. In the human being, we often speak of "voluntary responses" as constituting observed output. In other words, this kind of learning makes it possible for an individual to perform an action when he or she wishes.

Learning of this type, much like signal learning, requires participation, repetition, and confirmation. Repeated exposure to the response-provoking stimuli and participation by the learner with confirmation of correct responses will enable each learner to develop repetitive skills which are often necessary for many occupational areas. For example, the learning of new vocabulary words, which is an integral part of medical transcription, requires repeated vocal or written responding. Simply looking at the list of words is not enough.

Similarly, selection of the appropriate tool by the dental assistant requires response to a verbal stimuli.

CHAINING

In brief terms, chaining is a matter of connecting together in a sequence two (or more) previously learned stimulus-responses. The conditions for chaining are essentially the same as for stimulus-response learning; namely, participation, confirmation, and repetition. Chaining could be divided into two logical categories: (1) *motor chaining*, which is the linkage of a series of motor responses, and (2) *verbal chaining*, which is very similar, but occurs when a sequence or list of words is linked together by association.

The purpose of motor chaining is to carry out a sequence of motor responses which lead to a completed task or operation. With the help of external directions or prompting, the separate motions are performed in close sequence. The machinist, for example, while chasing threads on an engine lathe, must manipulate the various parts of the lathe in close sequence if the operation is to be completed successfully. Repetitions bring about progressively smoother performance by establishing a stimulus-response link between successive motions. Each motion provides confirmation of the motion which precedes it, and also serves as the stimulus for the motion which follows.

If the first motion is incorrect, or incomplete, then succeeding motions cannot be carried out. As a result, successful completion of the total chain is impossible. For example, the starting of many modern automobiles is dependent upon certain safety precautions, i.e., fastening of seat belts, etc. Thus, a key placed in the ignition all the way and turned without starting the automobile will provide the stimulus to fasten seat belts. Of course, the loud buzzer which one also hears tends to intensify the stimulus. Once this motion is completed, it will provide the stimulus for other motions which would complete the chain. Each separate move becomes the mediating link between each move that comes before and after it. Once the connecting linkages have been made, prompting, from verbal directions or a list of performance steps, is no longer needed.

The forming of each chain requires participation by the learner. It is highly unlikely that a student would learn to measure blood pressure by watching someone demonstrate the procedure or by being given a description of the process. While demonstrations and verbal cues are important at the initial phase of training, the learner must develop the feel for right motions through repetition to assure an acceptable level of competence.

VERBAL ASSOCIATION

The learning of verbal chains requires conditions which are similar to those of motor chains. First, the learner is dependent upon previous learning which can be associated with the external cues which will be used to evoke the verbal chain. Second, a connecting stimulus response must have been learned which will allow the learner to associate the new cue with the response sought. Third, a "coding connection" must be available. The experience and educational background of each individual will determine the availability of codes which may be selected in order to make the connection between the new stimulus and previously learned information. Fourth, the chain must be sequentially ordered, so that continuity and confirmation is achieved with each repetition.

As the chains are put together and practiced, the words become mediating links which prompt succeeding words. In many instances, the learner creates mnemonic devices which can be used to aid in the memory of certain verbal chains. In electronics, for example, many rhymes have been developed to prompt the recall of the color code on carbon resistors.

As the chain is established, the external cues usually lose their importance. The electronics technician working with carbon resistors and determining their values will soon stop using the rhymes. Well established verbal chains and prompting devices are often recalled many years after the initial learning.

In many cases, there are no external cues. Verbal chains are established primarily through repetition. The formula for determining the circumference of a circle, Πd, which is frequently used by the sheet metalworker, is an example of the verbal chain. The value of Π must be recalled, which, in turn, is multiplied by the diameter of the circle. Repeated application of this formula will establish the verbal chain. Multiplication tables are a further example of this kind of learning. Many hours are needed to commit to memory the multiplication tables. It is evident that repetition, confirmation, and participation are important if verbal chains are to be learned.

When motor and verbal chains are combined, complex procedures are developed. One need only to review the landing procedures of today's aircraft to realize the complexities of some motor and verbal chains. In such cases, because of the complexities, external prompts are utilized to ensure the safety of all persons on the flight. In repairing a carburetor, external prompts are necessary in the initial learning phase; but, as the chain becomes well established, the auto mechanic will be able to accomplish this task without the use of step-by-step directions.

Practice and repetition are important when it comes to learning and remembering a chain. Forgetting can become something of a problem with chains; while motor chains seem to be retained fairly easily over long periods of time, verbal chains are easily forgotten if interference takes place or if the chain is broken.

DISCRIMINATION

Discrimination learning involves distinguishing one stimulus from another. Simple discrimination may involve determining the manufacturer of certain automobiles, or distinguishing a square wave from a sine wave on an oscilloscope. This type of learning involves learning not only what an object is but also what it is not. Therefore, practice which provides a contrast between the correct and incorrect stimuli must be a part of the learning experiences of the student. Initial practice in discrimination must present stimuli in such a manner that emphasis is placed on their distinctiveness. For example, the cabinetmaker will be faced with the problem of selecting suitable materials for cabinets. A part of such a training program will be wood identification. Practice must be provided which will allow the individual to identify correct and incorrect materials. The initial experiences should involve wood samples which are distinctive, for example, oak and walnut. Continued and successful experiences will allow the learner to discriminate between western maple and alder. In many ways, discrimination is similar to specific responding in that participation, confirmation, and repetition are required to develop this type of learning.

The learner is frequently called upon to make discriminations. This often takes place on an informal basis. For example, students tend to compare the quality of work completed in a shop or laboratory.

On a formal basis, a student may be given a sample weld in a metals class and asked to compare that sample with the standard. If the learner is to learn to discriminate among various types of wood screws, various samples, pictures, or drawings of wood screws must be provided and learning experiences designed which require the learner to compare and contrast the items. Discrimination learning experiences should begin with the easiest, and gradually move to more subtle instances.

As with signal and chain learning, correct discriminations must be reinforced and the efforts of the teacher directed toward insuring that errors are as unlikely as the circumstances permit. Practice does not appear to strengthen discriminations involved in the task. Further, the ease or difficulty of learning does not appear to affect the recall of such learning. This type of learning is subject to forgetting; therefore, periodic practice should be included in the teaching/learning plan to prevent learning loss.

CONCEPT LEARNING

Concept learning is a process whereby the learner makes a response that identifies and categorizes an entire class of objects or events. The student must make generalizations about a whole class of phenomena that may differ from each other in outside appearance. For example, oak, walnut, and beech lumber and trees are outwardly very different; yet, all would fall into the category labeled deciduous trees. In classifying the trees into one category, the learner must respond to a wide range of properties, such as color, shape, density, and grain structure. A student deals with concepts when he or she becomes concerned about generalizations, relationships, and similarities among objects or events.

Particularly important parts of concept learning are organization, confirmation, and application. While concept learning can be acquired through trial and error, this process is not viewed to be a particularly effective method. If the prerequisites for concept formation have been fulfilled, i.e.: identification, motor and verbal chains, and discrimination, it is relatively easy for the student to learn the concept.

Concept learning is not necessarily a verbal matter; but, at the same time the learner is exposed to stimuli that are representative samples of a particular class, verbal guidance is necessary to assist the individuals in recognizing similarities among objects or events with wide ranges of apparent differences. When possible, it is better to provide concrete examples, even though concepts can be learned through verbal means. When the class of objects or events has been described only by words, only words are learned—not a concept with real application.

Learning to classify objects, and thus establishing a concept, involves discovering the similarities and differences between the objects. When enough similarities are found, a grouping is possible; its characteristics are distinguishable from another grouping which represents a different cluster of similarities. These groupings in turn may be compared and put into larger systems.

In developing classifications systems, students may be asked to develop groups or categories based on function, size, effect, form, rank, or some other criterion. The resultant learning is concept development. For example, given a list of the following items, the student will be asked to classify the following:

ammeter	light bulb
dry cell	storage battery
generator	voltmeter

The student may respond by classifying these items as:

1. producer or user of electricity

producer of electricity	*user of electricity*
dry cell	ammeter
generator	light bulb
storage battery	voltmeter

2. containing an electromagnet or permanent magnet
3. containing movable parts
4. presence of chemical action in its operation

chemical action	*no chemical action*
dry cell	ammeter
storage battery	generator
	light bulb
	voltmeter

The first step in acquiring a concept has be initiated through the classification system developed by the student. Each group or classification could be added to or reclassified to form a new concept. For example, as the learner would compare additional items with the producers of electricity, noting the similarities and differences, concept development would reach a higher level. With reinforcement of the correctness of each response, the concept is learned—tentatively formed concepts are put to the test and found to be adequate. If the range of samples has been broad enough in developing each concept, the learner should be able to generalize any new electrical item and classify it according to previously defined categories. Concept learning probably will not require repetition if prerequisite learning has been adequate.

RULE USING

For each individual, rule using or the application of principles constitutes the bulk of what is learned. In both formal and in day-to-day living, conditions are nearly the same. In its simplest form, rule using is the chaining of two or more concepts to form a meaningful relationship. An example of a very elementary principle is the simple statement that "like charges repel." Here, several concepts such as atomic structure, electron, proton, and charges are linked together. Therefore, when a principle is to be learned, the individual must first know and understand the concepts to be linked. The chain then represents the relationship between concepts.

Once the concepts have been learned, the process of chaining or learning a principle involves recall of all concepts which make up the rule. The resultant principle must be verbalized. The student should be encouraged to state the rule in his or her own words and to provide practical examples of the principle at work. The learning manager should also ensure that conceptual chains rather than verbal chains have been established. Confirmation of the rule by application is a very important step in this type of learning.

The previously cited example of a rule, "likes repel," could also be demonstrated through the use of electronic equipment or by using bar magnets.

The more elementary rules can be learned rather quickly and in many cases entirely from a verbal statement. Adults can often learn a new principle from a verbal statement of the principle. However, highly complex principles, such as Ohm's law or Newton's laws of motion, must be confirmed through concrete examples which may include some actual practice in applying the principle in a shop or laboratory setting.

The learning of a rule generally does not need to be repeated. Once learned, principles are highly resistant to forgetting. The rule learning usually takes place on a single occasion. However, practice may be necessary to develop skill in using the rule. For example, the student nurse may learn the methods for computing dosages of medication for patients, but will need to solve a series of problems before he or she becomes skilled in using the rule. Similarly, the electronics technician may learn Ohm's law; but, experience in computing the values of current, resistance, and voltage in a given series of circuits will be very helpful.

PROBLEM SOLVING

Problem solving occurs when the individual combines previously learned rules to form a higher-order rule. Learning of this type requires the learner to utilize previously learned principles in arriving at an answer to a problem which has not been previously confronted by the individual. When the learner knows an answer in advance, thinking tends toward the lower mental processes of recall, discrimination, or chaining.

Problem solving is often equated with research. In such cases, solution of a problem involves the use of deductive, interpretive, observational, and statistical techniques in bringing about a solution to the problem. Further, problem solving is basically a self-directed activity which involves little or indirect guidance from others while, on the other hand, rule using requires considerable guidance. Successful problem solving is, however, dependent upon the availability of previously learned rules and principles. The conditions and processes required for problem solving are quite similar to those required for rule using. Several conditions must exist if the learning situation is to become a problem solving learning experience:

1. A problem is not a simple statement of "how to do it," but implies that several alternatives are present. If there are no alternatives, there is no problem.
2. Problems are always questions; not all questions are problems, however.

3. A puzzle is not synonymous for the word problem. Solutions to puzzles usually depend on trial and error.
4. A problem is usually a personal matter, the individual must furnish the guidance himself and determine how best to attack the problem. Further, that which is a problem to one individual may not be to another.

What is true regarding a statement of a problem—that it is a personal matter—is also true of the kind of performance required to bring about a successful solution to the problem. The learner must organize and use various combinations of previously learned rules and principles. The efficiency developed in bringing about solutions to problems is an indication of the organizational ability of the individual.

It should also be noted that formalized steps in problem solving, like steps in a motor or verbal chain, are detrimental to this type of learning. One must recognize that there is no single scientific method; there are scientific *methods*. Problem solving does, however, depend upon previously learned strategies and techniques.

As the learner sets out to solve a problem, tentative solutions are arrived at and confirmation of the adequacy of the solution must be tested through trial application. Once tested and found to be adequate, the learner has developed a higher-order principle. Confirmation is usually accomplished by the individual rather than from an outside source. For example, an electronics technician troubleshooting a piece of equipment will confirm his or her actions when the circuit or equipment is placed in operation. Simply put, if it works, the solution to the problem is adequate.

The time needed to arrive at a solution is dependent upon the conditions present at the time the student engages in learning activities which require problem-solving abilities. The learning manager must carefully analyze the learning task and determine whether guidance is necessary. The learner must be able to recall the relevant rules or principles which will bring about a solution to the problem, and unless some verbal instructions are provided, the learner may spend an excessive amount of time solving a simple problem. It should also be noted that problem solving faced on the job is never solved in a vacuum. Most workers frequently consult and discuss various problems with other workers. Therefore, if the training situation is to be both practical and efficient, sufficient verbal guidance should be provided. This guidance may be provided in the form of a general goal for the learner which will enable the learner to discover the higher-order rule without specific help. There is evidence which indicates that self-discovery and self-direction in the problem-solving process enhances learning. Further, once learned, the solution can be readily remembered and applied to a wider range of similar problems.

SUMMARY

The occupational teacher who carefully analyzes the learning which is to take place in the shop or laboratory will discover that each type of learning requires a different set of conditions. The intent and purpose of the foregoing discussion is to establish the principle that different types of learning require different learning and teaching strategies. Further, each type of learning is dependent upon prior learning. For example, rule using is dependent upon concept development and problem solving is dependent upon rules and principles.

Good instructional design requires a careful analysis of the course content to determine the type of learning involved at various stages of the student's development. It should also be recognized that each learning type requires a previously learned capability on which to build. The resultant learning then produces a different type of performance, with each type of learning beginning and ending at a different level in the learning hierarchy (TABLE 6-1).

Each type of learning also requires different teaching strategies. For example, chaining requires a great deal of repetition, while learning of rules or principles requires verbal communication and guidance, and repetition has little effect upon the detention of the rule (TABLE 6-2). The learning involved in each of the student's courses is to learn in the most efficient and effective manner.

REVIEW QUESTIONS

1. How will the variety of learning types affect the amount of time allocated for learning?
2. How can verbal chains be maintained?
3. What kind of teaching tactic would or should be used when discrimination learning is involved?

TABLE 6-1

SUMMARY OF LEARNED PERFORMANCE

Learning Type	Definition	Examples	Capabilities
Signal	Making a precise response to a precise stimuli	A shout of "HOT" causes removing hand from an object	
Stimulus-response	Precise movements to specific stimuli	Learner repeats name of dental tool when handed instrument	Connections, identification
Motor chaining	Connecting two or more previously learned stimulus-responses together	Chasing threads on an engine lathe (motor)	Sequence of motions
Verbal association	Verbal responses which are linked to the previous word and the subsequent word	Listing from memory the steps involved in taking blood pressure	Verbal association and sequence
Discrimination	Distinguishing one stimuli from another	Distinguishing between different types of wood screws	Identifications and discrimination
Concept	Making a generalization about a whole class of objects or events	Sorting items into specific categories or reclassifying items into new categories	Discrimination and association
Rule using	The chaining of concepts to form meaningful relationships	Adjusting an automobile carburetor air/fuel ratio at high altitude	Concepts, discriminations, and chaining
Problem solving	Combining previously learned rules to form a higher-order rule	Diagnosis of a malfunctioning automobile	Concepts, rules, and associations

4. Learning the nomenclature for a specific piece of equipment involves what type of learning?
5. Which types of learning require considerable practice by the learner?
6. Which of the learning types are most resistant to forgetting?
7. Which learning type comprises the majority of what is learned in everyday living?
8. In view of the fact that there are several levels of learning, what effect will this have on the selection of learning activities for the student?

STUDENT ACTIVITIES

1. Review a task analysis for your occupational area and state the type of learning involved in ten of the tasks.
2. Select twenty performance objectives from a course of study related to your occupational area and determine the learning type involved and specify a learning activity for each objective.
3. Describe the prerequisites for rule using and problem solving.
4. Visit a shop or job-simulation laboratory and observe students engaged in the various activities. For each activity observed, specify the learning type which predominates and list the prerequisite learning.
5. Complete a case study of one youngster who is enrolled in an occupational program. Determine how often and to what extent the learner engages in problem solving.

REFERENCES

Bruner, J.S. *The Process of Education*. Cambridge, Mass.: Harvard University Press, 1965.

———. *Toward a Theory of Instruction*. Cambridge, Mass.: Harvard University Press, 1966.

Davies, I.K. "Structure and Strategy—Instructional Decision-making," *Royal Air Force Education Bulletin*. 6, 1969.

Gagne, R.M. *The Conditions of Learning*. 2d ed. New York: Holt, Rinehart and Winston, 1970.

———. "The Analysis of Instructional Objectives for the Design of Instruction." In R. Glasser (Ed.) *Teaching Machines and Programmed Learning, II*. Washington, D.C.: National Education Association, 21-65, 1965.

TABLE 6-2

SUMMARY OF FACILITATING CONDITIONS

Learning Type	Learning Activities	Resistance to Forgetting	Effect of Practice
Signal	Generally not utilized in most teaching/learning situations		
Stimulus-response	1. Repeated exposure to response-provoking stimuli — confirmation of correctness of response 2. Continuous practice	Marked resistance	Very important
Motor chaining	1. Present external cues 2. Provide a number of trials, to smooth out rough spots	Marked resistance	Important
Verbal association	1. Present a sequence of external cues 2. Teach mnemonic devices 3. Provide check lists, etc., to follow	Little resistance	Important
Discrimination	1. Provide items that are clearly different at initial phase 2. Present stimuli which are similar, but different	Little resistance	Little importance

	3. Present very similar items which require measurement as samples for comparison		
Concepts	1. Present a variety of stimuli and force students to make generalizations about all stimuli 2. Make stimuli and response as distinctive as possible 3. Confirm successful application	Marked resistance	Little importance
Rule using	1. Have student restate rules in their own words 2. Provide laboratory experiences which will enable students to confirm previously learned rules	Marked resistance	Important
Problem solving	1. Provide a problem to be solved 2. Allow students to plan their own method of solving the problem 3. Have students list several tentative solutions to problems	Marked resistance	Important

Leavett, H.J. and Scholsberg, H. "The Retention of Verbal and Motor Skills," *Journal of Experimental Psychology*, 3, 404-17. 1944.

Shriver, E.L. *Determining Training Requirements for Electronic Systems Maintenance.* Alexandria, Virginia: HUMRRO Technical Report, 1960.

Performance-Based Instruction

Regardless of the occupational program, each teacher, administrator, board member, and parent should focus attention on the student and his or her special needs. The primary educational concern should be that of making sure each learner possesses the competencies required for success in her or his next endeavor. Performance-based instruction is concerned with the competencies needed by each individual, as he or she enters the selected career field. Performance-based instruction also emphasizes learning activities which simulate on-the-job performance.

Upon completion of this chapter, the reader will be able to:

- Describe the nature and need for performance-based instruction in occupational programs.
- List the advantages and disadvantages of performance-based instruction.
- Describe the key elements of a performance-based instructional program.
- Describe techniques for revising present occupational programs to assure a performance-based approach.

INTRODUCTION

American education, today more than ever before, is being called upon to provide each person leaving our schools with skills which will enable that person to assume a productive role in society.

The decade of the 1960's brought about a changing emphasis in education in the United States. The impact of unfilled jobs which require technical skills and knowledges and the realization that high school graduates were leaving our school systems without salable skills forced a reevaluation of the total educational system. Furthermore, there has been a change in the composition of the nation's work force. The United States, at one time a nation of blue collar and agricultural workers, now has a work force composed predominantly of white collar and service employees. The shift in employment has brought about new training requirements. Technological advances have brought about the need for longer periods of training and for continuing education and updating of skills through each individual's working life. The changing nature of major occupations and employment distribution is diagrammed in FIGURE 7-1.

It can no longer be assumed that the completion of the requirements for a high school diploma, or in many cases a baccalaureate degree, prepares an individual to enter the work force. The complexities of skills required by today's labor force demand that some assurance of competence be given to both the learner and the employer.

The United States and other highly developed technological societies cannot operate on the assumption that secondary and advanced education is only for the few, but must develop school systems which enable each individual to assume a productive role in society.

Many societies cannot provide the economic support for a major proportion of the student population to complete secondary or post-secondary education. These same societies are also able to utilize only a small number of highly educated people in the work force. When such conditions exist, considerable effort is devoted to rejecting a majority of students at various points in the educational system and to select the few who are to be given advanced educational opportunities.

The complexity of skills required by the work force in the United States mandates that all program completors at all educational levels possess the competencies necessary for entry into the world of work.

Education and training now represent the single largest expendi-

OCCUPATIONAL GROUP

EMPLOYMENT
(Millions)

1968	1980	
75.9	95.1	All occupations
10.3	15.5	Prof. & tech. workers
7.7	11.1	Service workers, except private household, e.g., hospital attendants, policemen, waitresses
12.8	17.3	Clerical workers
4.6	6.0	Sales workers
7.8	9.5	Managers, officials, proprietors
10.0	12.2	Craftsmen & foremen
1.7	2.0	Private household workers
14.0	15.4	Operatives, e.g., assemblers, truck drivers, bus drivers
3.6	3.5	Nonfarm laborers
3.5	2.6	Farm workers

Source: U.S. Manpower in the 1970's — Opportunity and Challenge
Washington, D.C.:   U.S. Department of Labor, 1970, p. 13.

FIGURE 7-1

The Changing Nature of Occupations

ture in the United States. While many economists (Bowman; Schultz) and politicians believe that it is doubtful whether society can afford the high costs and low productivity associated with instruction, there is increasing evidence that investment in the education of humans pays off at a greater rate than does capital investment.[1] Furthermore, those findings indicate that we cannot afford an economy typified by a scarcity of educational opportunities. The problem is no longer one of finding the few who can succeed. The basic problem is to determine how the majority of students, enrolled in each occupational program,

[1] J.J. Bowman, "The New Economics of Education," *International Journal of Educational Sciences* 1 (1966): 29-46.

can learn the skills and subject matter regarded as essential for that occupation. Schools must strive to assure all students successful learning experiences.

Furthermore, the consequences of student success in learning tasks will have a profound effect upon the willingness of each individual to continue learning throughout life. It has become necessary for a larger segment of the work force to reenter the educational arena. As new technologies are developed, new skills are needed. Education and training can involve workers in the educational process for a few hours to several weeks. If learning is regarded as an activity which was previously met with little success and should consequently be avoided, then little can be done to change this concept later in life. In order to insure that learning can continue throughout life, each young person must be successful while in school and prior to entering the world of work.

There is little doubt that today's schools do provide successful learning experiences for some students, perhaps as many as one-third. However, we live in a society where as much as 80 percent of today's young people will enter the work force with educational experiences at less than the bachelor's level. It is essential that these students be provided instructional experiences which will ensure the development of the competencies which are required on the job. If the schools are to provide successful satisfying learning experiences, major changes must take place in the attitudes of students, teachers, and administrators. The focus of the teaching/learning process must be upon learning and the performance of the student, rather than on the activities of the instructor and the amount of time spent in the classroom. Further, the purposes of evaluation must be reexamined. Performance-based instruction implies a specified acceptable level of performance. This being the case, students can no longer continue to be judged or evaluated on the basis determined by measures of difference among groups.

The use of the normal curve as a method whereby grades are assigned has existed for so long that to use some other method appears to be a violation of a sacred trust. Many achievement tests have been designed to determine the differences among students. The assignment of grades is then based upon the normal curve, with the number of "A" grades being approximately equal to the number of failing grades. This method of assigning grades also predetermines that a large number of students will fall within the average or "C" grade range. Failure, frequently, is determined by the rank order of students, as classified in levels of performance, and grades are assigned according to the established levels.

A major premise of a performance-based instructional program is that most students can develop competencies in their occupational specialty. This implies that some specific criteria will be utilized in assessing these competencies and students will be evaluated against the criteria rather than by their standing within the group. Further, "individual differences" in learners are facts that can be demonstrated in many ways. This concept cannot be forgotten when developing performance-based instructional programs. The variations of individual differences must not determine the learning standards and achievement criteria. Such policies and practices are based upon the previously held belief that in any group of students, their achievement levels will be distributed in a normal distribution and that grades should be assigned in a similar manner. The basic task in performance-based education is to find strategies which will take individual differences into consideration and which will also promote the greatest development of the individual. This insures that each person will have the competencies required for their occupational specialty.

The theoretical basis for performance-based occupational education can be found in the mastery learning concepts as formulated by Bloom and Carroll.[2] Carroll states "that if students are normally distributed with respect to aptitude for some subjects and if all students are provided exactly the same instruction (same in terms of amount and quality of instruction and time available for learning), the end result will be a normal distribution on an appropriate measure of achievement. Conversely, if students are normally distributed with respect to aptitude but the kind and quality of instruction and the amount of time available for learning are made appropriate to the characteristics and needs of each student, the majority of students may be expected to achieve mastery of the subject."

Carroll identifies five variables which determine the strategy for mastery of a learning task: *aptitude, quality of instruction, ability to understand instruction, perseverance,* and *time allowed* for learning. "The concept of the learning task is defined to include the attainment of that degree of competence which will make transfer essentially as

[2] B.S. Bloom, ed., *Taxonomy of Educational Objectives.* Handbook 1: Cognitive Domain. New York: McKay, 1956; J.B. Carroll, "A Model of School Learning," *Teachers College Record* 64 (1963): 722-33.

automatic as demonstration of performance in the original setting." "Transfer," correctly viewed, is a term in a metalanguage which states the conditions under which particular learnings occur or manifest themselves. Thus, we say that "learning which occurred in situation A transfers to situation B," there being sufficient commonality between the two situations to elicit the learned performance in both.

Aptitude is defined as the amount of time required by the learner to attain mastery of a learning task. Implicit in this formulation is the assumption that given enough time, all students can conceivably attain mastery of a learning task. Support for this view is to be found in the grade norms for many standardized achievement tests. These norms demonstrate that selected criterion scores achieved by the top students at one grade level are achieved by the majority of students at a later grade level. Although most students reach mastery of each learning task, some achieve it much sooner than others.

Quality of instruction has been defined in terms of the degree to which the presentation, explanation, and ordering of the elements of the task to be learned approach the optimum for a given learner.

Ability to understand instruction may be defined as the ability of the learner to understand the nature of the task he is to learn and the procedure he is to follow in learning the task.

Perseverance is the time the learner is willing to spend in learning.

Time allowed for learning has been defined as the amount of time allowed by the school and the curriculum for particular subjects or learning tasks.

Performance-based instruction, therefore, must take into account the variables which affect mastery of the tasks required of each worker in her or his occupational specialty.

Occupational education has historically been concerned with the actual performance of each individual enrolled in the multitude of programs. A review of apprenticeship programs, clinical experiences of allied health students, and cooperative work experience programs associated with distributive education and other vocational specializations indicates these activities have been designed to ensure satisfactory performance of the tasks required of the particular occupation involved.

The learning experiences of students engaged in the various occupational programs described above have been guided in most cases by a "master" worker in the occupation. For example, an apprentice carpenter works with and under the direction of a journeyman carpenter. Similarly, the dental assistant will work under the direct supervision of another dental assistant, or with the dentist. This training is essentially a tutorial system. The "master" worker becomes the tutor and demonstrates to the learner the correct and efficient method of accomplishing each task. While the tutor-student relationship is a highly desirable method of instruction, the need for increasing the number of competent individuals in many career fields requires a less costly method, yet one which will permit the student to learn at his or her own pace, and a method which will ensure each student's performance is at a specified criterion level upon completion of the learning task.

Performance-based education would emphasize the expected knowledge, skills, understandings, and behaviors (terminal behavior) of students. Emphasis must be placed upon developing teaching strategies and learning experiences which will bring all or almost all students to the specified criterion level of performance. Such an approach to occupational education will require that regular group instruction be supplemented by using diagnostic procedures and alternative instructional methods and materials in such a way as to bring a large portion of students to a predetermined standard of achievement. In this approach, the goal is for most students to reach mastery levels of achievement within the regular term, semester, or calendar period in which the course is usually taught. Undoubtedly, some students will spend more time than others in reaching the desired performance. It is also anticipated that a portion of the students will be able to reach the desired performance level in a shorter period than required for a majority of the group.

In developing and implementing a performance-based occupational program, the following components must be included in the system:

1. Performance objectives which are specific enough to inform both the teacher and the student of the learning that is to take place.
2. A system for diagnosing the readiness of each individual for learning the specific performance objectives and provisions for more than one mode of learning.
3. An arrangement which provides each student with the amount of time needed to learn.
4. An evaluation system which will include the criterion level of performance that the teacher and the learner understand,

and both will be able to secure evidence of progress toward the specified criteria.

PERFORMANCE OBJECTIVES

Motivation for learning is established by setting standards of excellence toward which student and teacher energies are directed. Rather than a competitive system whereby grades are allocated upon the basis of rank order, it is conceivable that all students in a program could reach the A-B level upon reaching the mastery level in a performance-based program. It is important that students feel they are being judged in terms of level of performance rather than on a normal curve. Realistic performance standards must be developed for each performance-based occupational program. This approach to education will enable students to work with each other without being concerned about competition for grades at the end of the instructional period.

To develop the performance of students to the acceptable level or a standard, one must determine that level. The performance level must be carefully defined, and once engaged in the teaching/learning process, both the student and the teacher will be able to obtain evidence of attainment. There is probably no single procedure in education which is more important than writing learning objectives, or what more accurately could be described as prescribing the desired performance of the learner. Specification of objectives is a necessary means of informing both the teacher and learner of the desired performance. Both skills and knowledges, which are expected as a result of the specifications into evaluation procedures, help define what it is that the student should be able to do when he or she has completed the course.

The main emphasis of a performance-based educational system is to develop the competencies of each student. The basis for selecting and developing performance objectives for any occupational program is a detailed analysis of the tasks involved in the particular occupation being studied. Some tasks will be cognitive in nature and others will require the development of physical skills. Regardless of the nature of the tasks, it is necessary to determine the ingredients and characteristics of the topic or job the student must be able to perform. When these characteristics are known, training needs can be established and performance objectives written. The process of conducting a task analysis of the various occupations is beyond the scope of this text; however, the learner should be aware that performance objectives are, in fact, derived from identified competencies of workers in the field. Once the task analysis has been completed and those parts of the task which require formal training have been identified, performance objectives can be written.

Professional occupational educators have always been concerned with student performance. Their interest in performance objectives does not represent a concern for today's interest in accountability, but represents a genuine desire to develop each student's potential to the maximum.

CHARACTERISTICS OF PERFORMANCE OBJECTIVES

The process of writing performance objectives has been given considerable attention by educators for the past decade. A review of the works of such authors as Mager, Bloom, and Gronalund will provide the reader with the specifics of writing performance objectives. However, a brief review of the characteristics of well-formulated performance objectives is in order. *First*, they are stated in precise language and clearly define the desired behavior. *Second*, observable and measurable proficiency levels for this behavior are established. In so doing, it may be either necessary or desirable to describe the behavior in some detail, using qualifying phrases or statements of behavior that describe conditions under which the terminal behavior will be observed, tested, or judged. *Third*, performance objectives may also describe procedures for determining whether the students can perform at an established level of proficiency.

The occupational educator must have this information if logical decisions regarding content, sequence method, and media are to be made. The information and standards of performance established in performance objectives serve as the basis for development of criterion tests which will be used to assess the performance of students as well as the program itself. If procedures are included for determining whether levels of proficiency have been obtained, they can vary from observation by a skilled observer to measurement by precise instruments.

WRITING PERFORMANCE OBJECTIVES

The task of writing clear, concise performance objectives is not an easy one. A primary consideration in accomplishing this task is the learner. Each student must have access to the information and all performance objectives must be written in a manner that there is no doubt about who is to perform—the *student*. Too often, either objectives are not made known to the student or they are written in a manner that it is unclear as to who the performer will be. If learning is to be efficient, and rewarding, the learner must know what is expected of her or him. Motivation of the student, and the quality of performance, is directly related to knowing what is to be done and to knowing how well it has been done upon completion. Therefore, when writing performance objectives, it must be clearly evident to the reader that the student is to be the performer.

TASK DESCRIPTION

A second component of a well-written performance objective is the behavior required of the student. It is important to describe the behavior required in clear precise terms which are observable and measurable. To say a student will be expected to "understand" or "appreciate" something at the end of instruction is an unsatisfactory basis for determining mastery of a task or subject. Performance must be described as the visible actions of the students. Evaluation can then be accomplished by observing the behavior, or by evaluating the product of such behavior. Some words commonly used in writing objectives are vague and ambiguous. This leaves these statements open to many interpretations, whereas more precise terms tell the learner what is expected. Some of the commonly used words which tend to create ambiguity and are open to many interpretations are:

know	enjoy	apply
understand	believe	master
appreciate	perceive	become
interpret	comprehend	want
grasp	learn	

Other verbs which could be accepted as evidence of satisfactory performance are much more descriptive of behavior. A partial list of these words is included to provide an example:

write	compare	load	replace
recite	contract	measure	describe
identify	compute	select	order
construct	diagram	remove	name

These verbs are less ambiguous because they are subject to fewer interpretations by the learner and the instructor. The above list represents only a small sample of the words which could be used to describe performance which can be observed and measured. The verb used in each performance objective statement should clearly indicate what the learner is to do. Furthermore, there should be agreement among observers of learner behavior on whether the objective has been met.

CONDITIONS

In addition to a precise statement of what the student is to be able to do, conditions under which the performance will occur must also be described. Generally, a teacher has a very clear idea of the conditions under which the student is to perform at the time of assessment. These conditions are usually dictated by the job itself and to a great extent has been determined through the task analysis. It has been an underlying principle for occupational education that the performance required of students in the various job-simulation laboratories be as realistic as possible to ensure transfer of competency gained through instruction to the job situation.

Tools and materials needed to accomplish the objective must be specified. Special aids, such as manufacturers' manuals, slide rules, calculators, and charts should be listed. If occupational teaching is to prepare students for job-like situations, information and reference materials found on the job must be available.

In attempting to simulate the work environment in job-simulation laboratories, a variety of experiences must be available to the student. Therefore, when writing objectives, the range of conditions under which students' performance will be tested must be stated. This does not mean that all possible conditions need be in-

cluded; but, it may be necessary to specify particularly difficult physical demands of the job, if the student is to be prepared to accomplish
the task on the job.

Some reasonable limitation must be set on the range of knowledge the student is expected to demonstrate. By limiting the expected
performance to specific situations, the student would not be required
to be knowledgable of all applications. For instance, would the
learner be required to operate all types of calculators or only a Texas
Instrument, Model 51A? Would the learner be required to measure
any frequency, using an oscilloscope, or only to measure frequencies
in the audible range? In summary, the learner must perform skills
under realistic on-the-job conditions. Performance objectives must
require realistic job-like conditions to assure a reasonable degree of
transfer from the job-simulation laboratory to the job itself.

PERFORMANCE STANDARDS

A clear objective must also include a statement of the standards
expected of the learner. Two standards, which taken together are a
measure of efficiency of performance, are accuracy and time. Accuracy is generally indicated in terms of the percentage or number of
problems which must be answered correctly, the percentage or score
to be obtained on a measurement instrument, or the tolerances within
which the learner must work. Again, the standards specified in performance objectives must reflect the realities of the work situation for
which the student is preparing. For example, there are some instances
where performance must be absolutely error-free because of the
danger to personal safety, or when an error could cause serious damage to the equipment being used. In cases where errors in performance
are not critical, a lesser percentage of correct responses could be used
as the standard. For example, being able to name the parts of an
automobile brake system is less critical than being able to correctly
assemble the brake unit. Similarly, naming the parts of a sphyg-
momanometer is less critical than accurately taking and recording the
blood pressure of a patient.

As performance objectives are developed for occupational programs, one additional standard must be considered. The speed at
which the task is to be performed is extremely important. If a learner
cannot perform a specified task within a time limit similar to most
new entrants in the occupation, the possibility for employment or

continued employment will be severely limited. Time is an important element on the job, and this standard should be reflected in performance objectives where this standard is appropriate. Time standards are also an indication of the degree of mastery developed by the learner. Some tasks can be allocated lenient time limits, other tasks require more rigid time criteria. The acceptable time frame may be imposed by the requirements of the job, safety factors, and economic concerns. A complete performance objective must clearly state the realistically acceptable performance, both in quality and performance time.

The following are sample performance objectives which meet the criteria established above:

Allied Health Careers

Upon completion of this lesson, the student will be able to:

1. Calculate and perform a white blood count with 95-percent accuracy within 20 minutes.
2. Make an open surgical bed, to the satisfaction of the supervisor, within 5 minutes.

Business and Office

Upon completion of this lesson, the student will be able to:

1. Use a 10-key adding machine to solve 25 subtraction problems with 95-percent accuracy within 10 minutes.
2. Given a 10-key adding machine and a list of 20 addition problems, find the correct sums using the subtotal, nonadd and repeat keys within a 15-minute period of time with 100-percent accuracy.

Mechanical Drawing

Upon completion of this lesson, the student will be able to:

1. Given a set of 10 lines, measure the length of each line with an accuracy of $\pm$ 1/16 inch in a 5-minute period.
2. Draw the end and side view of a 3-inch diameter cylinder, including the appropriate center lines, within a 10-minute period of time.

Auto Mechanics

Upon completion of this lesson, the student will be able to:

1. Assemble a given set of eight pistons to their individual rods in 25 minutes, according to the manufacturer's specifications.
2. Perform a compression test on a four-cylinder engine and check and interpret readings in a 25-minute period.

Electronics

Upon completion of this lesson, the student will be able to:

1. Calibrate a VTVM and measure AC voltage of 5 test points in a given electronic circuit with 95-percent accuracy and within a 20-minute period.
2. Determine the resistive color value of 15 carbon resistors within a 10-minute period.

Detailed performance objectives like those listed above simplify the instructional planner's task of determining the types of learning involved and conditions necessary for this learning to take place. For example, if the objective is to take a patient's blood pressure, a motor/verbal chain must be learned. If the objective is to match the appropriate names with their respective dental tools, discrimination learning is involved. Ringing up items on a cash register calls for rule using, as well as motor chaining. Isolation and repair of a malfunctioning television involves rule using and problem solving.

TERMINAL AND PERFORMANCE OBJECTIVES

The job tasks or competencies possessed by the entry-level worker are the focus for developing terminal objectives. In many cases, several intermediate objectives are required if the learning manager is to certify the competence of the learner for a particular task. A hierarchy ranging from general duties to very specific detailed tasks can be developed as the components of a job are analyzed. Similarly, as the curriculum developer translates these components into objectives, a hierarchy of objectives is formed. Identified tasks can be equated to rather general objectives, while performance objectives would be equated to the task details. For example, the task of taking a chest x-ray would convert to a general course objective as a statement of competence. However, the competence of the learner would be determined by observing the learner as he or she follows the proper steps for performing the task. Therefore, sub-objectives or specific performance objectives are required, since these objectives have a direct relationship to the development of the specific competencies of an occupation.

Affective objectives, on the other hand, are concerned with attitudes and emotions. *Psychomotor objectives* describe muscular and motor skills. While each occupational education instructor will be concerned primarily with cognative and psychomotor objectives, affective objectives should not be overlooked. Feelings and emotions become internalized. "Attitudes" are developed by each learner over a period of time, and represent a very real component of any job or occupation. The "professional" attitude developed by allied health personnel, for example, is not taught in a single course, but is made a part of all learning experiences. Similarly, attitudes toward safety and group responsibility must be developed throughout a course or program. Affective objectives are difficult for many teachers to write. However, these objectives must reflect some observable behavior of students. Where cognative and psychomotor objectives can be measured by a written test or a product of behavior, the affective performance is usually determined by observation.

The development of performance objectives is an important and essential aspect of performance-based education. Instruction is basically the management of the learning environment in a manner that will bring about the greatest amount of learning in the shortest possible time. Clearly stated performance objectives complete with specified acceptable standards of performance are the first step toward establishing a sound performance-based program.

PERFORMANCE-BASED INSTRUCTION, OPERATING PROCEDURES

Performance-based education consists of several desirable components which will assist the learner to exit the many occupational programs with salable skills or with upgraded skills which will enable him or her to enter and to advance in the chosen career field.

First, each course or program will be divided into small units of learning. These units may correspond to the identified competencies, a chapter in the textbook, or a particular unit of time. As the student proceeds with the learning tasks, diagnostic progress tests will be utilized to determine mastery of the unit or achievement of specified competence. If competence is not reached, the alternative instructional methods may be prescribed. Formative evaluation tests tend to pace learning and to motivate learners.

Further, as the group progresses through each unit, the teacher will find it necessary to adjust the learning time for some students. There will be students who need additional time to complete the required tasks, while some students will achieve competence in a shorter period of time than that which was initially allotted for the unit.

Frequent use of progress tests will increase motivation and can improve achievement to a small degree. If the student can be motivated to spend additional time at the learning task, further gains can be expected. Generally speaking, if students are provided with alternative methods of learning, they then become willing to work on those objectives which are causing difficulties. This may require students to work in small groups to help each other overcome their weaknesses. Tutorial assistance could be provided external to or within the job-simulation laboratory. For example, the slower learner may be teamed with a student who shows greater aptitude. Such a method generally proves beneficial to both students. Other learning resources should also be prescribed for students. Alternate textbooks may be utilized. Audiovisual materials may be used to supplement the textbooks. Audio tapes, which will correspond with each job sheet, assignment sheet, or learning activity should be utilized, when it would aid in the learning process. It should be noted that teacher-produced audio tapes are quite effective.

Provision for a great variety of instructional methods and procedures will suggest to the student that there is more than one way of learning.

PROBLEMS OF ESTABLISHING A PROGRAM

The most desirable outcome for any performance-based occupational program is learners who have developed the competence necessary for entry or advanced levels of employment. Establishing and operating such a program cannot be established without encountering some problems. Each occupational educator needs to recognize that large group instruction will be more difficult. While such a program is directed toward the individual needs of each person entering the learning environment, large group instruction must be available to the students as they need it. In fact, the development of some affective objectives may very well dictate large group instruction.

Tutorial assistance which might become a vital part of performance-based instruction may be very costly and, in many cases, impossible to provide. Experiences such as those found on the job could be utilized in lieu of special tutorial assistance.

Additional instructional materials may also pose a problem. These include alternative textbooks, workbooks, and programmed instruction materials. Appropriate audiovisual materials also present a few problems for the learning manager of a performance-based instructional program, primarily because such materials often are unavailable or are too costly. However, teacher-made audio tapes will enable students to review the instruction received in demonstrations, short lectures, etc. Audio tapes may also provide concurrent verbal instructions for students engaged in the various laboratory activities. Audio tapes can also be very effectively utilized where a timed sequence of events is to take place. For example, in the process of developing color film, prints must be made in total darkness. By using an audio tape, with carefully timed instructions, the learner may successfully accomplish this task.

Perhaps one of the foremost barriers to the establishment of a performance-based occupational program is the amount of time which has been allocated for instruction. School administrators are often faced with the problem of allocation of specific amounts of time for each class. In many cases, the time frame is established by law, or at the post-secondary level, by accrediting agencies. However, most educational planners are aware of these problems and a variety of techniques have been tried to overcome the scheduling problem, i.e.: modular scheduling, open-entry/open-exit programs, individualized instruction packages, etc. All such strategies have been directed toward developing the competence of each individual enrolled in occupational programs.

SUMMARY

Performance-based instruction is concerned with the competencies developed by each person enrolled in the occupational program. A primary concern is the insurance that upon completion of each occupational program, the student will have the necessary skills and knowledges which will ensure employability. This will include writing performance objectives for each identified competency. Performance-based instruction also includes objectives written in the cognative, psychomotor, and affective domains. The objectives written will determine the teaching methods which should be available to all students. This will include large group instruction, programmed learning, tutorial, and various audiovisual media presentations. Regardless of the instructional techniques utilized, the success of the program will be determined by the competencies developed by each student.

REVIEW QUESTIONS

1. What social conditions caused Americans to examine the intent and purpose of education in the 1960's?
2. Which occupational groups declined in total numbers of workers in the past decade?
3. What are the implications for training needs in the future?
4. How has the expenditure of tax funds affected the educational systems in America?
5. How has the traditional-normal course-method of grading affected the distribution or assignment of grades?
6. What are the five variables which determine the strategy for mastery learning?
7. What are the three characteristics of a well-written performance objective?
8. How do terminal objectives and performance objectives differ?
9. What are the advantages of performance-based occupational programs as contrasted to traditional programs?
10. What obstacles must the teacher overcome in developing performance-based instruction?

STUDENT ACTIVITIES

1. Interview three students who are graduates of an occupational program to determine their need for additional training on the job.
2. Survey teachers in four occupational areas to determine how competence is determined.

3. Interview three personnel managers to find out how the costs of too little training are passed on to the employers.
4. Compare or contrast the cost of too little training and too much training.
5. Using an occupational program course outline, write five objectives which meet the three criteria.
6. Using a psychomotor program course outline, write five objectives which meet the three criteria.
7. Explain the differences between a competence and a performance objective.
8. Explain in your own words the differences between performance-based instruction and traditional instruction.

REFERENCES

Aerasian, P.W.; Bloom, B.S. and Carroll, J.B. *Mastery Learning: Theory and Practice.* J.H. Block, ed. New York: Holt, Rinehart & Winston, 1971.

Allen, L.A. *The Management Profession.* New York: McGraw-Hill, 1964.

Bloom, B.S. ed. *Taxonomy of Educational Objectives: The Classification of Educational Goals.* Handbook 1: Cognitive Domain. New York: McKay, 1956.

Bowman, J.J. "The New Economics of Education," *International Journal of Educational Sciences.* 1966 1, 29-46.

Bruner, J.S. *Toward a Theory of Instruction.* Cambridge, Mass.: Harvard University Press, 1974.

Carroll, J.B. "A Model of School Learning," *Teachers College Record,* 64 (1963): 722-33.

Kibler, R.J.; Barker, L.L. and Miles, D.T. *Behavioral Objectives and Instruction.* Boston: Allyn and Bacon, 1970.

Krathwohl, R.; Bloom, B.S. and Masia, B. *Taxonomy of Educational Objectives.* Handbook 2: Affective Domain. New York: McKay, 1956.

Mager, R.F. and Beach, K.M. *Developing Vocational Instruction.* Belmont, Calif.: Fearon, 1967.

Mechner, F. Analysis and Specifications of Behavior for Training, in R. Glassner, Ed. *Teaching Machines and Programmed Learning II: Data and Directions.* Washington, D.C.: National Education Associates, 1965.

Popham, W.J. and Baker, E.J. *Establishing Instructional Goals.* Englewood Cliffs, N.J.: Prentice Hall, 1970.

8

Individualizing Instruction

Most teachers will agree that motivation is the key to helping a student learn. However, each person is a unique individual with personal needs, interests, and abilities. Individualized instruction is designed to put the student's interest at the very heart of the instructional process, thus enhancing motivation. The purpose of this chapter is to instruct preservice and in-service teachers in the elements of individualized instruction, thereby enabling them to:

- Identify the unique features of an individualized instructional system.
- Alert them to the changes in emphasis of the role played by students and teachers.
- Identify types of individualization.
- Develop appropriate materials necessary to support an individualized program.

The in-service or preservice occupational education teacher will be confronted with many organizational patterns. Among these are modular scheduling, flexible scheduling, and nongraded classrooms. Nearly all these organizational patterns are designed to provide for the unique individual differences of each student.

Occupational programs and the nature of the learner have changed rather drastically in the past several years. New programs exist, which prior to the *Vocational Education Amendments 1968*, were nonexistent. In addition to new programs, enrollment in nearly all occupational programs has increased. These factors, coupled with the changing nature of the occupations themselves, present many problems for the occupational teacher in the job-simulation laboratory and classroom. Further, as a result of a wider selection of course offerings and an increased emphasis on vocational education, greater numbers of individuals are finding their way into the various shops and laboratories at all levels of instruction, whether it is a secondary, community college, or proprietary school.

Each individual presents a unique set of needs, abilities, and competencies. The occupational teacher is, therefore, faced with a group of students who wish to learn a specified set of objectives. Due to the varying levels of competencies and motivation of each student, it is extremely difficult to design a program that will meet the needs of the entire group. A variety of alternatives for developing the competencies must be provided. Occupational educators cannot afford a "shotgun" approach to education. A program must be designed which will:

1. permit students to begin work at their actual level of accomplishment and to move them ahead as soon as they master the prerequisites for the next level
2. have a well-defined sequence of progressive, measurable objectives which serve as guidelines for establishing the individual student's program of study
3. monitor progress through a curriculum composed of adequate methods and instruments for assessing individual abilities and accomplishments
4. provide appropriate instructional materials for use by students so that they acquire increasing competence in self-directed learning
5. establish standards of performance which will enable each student to evaluate his or her own competencies
6. provide specialized training for professional educators; then they can accomplish the evaluation, diagnosis, and guidance of student performance on an individual basis

With the above concepts in mind, it is appropriate that an individualized instructional system be utilized in most occupational education programs.

INDIVIDUALIZED INSTRUCTION DEFINED

Individualization of instruction has been defined as the use of information about individual differences to prescribe appropriate educational environments (Bolvin and Glaser).[1] The individualizing process includes specification of objectives in terms of observable competence, a detailed diagnosis of learner characteristics, provision of alternative instructional procedures, and continuous assessment of learner progress.

The key word in this type of program is *individualized.* Each student is a unique person, and as such, should have the opportunity to progress at a pace which is best suited to his/her learning style. By recognizing the unique differences of each individual, each person will be allowed to work on objectives which are appropriate for that person. It is not uncommon for students to enter occupational programs with previously developed skills and knowledges. In an individualized occupational program, these students would be given a preassessment evaluation and then placed at the appropriate level. For example, a licensed practical nurse entering a registered nursing program should be placed at an appropriate level; and as a result, considerable instructional time will be saved, because they would not have to relearn skills learned previously.

In a system which allows the student to learn at an individual pace, entrance to and exit from the program must, of necessity, become more flexible. The open-entry/open-exit concept should become a reality in a totally individualized system. That is, the student would be able to start learning at any time during the year and also would be able to complete and exit from a course or program when competence had been achieved for the specified objectives.

The Teacher

Education in an individualized job-simulation laboratory or classroom will be similar in many ways to a group-centered classroom. However, since the basic premise is that each student should be treated as an individual, and learning activities will be selected to meet individual needs, the role of the teacher will be changed. The occupational teacher who develops an individualized instructional

---

[1] J.O. Bolvin and R. Glaser, "Developmental Aspects of Individually Prescribed Instruction," *Audio Visual Instruction* Vol. 13 (October 1968): 829.

system will find that more time can now be spent with each individual student. Less time will be spent in large group instruction and demonstrations. The teacher will now be able to direct energies toward providing new and different ways for students to learn, rather than utilizing a single teaching method which all must follow. Motivation will become the place of emphasis in such a system. Further, the teacher will function as a curriculum counselor, a tutor, and a behavior modifier.

The Administration

The school administrator will also find that an individualized occupational program has some unique features which will simplify the administrative task. Specific learning outcomes will be carefully defined. These outcomes can then be easily communicated to parents, students, and prospective employers. It is more effective to talk about the competencies each student has developed, rather than the number of courses taken. Scheduling of students is a major problem for most school administrators; however, with an open-entry/open-exit system, students could be enrolled in classes with the knowledge that they will "fit in" and profit from the educational experiences provided. A third feature of an individualized instructional program, which is important to the student and teacher, as well as the school administration, is articulation. Students are able to proceed from one level to another with a written record of exactly what they know and can do. Where the secondary school and post-secondary institutions are individualized, continuous progress becomes a reality.

The Counselors

An individualized instructional program also has an effect upon the counselor's role. Placement and assurance that students will be able to perform in such a program is greatly enhanced. Where students have a choice of learning styles and the rate at which they can proceed through a course, counselors can be confident that a student will be successful. Course content is carefully defined and as a result the student does not have to enroll in a course "blind." Too often, students enroll in occupational programs with little knowledge of the general requirements for a course and no knowledge of the specific requirements.

Individualized instruction is a teaching method which places the needs, abilities, and aptitudes of the student at the heart of the program. It also shifts some of the responsibility for learning from the teacher to the student. The teacher's role becomes one of curriculum counseling, tutoring, and motivating students.

TYPES OF INDIVIDUALIZED INSTRUCTION

Individualized instruction as an educational process can have various definitions. Several major types of individualized programs have been identified. The following discussion describes the major types of individualized instruction and the basic components of each type. Four identified types of individualization are provided in FIGURE 8-1.

TYPE I		
Individually diagnosed and prescribed. (Usually used in a required course.)	Objectives are determined by the teacher.	Teacher selects the media to be used in learning.
TYPE II		
Self-directed instruction	Objectives are determined by the teacher.	Student selects the media and method of learning the objectives.
TYPE III		
Personalized	Student determines objectives with the assistance of the teacher.	Media and method of learning are selected by the student and teacher.
TYPE IV		
Independent study	Student determines the objectives.	Media and method of instruction are selected by student.

From *Considerations in Implementing an Individualized System* by James W. Hargis. Copyright 1972 by Educational Associates. Reprinted by permission.

FIGURE 8-1

Four Identified Types of Individualizing

In addition to the types of individualization identified in FIGURE 8-1, one other factor must be considered, that is, the time available for the students to meet the criterion level of performance specified in the performance objectives. The amount of time allowed or provided to master a given competency is crucial to an individualized program. Some individuals are able to learn the prescribed content rapidly; others learn it more slowly. Yet, once learned, each person can demonstrate the same or similar level of skill and knowledge about that which they have studied. In the Type I individualized instructional system, the student enters the program or course, strengths and weaknesses are evaluated, and the results of the evaluation are utilized to diagnose and prescribe appropriate learning objectives according to abilities, needs, and interests. Further, the teacher determines the methods and media that will facilitate student learning. This type of learning will differ from group instruction, in that for a given group of 20 to 30 students, it is theoretically possible for each individual to be working under the teacher's guidance, but on different competencies and at various rates.

The self-directed method of individualizing instruction (Type II) is somewhat more flexible. In this program, the objectives of the course or program have been determined and specified by the instructor. The student, however, selects from the available media and teaching methods the procedures used to accomplish the objectives. Where there are specific skills and knowledges to be learned, this approach appears to be most appropriate. The student can utilize learning modules, work in small groups, use audiovisual materials, or watch a demonstration. The emphasis is placed upon student selection of the method that will be most appropriate for the individual style.

Type III, personalized individualized instruction, usually functions best in an elective course. In most cases, the student and the teacher work together to determine the objectives of a course. Once the objectives have been selected, the teacher and the student then plan or select the media and methods of learning. In this type of individualizing, a variety of methods might be employed. For example, individual tutoring—a person from the community with special skills could be used as a resource person. The appropriate method for a particular student would be determined by both the teacher and the student.

The fourth type of individualization (Type IV) is described as independent study. In this method, both objectives and methods of learning are determined by the student. The student is required to provide structure and organization for the learning which is to occur. Such a program requires that each person be capable of establishing goals, and that they also be self-directed and have the motivation necessary to bring about closure on identified problems. To further clarify the four types of individualized instruction, refer to FIGURE 8-2.

NECESSARY CHANGES

The decision to implement individualized instructional methodology in the classroom or laboratory is one which should be accomplished with the aid and assistance of other teachers, school administrators, and, of course, the students themselves. Certain changes in the traditional school setting are necessary.

The Teacher's Role

The occupational teacher becomes a learning manager. This entails serving as a consultant, diagnosing learning problems, suggesting alternative learning activities, and performing evaluation activities. In this system the instructor recognizes that each student enters the classroom with a different set of competencies, a different rate of learning, and often possessing different preferences for instructional methods. Recognizing the variability among students, the teacher must deal with each person separately. The key to a successful program is the interest and motivation generated by the instructor.

Advance placement and credit for previously developed competencies will result in a wide range of performance objectives that must be accomplished. The teacher must be prepared to give instruction ranging from the basic concepts to more advanced levels during a single class period. The implication this has for the instructor is that he/she must have a firm grasp of the full range of concepts covered by the course. Immediate feedback has proven to be of great value in helping students learn. The instructor needs to provide immediate confirmation of proper behavioral changes when the information is not available in the media being used.

The Student's Role

It is also important that each student understand his/her role in the individualized occupational program. Where the general program goal is to produce competent workers for productive employment, each student must become an active participant in the educational process. Therefore, each student must function as an independent learner. Other responsibilities, such as tutoring other students and assuming responsibility for the maintenance of a proper learning environment, must be assumed by each learner. Students must also learn to manage time and to participate in the decision-making process by selecting instructional methods which will enable them to accomplish their objectives.

ELEMENTS OF AN INDIVIDUALIZED PROGRAM

The teacher in an individualized classroom or job-simulation laboratory will be required to prepare for instruction differently than for a group-centered classroom. The major components of an individualized course deal with curriculum materials and interaction between the teacher and student. The initial step in developing an individualized instructional system is to write terminal and performance objectives. These objectives must be written in measurable terms and state the expected behavior, the conditions under which the objective is to be accomplished, and the mastery level or criteria of performance. For specific techniques and instruction in writing performance objectives, refer to the references listed at the end of this chapter. Performance objectives become the basic part of each unit of instruction.

The second element of an individualized course is the learning activities which are to be incorporated into each learning unit. A wide variety of resource materials must be readily available to the student, and a system which will allow full utilization of all available resources must be developed and implemented. Every student does not need the same type of activity, nor will all students need the same number of activities. Free and easy access to materials is essential if students are going to make effective progress in achieving objectives. Considerable emphasis should be placed upon the use of nonbook materials such as audio tapes, film strips, closed-loop films, and perhaps videotape learning modules.

The room should be arranged in a manner that audiovisual equipment can be operated by either a single student or a small group. Space should also be provided for small groups of students to work. Storage and retrieval of instructional materials can cause a class to function properly, or it can create chaos and frustration on the part of both the teacher and the student.

TYPE I

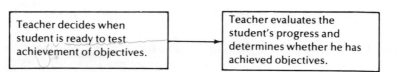

| Teacher selects objectives which have been identified as appropriate for identified abilities and needs. | → | Goals are set by the teacher for the student to complete work on objectives. | → |

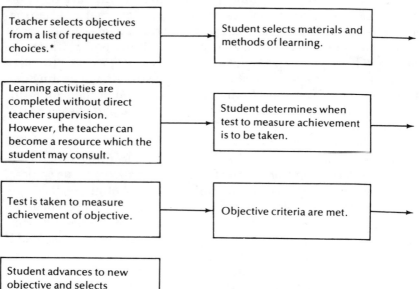

| Media, methods, and materials necessary for learning are selected by the teacher. | → | Student's work is evaluated and supervised by the teacher. | → |

| Teacher decides when student is ready to test achievement of objectives. | → | Teacher evaluates the student's progress and determines whether he has achieved objectives. |

TYPE II

| Teacher selects objectives from a list of requested choices.* | → | Student selects materials and methods of learning. | → |

| Learning activities are completed without direct teacher supervision. However, the teacher can become a resource which the student may consult. | → | Student determines when test to measure achievement is to be taken. | → |

| Test is taken to measure achievement of objective. | → | Objective criteria are met. | → |

| Student advances to new objective and selects materials. |

*Usually based upon an analysis of the occupation to be taught.

FIGURE 8-2

Classification of the Four Types of Individualized Instruction

TYPE III

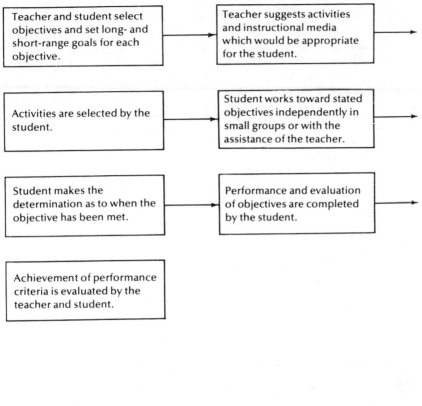

| Teacher and student select objectives and set long- and short-range goals for each objective. | → | Teacher suggests activities and instructional media which would be appropriate for the student. | → |

| Activities are selected by the student. | → | Student works toward stated objectives independently in small groups or with the assistance of the teacher. | → |

| Student makes the determination as to when the objective has been met. | → | Performance and evaluation of objectives are completed by the student. | → |

| Achievement of performance criteria is evaluated by the teacher and student. |

TYPE IV

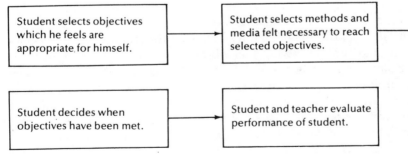

| Student selects objectives which he feels are appropriate for himself. | → | Student selects methods and media felt necessary to reach selected objectives. | → |

| Student decides when objectives have been met. | → | Student and teacher evaluate performance of student. |

FIGURE 8-2 (Cont'd)

Once the individualized system is implemented and operating, students will be working on a variety of objectives, various types of media will be utilized, and a variety of learning techniques will be in operation. The teacher will find it necessary to develop a student record system in order to adequately monitor each student's progress. It is quite valuable to have each student record the achievement of each terminal or enroute objective accomplished. FIGURES 8-3 and 8-4 are provided as samples to guide the reader in developing similar competency records. Duplicates of the student record should be maintained by the teacher and would become a part of the student's permanent record.

EVALUATION/GRADES

The learning manager of an individualized occupational program will continue to be concerned with evaluation. Evaluation can and should serve two main purposes. First and foremost, evaluation is a means whereby the student and teacher determine whether the learner has developed the competencies considered to be essential for the occupation being studied. Several types of evaluation are possible and must be conducted at different points in the student's progress. The pretest should be utilized prior to beginning any unit of instruction. Such a test may require student performance, or it could simply be a paper-pencil examination. Other devices for pretesting could be utilized. However, the primary purpose of a pretest is to determine whether the learner can meet the stated objectives before he or she engages in any learning activities. A second evaluation process following each activity is the self-check. This evaluation is accomplished prior to taking the post test. If the student feels a need for additional time following the self-check, he or she may select and complete another learning activity. After completing one or more learning activities and answering the self-check questions, the student will then take the post test. All test items, whether they are questions or performance activities, must be based on the performance objectives stated at the beginning of the unit of instruction. The complete evaluation process will include performance problems; paper-pencil tests, as pretests, self-checks, or post tests; and diagnostic tests for specific difficulties.

Evaluation and assignment of grades has been a problem for teachers. However, grades are important to students, as well as parents, and some method must be devised to assign them. Several grading systems have been tried with individualized instructional systems. The following systems are provided to give some guidance in this area. It should be noted, however, that basic to the concept of individualized instruction is the idea that each student should reach a mastery level for each unit of instruction.

A-B or No Grade. In this system, the mastery level of specified objectives is equated to an "A" or "B" letter grade. If the individual does not reach mastery, no grade is assigned. If there is a required grading period, no grade would appear on the grade report. An "A" or "B" grade would be assigned at the time the student satisfactorily completes the work.

A-B or Incomplete. This system also stresses mastery of skills and knowledge essential for an occupation. Because time is a factor in teaching specified competency level, incompletes are given to allow additional time for the student to complete his work.

Pass-Fail. This grading system places an emphasis upon learning the material in a specified period of time. If an incomplete is possible, it would extend the students learning time period.

A, B, C, D, F. This system can be used if each grade is carefully defined. Those individuals who start a course and never return or drop the course through the proper procedure would be assigned an "F." A contract system would be used with the student. In this method, the student would determine the desired grade. Provisions should be made to allow the student to change. A flexible time schedule will also provide for incompletes.

LEARNING MODULES

A basic component of an individualized instructional program is a prewritten learning module. Learning modules have been called by various names and can have different formats. Terms such as learning packets, learning units, operation sheets, job sheets, and job plan sheets are commonly used. Many of the above-mentioned guides have been used by occupational education teachers for some time.

The essential elements of all learning modules are as follows:

STUDENT PERFORMANCE RECORD

Name_____ Grade _____

School_____ Period _____

Directions: Fill in the circle after you have completed the task.
Example: DESCRIBE STARTING SALARY.

DESCRIBING WORKERS

0 Worker requirements
0 Special vocational preparation
0 General educational requirements
0 Required aptitudes
0 Required attitudes
0 Desirable interests
0 Required temperaments
0 Physical demands

UNDERSTANDING YOURSELF

0 Personal goals
0 Interests
0 Aptitudes
0 Attitudes
0 Temperament
0 Educational background
0 Work experience
0 Family background
0 Career plan

JOB OPPORTUNITIES

0 Jobs related to this class
0 Jobs in this town
0 Jobs in this school
0 Jobs in the state
0 Nationwide job openings
0 Worldwide job openings
0 Advancement opportunities
0 Employment trends

CAREER CLUSTERS

0 Key occupations in communications
0 Key occupations in metals
0 Key occupations in industrial
    mechanics
0 Key occupations in forestry
    products
0 Key occupations in electricity/
    electronics
0 Key occupations in construction

JOB DESCRIPTIONS

0 Work performed
0 Working conditions
0 Work locations
0 Job hazards
0 Special clothing, tools, equipment
0 Job dissatisfaction
0 Job satisfactions
0 On-the-job tasks

EDUCATION AND TRAINING

0 Job training time
0 Apprenticeship requirements
0 Licensing requirements
0 Union membership requirements
0 Trade/technical schools
0 Community Colleges
0 Military schools
0 Colleges/universities
0 High school courses
0 Job training costs
0 Admission requirements
0 Entrance procedures

ECONOMICS OF WORK

0 Starting salaries
0 Fringe benefits
0 Seasonal jobs and layoffs
0 Personal budget
0 Consumer awareness

GETTING AND KEEPING A JOB

0 Write a letter of application
0 Write a resume
0 List "Do's & Don'ts" for job interview
0 Simulate job interview
0 Fill out job application
0 Fill out social security application
0 List work rules
0 Conduct self appraisal
0 Prepare self-improvement plan

From Kenneke, L. et. al. *Industrial Arts Program Goals and Competencies.* Oregon State Department of Education. Project #RE-3-74, 1974. Reprinted by permission.

FIGURE 8-3

STUDENT PERFORMANCE RECORD
Electricity/Electronics

Name _____ Instructor _____

Directions: Fill in the circle after you have completed the task.

HAND TOOLS — Properly uses:

0 conventional tools
0 soldering tools
0 hand drill
0 taps and dies
0 box and pan brake

POWER TOOLS — Properly uses:

0 drill press
0 grinder
0 small lathe

TEST EQUIPMENT — Properly uses:

0 signal generators af/rf
0 oscilloscope
0 single trace
0 dual trace
0 capacitor analyzer
0 volt-ohm-milliammeter
0 vacuum tube voltmeter
0 transistor tester
0 rc substitution box
0 low voltage power supply
0 high voltage power supply
0 variac
0 isolation transformer
0 digital meters
0 grip dip meter
0 megger
0 amprobe
0 growler

FUNDAMENTALS — Can properly:

0 apply basic dc/ac theory
0 use color codes
0 convert basic electrical units
0 use transistor/tube/instrument manuals

ELECTRO MECHANICAL
MAINTENANCE/REPAIR —
Demonstrates techniques in:

0 identifies electrical components
0 tests/evaluates components
0 substitutes/installs components
0 identifies function of components
   in circuit

0 installs electrical cable and
   conduit to code
0 makes correct wire splices and
   connections
0 solders wire, components, tubing
0 replaces/services contacts
0 services electro-mechanical components
0 services domestic refrigeration systems
0 identifies abnormal signals
0 lubrication
0 installs holding devices
0 installs fittings
0 aligns, adjusts, calibrates equipment
   to manufacturers specifications
0 installs, tests, constructs PC boards
0 protective devices
0 chassis wiring
0 laces and forms harness cables
0 measures parameters using test
   equipment
0 installs electrical receptacles
0 proper grounding
0 belt and pulley arrangements
0 trouble shoots faulty equipment/
   malfunction using senses
0 breadboarding
0 maintains/repairs simple ac/dc motors

COMMUNICATIONS — Can properly:

0 instruct customer on use of controls
0 keep time, material, cost records
0 use diagrams, schematics,
   pictorials, abbreviations
0 prepare graphs and charts
0 use parts catalogs for orderings
0 follow verbal instructions
0 work well with others
0 display desirable work attitudes
0 write reports clearly and legibly
0 follow blueprints
0 interpret nameplate data

RELATED SKILLS — Can use:

0 scientific notation
0 electrical code
0 calculation for electrical circuit
   characteristics
0 slide rule
0 safety procedures

FIGURE 8-4

Title. A short descriptive statement about the contents of the package. If a number of packages are used, each should have a number.

Purpose. This is an explanation to the student, indicating why he should learn the contents of a guide. It should be written at a student comprehension level.

Pretest. The pretest should be a regular part of the learning module, and is taken before the student starts the package. If the student scores at the criterion level, he or she may skip the unit. The individual teacher may set the criterion level. Criterion levels of 80 percent may be sufficient for some modules, at other times, however, 100 percent accuracy may be required. The required performance level must be clear to the student at the start of each learning module. The test should reflect the objectives of the guide.

Performance objectives. The performance objectives should be stated in behavioral terms and contain three basic elements:
1. the performance expected of the learner
2. the conditions under which the performance will be measured
3. the criterion level of performance expected of the student

Directions. Instructions for proceeding in each individual learning module.

Enabling activities. A listing of the activities a student may select to learn the stated objectives is provided. The activities should be as diversified as possible to provide many alternatives which will cover the range of abilities and interests of the students.

Summary of methods and sources. Provides the learner a brief review of what to expect.

Sources	
Materials:	textbooks, periodicals, pamphlets, laboratory experiments, work sheets, job sheets, information sheets, projects, charts
Media:	films, filmstrips, records, tape recordings, film loops, videotapes, pictures
Methods:	large groups for media, small groups for discussion, student tutoring, teacher tutoring, individual research

Summary
Present a brief summary of what is presented in each activity.

SAMPLE

Sources	*Summary*
1. View a filmstrip and listen to recording "Laying Out Foundations of a Building."	Provides an overview of the process of laying out foundations.
2. View 8mm loop—The Spirit Level.	Demonstrates the uses of the spirit level

Self-test. A self-test should be an equivalent form of the pre-, post test. It should be included as a regular part of each learning guide. Answers to the self-test should be included to provide the student immediate feedback regarding the correctness of responses.

Post test. An alternate form of the pretest would become the post test with similar levels of mastery, as well as conditions under which the student must perform. It is also suggested that alternate forms of post tests be used when the student retakes the test.

Other formats for learning guides may be used, however, regardless of the format selected, the eight basic elements should be contained in each module. That is, a descriptive title, a stated purpose, specific performance objectives, directions, a list of alternatives for learning activities, a pretest, self-test, and post test.

The instructional package or learning module may also contain other information and aids to learning such as job sheets, information sheets, and operation sheets. In many occupational programs, there are certain processes and operations which must be followed in an established sequential order, if the operation is to be performed correctly. Therefore, an operation sheet would be very valuable and helpful to the student in learning to perform a given operation. Similarly, job sheets, which provide the essential information to complete a job, may be a part of the learning module. Occasionally, the available textbooks and reference books available do not provide all the necessary information for the completion of a learning module. It, therefore, becomes necessary to provide the student with the necessary information. The content of information sheets may be found in service manuals, pamphlets or brochures, trade and professional journals, as well as selected reference books which are not readily available for student use.

All supplemental materials, such as the operation sheet, job sheet, etc., are designed to provide alternate sources of information to the student rather than utilization of the instructor in this role.

SUMMARY

Individualizing instruction as a teaching method has the potential for assuming that each person entering an occupational program will exit that program with some specified degree of competence. Such a system should be designed which will take into account those competencies developed prior to entering the laboratory or classroom. Provision should also be made for students to learn the specified competencies at a pace which best suits their learning style. This would mean that some individuals would need less time than has traditionally been allocated, and other students would need additional time. But the primary emphasis would be upon the performance level of each person.

REVIEW QUESTIONS

1. How is the teacher's role changed in individualized instruction?
2. What are the advantages for a student enrolled in an individualized instructional program, as compared with the traditional group-centered classroom?
3. What are the basic elements of an individualized program?
4. You wish to individualize your occupational program. What arguments would you use to convince the school administration that this should be done?
5. Four types of individualizing have been presented in this chapter. Which type appears most appropriate for your occupational specialty?
6. How and when would the other types of individualizing be used?
7. Assuming you would be able to change grading systems, which method would you utilize and why?
8. What are the advantages and disadvantages of maintaining a student performance record?

STUDENT ACTIVITIES

1. Prepare a proposal and budget to implement individualized instruction in your occupational program.
2. Secure individualized instructional materials from other education agencies, such as State Vocational Education Department, colleges and universities, or regional curriculum materials centers.
3. Arrange to visit an operating individualized instructional program. This could be a reading, mathematics, or another occupational program such as nursing.
4. Review available media and materials, and determine the availability of materials and equipment which could be used in a learning resource center.
5. Prepare a written plan which would include a time line for implementing an individualized program into your job-simulation laboratory.
6. Develop a student progress record form which is suitable for your occupational specialty.
7. Design a classroom and job-simulation laboratory which could be utilized for individualized instruction. Ask your instructor or a colleague to critique your plan.
8. Develop an audio tape for use with the previously developed learning modules or operation sheets.
9. Develop a series of slides for use with audio tape and learning modules.

REFERENCES

Baker, R.L. and Schutz, R.E. (Ed.) *Instructional Product Development.* New York: Van Nostrand Reinhold, 1971.

Bloom, B.S., *et al. Taxonomy of Educational Objectives.* New York: McKay, 1956.

Bolvin, J.O. and Glaser, R. "Developmental Aspects of Individually Prescribed Instruction," *Audio Visual Instruction,* Vol. 13, October, 1968. p. 829.

Carroll, J.B. "A Model of School Learning," *Teachers College Record,* 64 (1963): 722-33.

Combs, A.W. and Snygg, D. *Individual Behavior.* New York: Harper & Row, 1959.

Dell, H.D. *Individualizing Instruction.* Chicago: Science Research Associates, 1972.

Doll. R.C. (Ed.) *Individualizing Instruction.* Washington, D.C.: Association for Supervision and Curriculum Development, 1964.

Drumheller, S.J. *Handbook of Curriculum Design for Individualized Instruction.* Englewood Cliffs: N.J. Educational Technology Publications, 1971.

Ebsensen, T. *Working with Individualized Instruction.* Belmont, Calif.: Fearon, 1971.

Flanagan, J.C. "How Instructional Systems Will Manage Learning," *Nations Schools,* 86: October, 1970.

Gagne, R.M. *The Conditions of Learning.* 2d ed. New York: Holt, Rinehart & Winston, 1970.

Knirk, F.G. and Childs, J.W., eds. *Instructional Technology.* New York: Holt, Rinehart & Winston, 1968.

Mager, R.F. *Developing an Attitude Toward Learning.* Belmont, Calif.: Fearon, 1968.

Prescott, D.A. *Factors That Influence Learning.* Pittsburgh: University of Pittsburgh Press, 1958.

Pucel, W.J. and Knaak, W.C. *Individualizing Vocational and Technical Instruction.* Columbus, Ohio: Merrill, 1975.

Demonstrations

The instructional demonstration is no doubt the most used instructional method in occupational education. It is the principal instructional method found at the exploration and preparation levels. It permits the instructor to describe in step-by-step detail the various processes, procedures, and techniques involved in various tasks associated with specific occupations.

Upon completion of this chapter, the reader will be able to:

- **Define the demonstration method of instruction.**
- **Describe several techniques that will maximize the effectiveness of the demonstration method.**
- **Define advantages of the demonstration method.**
- **Identify and overcome potential disadvantages associated with instructional demonstrations.**

The demonstration is an instructional method through which students can observe various procedures and techniques being correctly implemented to produce some end product or to illustrate a specific principle. For example, students in an automotive mechanics program can best learn the correct procedures for replacing a set of brake shoes by watching someone familiar with the procedure performing the task. The instructor, while demonstrating the correct procedure, will carefully explain each separate step involved and may discuss various techniques that will work best on a particular type of brake system or make of automobile.

MANAGING THE INSTRUCTIONAL DEMONSTRATION

There are several techniques that should be utilized to assure that a demonstration will be effective. Each of these components is important and related to the overall value that learners can derive from the demonstration. The techniques or components can be divided into three primary categories. These include predemonstration preparation, the demonstration itself, and post demonstration followup and evaluation.

Predemonstration Preparation

As with any instructional method or procedure, preliminary planning and organization are essential. The demonstration is not different. The successful demonstration demands planning, organization, and practice.

Plan the demonstration.   The occupational education instructor must carefully analyze his or her instructional objectives to determine whether the demonstration is the best instructional method that can be utilized. In most cases where a specific procedure or process must be learned, the demonstration will be an appropriate method. An exception to this might be where major industrial processes are involved. For example, the production of steel by the Basic Oxygen Process may best be learned through a field trip or instructional film. However, the procedure used in catherterizing a patient may best be learned by a demonstration.

Once a determination has been made to use the demonstration method, the instructor must consider the materials and equipment that will be needed and the specific techniques that must be employed. Perhaps the best approach to this planning problem is to practice the entire demonstration prior to actual implementation in the classroom, laboratory, or shop. The trial or practice run will help the instructor to identify needed supplies and to determine specific time requirements.

Arrange the demonstration site.   The arrangement of the demonstration site is an important predemonstration activity. Care should be given to assure that learners will be able to view the demonstration with ease and from safe viewpoints. In some industrial-related occupations where heavy immovable equipment is used, this can become a difficult task. The size of the learning group will dictate much of what can be done. In some cases, the instructor will have to repeat the demonstration several times to small groups of students.

Prepare the learners. Prior to the actual demonstration, the learners should be provided with essential related information and an orientation to that which is about to happen. The related information might be presented during the class session immediately preceding the demonstration. An orientation, including objectives, specific techniques to be observed, and additional related information, should be made directly preceding the demonstration. This preparation of the learners will assure fewer interruptions during the actual demonstration that may occur because students did not possess the necessary learning readiness.

The Demonstration

During the demonstration, there are several procedures that may be utilized to assure its effectiveness. These procedures coupled with both pre-demonstration and post-demonstration activities will help guarantee the effectiveness of this often used instructional method.

Use regular laboratory materials and equipment. The instructional demonstration must be conducted with minimum error on the part of the instructor. Students are viewing the demonstration with the objective of learning the correct procedures involved. Likewise, they should expect to achieve similar success when they undertake the procedures that are being demonstrated. For this reason, it is important that the same tools, equipment, and materials are used during the demonstration that the students will be using. This is an error often made by occupational education instructors, and this approach has ramifications on such topics as general laboratory equipment care and maintenance. That is, the tools and equipment made available to students should be of the same quality and in the same condition as those used by the instructor during demonstrations. If the instructor uses his or her own "special" tools and equipment, the learners will automatically assume that the materials available to them will not permit the same quality of work.

Permit free interaction.   Students must be permitted the opportunity of asking questions at any time during the course of the demonstration. Therefore, it is important that the instructor establish an air of openness with regard to this concern. Too often, students are not willing to ask questions during a demonstration for fear of ridicule by peers or by the instructor, or because they feel that they should not interrupt. For the demonstration to be effective, this feeling should not exist. Do not assume that this freedom of interaction with the teacher automatically exists. By the time students reach the exploration or preparation level, they have been thoroughly "schoolized." In most cases, this means keeping quiet while the instructor is talking, regardless of whether they understand.

Post-Demonstration Procedures

After completing the demonstration, follow-up activities should be conducted. These will assure reinforcement for the learners and evaluative information for the instructor. Both of these outcomes are essential to the learning process. Without these post-demonstration activities, much of the potential associated with this method of instruction will be lost.

Review the basics.   Review the basic processes covered during the demonstration. An instructional handout describing these is very helpful. This handout might be in narrative form or prepared as a process flow chart. Entertain student questions and discussion items. Follow the demonstration with an evaluative device or activity. For example, if the demonstration consisted of showing students the correct technique of applying frisket materials for airbrush illustrations, have them prepare an illustration with frisket material. This may be used in further activities involving actual airbrush usage. However, if the demonstration were used to illustrate Bernoulli's Principle, a brief examination involving sketches of the cross section of an airfoil would be appropriate.

Self-evaluation.   Spend a few minutes after the demonstration and after other post-demonstration activities have been completed to note both the strengths and weaknesses associated with the demonstration. Consider possible procedures that would strengthen the presentation. List any problems that students might have had in understanding the material as presented. Attach these evaluative notes to your lesson plan for future reference. This self-evaluation technique will greatly improve future demonstrations. If possible, invite a faculty colleague to watch and make recommendations for ways in which you might improve your demonstration techniques.

ADVANTAGES OF THE INSTRUCTIONAL DEMONSTRATION METHOD

There are three primary advantages in using the demonstration as an instructional method. First, the demonstration permits the learner to observe a process or procedure as it actually happens through the use of equipment, tools, and materials that he or she will be using to duplicate the activity. Second, this instructional method is an ideal approach for teaching students correct and *safe* procedures that must be followed in the accomplishment of a task or experiment. The instructor can emphasize all safety precautions as the demonstration progresses. Finally, by showing the students the correct techniques, the materials and supplies that they will be using in their activities can be conserved. Since initial instruction will focus on the correct procedures, material waste and equipment abuse will be kept at a minimum.

DISADVANTAGES OF THE INSTRUCTIONAL DEMONSTRATION METHOD

The disadvantages commonly associated with the demonstration can be kept at a minimum by the alert instructor. The following three disadvantages are followed by suggestions that will minimize the negative effects on learning that might occur because of these potential problem areas.

Difficult for all to see. Often, a demonstration involving the use of a particular piece of equipment will require the students to crowd around the work station where the demonstration is being conducted. Learners may have difficulty in actually seeing the specific procedures and techniques that might be involved, because of their view relative to the position of the equipment, size of the workpiece, or speed of the operation. In many cases, this potential disadvantage can be reduced by dividing the learners into small groups for viewing the demonstration, or by permitting them to file past the operator's station so that they can see the relationship between the operator and the work at hand.

Time consuming.   Involved processes and procedures or activities requiring considerable time for completion often pose a time-related problem with regard to the instructional demonstration. However, if the instructor will prepare demonstration materials in various phases of completion prior to the actual demonstration, these materials can be utilized to illustrate how the completed phase will look after specific procedures have been completed. These materials can then be substituted for the originals as the demonstration progresses. Considerable time can be saved through this approach.

Limited student interaction and feedback.   Often, an instructor will be so involved in conducting a demonstration that he or she will neglect to provide opportunity for student questions or comments. Specific opportunities for such student interaction must be provided throughout the course of the demonstration. In most cases, there will be natural breaks in the process that will permit the instructor to discuss any questions that the student might have. Except where processes or procedures are extremely noisy, students should be encouraged to ask questions at any time throughout the course of the demonstration.

SUMMARY

The instructional demonstration is a method which permits students to observe the conduct of various procedures and techniques utilized to produce some end product or to illustrate a specific principle.

Three essential components of the demonstration include:

1. Predemonstration preparation
2. The demonstration itself
3. Post-demonstration procedures

Predemonstration procedures involve planning the demonstration activity, arranging the demonstration site, and preparing the learners. During the demonstration, the instructor should utilize regular laboratory materials and equipment and must permit free and open interaction with students. After the demonstration, the students should review the basics, and the instructor should evaluate the effectiveness of the learning activity.

REVIEW QUESTIONS

1. What are the three primary concerns associated with predemonstration activities?
2. Why should the instructor utilize materials and equipment available to students when conducting a demonstration?
3. What procedures can be followed to provide adequate post-demonstration review activities for students?
4. Why should the instructor conduct a self-evaluation after each instructional demonstration? How can professional colleagues help in this assessment?

STUDENT ACTIVITIES

1. Develop a demonstration check sheet that can be used by an occupational education instructor in planning, implementing, and evaluating this type of instructional method.
2. Prepare a "mini" demonstration of about five to ten minutes in duration for presentation to classmates. Discuss the presentation with your instructor and other class members. Repeat the demonstration following their input.
3. Contact a local occupational education program and ask whether you can view a demonstration by one of the instructors. Observe those techniques that he or she follows to assure adequate opportunity for student feedback and questions.

CHAPTER

10

Discussion and Questioning

The discussion and questioning techniques are two closely related instructional methods. Both procedures actively involve the students in the learning process. This involvement is in the form of verbal interaction among students or between students and the instructor.

Because of the extensive amount of psychomotor learning involved in occupational education programs, most instructors concentrate on refining methods that facilitate this type of learning. However, little emphasis is placed on methods that will permit students to assimilate information. Both discussion and questioning techniques can be effectively utilized in the teaching and learning of related information topics. Therefore, the occupational education instructor should become skilled in utilizing these two approaches to teaching.

Upon completion of this chapter, the reader will be able to:

- Define the discussion method of instruction.
- Describe several procedures that assure effective utilization of the discussion method.
- Define the questioning method of instruction.
- Identify specific techniques that can be utilized to implement the questioning method.

DISCUSSION

The discussion method of instruction may be defined as an organized system of verbal interaction among and with learners and directed toward a predetermined instructional objective. Discussions can be both formal and informal. They can include large groups of students, small groups of learners interested in special topics, or individual students who are experiencing very specialized learning needs. In any case, the discussion method of instruction can be discriminated from idle talk on the basis of the presence of a formal instructional objective.

Often during laboratory or shop activities, students will engage in various kinds of discussions with one another or with the instructor. When these discussions center about extracurricular activities or are not concerned with items associated with the shop or laboratory assignment, they must not be considered as instructional discussion techniques. An instructional discussion is a planned instructional method and is developed to meet a specific objective.

Formal Discussions

As mentioned earlier, the discussion method may be either formal or informal. Formal discussion methods include large groups, small groups, panels, and individuals. The formal discussion is characterized by the intent of the discussion activity. That is, when the instructor determines that an instructional objective can best be met through a discussion approach and implements that approach, a formal discussion occurs.

For example, if a preparation-level program in health occupations includes objectives related to human relations with patients, the instructor may elect to employ a large group discussion as the primary instructional method. During a given class session, the instructor will plan to use the discussion approach to meet the objective. Students may discuss the importance of human relations skills and try to determine through interaction among themselves and with their instructor specific traits that the health occupations professional must possess.

If a formal discussion is to be effective, several considerations are important. These include such concerns as the size of the group, the arrangement of the discussion area, the nature of individual students in the discussion group, and who will be responsible as the discussion leader. These concerns deserve individual attention.

Group size.   As with most instructional methods, the size of the group is inversely proportionate to the effectiveness of the method. However, a discussion group can be too small. Most discussion leaders will agree that a group should consist of at least seven or eight participants. Fewer participants tend to be less able to carry on continuous interaction and painful pauses will occur. If the group becomes too large, many students will not be able to participate because of a lack of time or because of fear. An ideal group size would consist of seven to twelve members.

If the group size exceeds fifteen or sixteen students, consider the use of a panel discussion approach. Select six or seven students to serve on a panel charged with the responsibility of discussing the instructional topic. Have the students research the topic and be prepared to discuss it. Establish a time limit for the panel and open the entire class to questions regarding the panel's topic. This approach is extremely effective where larger groups of students are concerned.

Arrangement of the discussion area.   The organization of the space in which the discussion is to be held is an extremely important factor. If the instructor wants to be assured of his or her role as discussion leader, the regular classroom arrangement of rows of seats might be maintained. This arrangement will tend to prevent some possible interaction from those near the rear of the room, because they may not feel they are part of the group. A better arrangement would involve placing the chairs in a large circle with the instructor seated in one of the chairs in the circle.

If a panel is to be used, place the panel at a table in front of the room facing the rest of the students. Form the chairs of the nonpanel members in a semicircle, with the panel near the opening. All students will be able to watch the panel discussion and have less hesitancy about questioning panel members.

A portable chalkboard is a handy device to have available for use with discussion groups. It can be placed near the panel table or near the discussion leader for sketching, note-taking, and brainstorming. It can also be used to summarize the outcomes of the discussion.

Individual student differences.   As with all learning, the individual differences of students can greatly affect the amount and quality of individual interaction. Many students will be at ease with their fellow students and will not hesitate to speak out during a discussion lesson. However, many secondary and post-secondary students will be extremely hesitant about saying anything during a class discussion. It is the instructor's responsibility to be aware of those students who have difficulty talking with the group and provide positive feedback when these students do speak. Conversely, many students like to talk and will try to dominate the discussion. In most cases, the group will exert enough pressure to keep this individual in line. If the remainder of the discussion group cannot control talkative members, the instructor may have to intervene.

Discussion group leader. The role of discussion group leader requires real skill. Some instructors have never been able to lead effective classroom discussions. The discussion group leader, whether it is a teacher or student, has the responsibility of keeping the discussion going by encouraging students to express their various points of view. This involves establishing a rapport with the class that will permit students to feel at ease in the discussion situation. The discussion leader must be well informed about the topic and be willing to accept various points of view without being judgmental. He or she must be able to keep the discussion on target and operating within an initial group of preestablished discussion rules.

If a student is to serve as a discussion leader, there are several functions that can be performed by the teacher that can increase the effectiveness of the student leader. The teacher can set the stage for the discussion by clarifying the topic to be discussed and the rules that are to be followed. By serving as a member of the discussion group, the teacher can concentrate the discussion on important points that arise. If, however, the teacher does elect a role in the discussion process other than leader, this role must be maintained. The instructor must follow those rules established for students in the discussion process.

Informal Discussions

Informal discussions may arise as a result of interaction growing out of some other instructional activity. For example, an instructor may determine that a given instructional objective can best be accomplished through the demonstration method. However, as the demonstration progresses, certain topics may surface that require discussion. When the students enter discussions as spinoffs of other instructional approaches, and these discussions are directly related to the instructional objective, an informal discussion results.

This type of student interaction must follow the same basic guidelines as formal discussions. The only real difference being that the informal discussion approach may not be a formally planned teaching method.

QUESTIONING

Questioning, as an instructional method, is a very effective approach to increasing interaction between the teacher and students or among the students themselves. The instructional questioning approach can be used to elicit recall information, to help students better understand specific processes and procedures, and to establish the basis for further analysis of various effective learning activities.

An instructional question is simply a carefully structured series of words that direct the learner toward a response that has been predetermined by the instructional objectives as appropriate. For example, the orientation-level instructor may ask, "How does the open-hearth method of steel production differ from the basic oxygen process?" The question requires a respondent to contrast the two processes. It also requires that the respondent be able to describe both processes so that a contrast can be made. The question can also serve as a springboard from which the class can be launched into the study of further information regarding the iron and steel industry.

Questioning can also be used to increase student involvement in the teaching/learning process. Toward this end, a general question regarding a particular subject being presented can bring students into the discussion in an active way. They can draw from information already gained in previous lessons in an attempt to respond to a particular question. For example, the machine shop instructor might ask, "Based on what we have already learned about the engine lathe, what to you think would be some basic rules governing the installation of a three-jaw chuck?" This kind of question would involve the students in rule making, rather than simply having the instructor present a list of procedures.

Questions can be extremely valuable as tools for summarizing an instructional unit. After a unit has been presented, key questions can be asked which will serve to help the learners summarize that which has happened and to crystallize their concepts about the material covered. The distributive education teacher might ask the following questions after completing a unit on the interactive effects of various items in a product line:

> "Why is it important to carefully select each sales item that composes a product line?"

> "What is meant by synergistic effects?"

> "What are some large companies that have been successful in determining a good product mix?"

Instructional Questioning Techniques

As an instructional method, questioning is generally used as a supportive or secondary approach to the teaching/learning process. In most cases, the questioning method is used in conjunction with other instructional methods. It may be part of a demonstration, field trip, discussion, or a number of other methods.

Carefully constructed questions should be included as part of any lesson plan. These questions should be keyed to various important components of the material used during the lesson. Many instructors prepare four or five questions for each instructional activity. These questions can be written directly on the lesson plan and can be used when students begin to show a lack of interest, when brief summarization is needed, or as an introductory approach to a specific topic or unit.

Following are several important points that must be considered when the questioning method of instruction is to be utilized.

Use care in constructing questions. The instructional question must be easily understood by the student. Spend time preparing instructional questions to assure that the terminology used is understandable. Keep the question short and to the point. Do not use questions that can be answered by a simple "yes" or "no" response. Instructional questions should be leading. They should permit the respondent to verbalize the information needed for a positive response. The instructional question should not be complex. That is, it should represent a single response. Where multiple responses are in order, construct separate questions directed toward each response.

Provide positive feedback.   When a student correctly answers a question, be certain to compliment him or her on the response. Do not simply nod and proceed to the next question. Students will respond to praise. Similarly, do not be excessively negative when a student gives an incorrect response to a question. Try to find something in the response that can be used as a positive focal point for others to continue with the correct response. If a student responds to a question with, "I don't know," then return to that student later with a question that you think he or she may be able to answer. If possible, try to assure that every student exits the class session having contributed a correct response to at least one question. If a student answers a question correctly, do not repeat his or her response to the class. The correct response should stand as the student's contribution to the class. If repeated by the instructor, the student will think that his or her response was not entirely correct. When the instructor repeats correct responses, other students may begin to decrease their emphasis on listening to peers.

Redirect questions aimed at the teacher.   During questioning sessions, when questions are directed toward the instructor, try to redirect these questions to the rest of the class. If other students can answer a question posed from within the group, the questioning student may be better able to retain the information. Be certain to ask the student who originally posed the question whether his or her question has been satisfactorily answered.

The nonresponder.   In nearly every class the instructor will have one or two students who simply will not volunteer responses to questions. In many cases, these nonresponders will not attempt to answer questions directed at them. Give them time to become adjusted to the questioning procedure. If the teacher provides positive feedback to all responses, this student may begin to get involved. If, after several sessions, the student continues to shy away from responding, a personal discussion with the individual will be in order. During the discussion, try to instill confidence in the student. Try to determine why the student is not responding. In some cases, these students may suffer from speech impairments or hearing difficulties. For these students, it would be improper to base evaluation on their classroom participation during questioning sessions.

SUMMARY

Instructional discussions and questioning are two closely related methods of teaching. Both involve students in the learning process through verbal interaction.

Discussion methods may be both formal and informal. In either case, this method of instruction may be defined as an organized system of verbal interaction among and with learners and directed toward a predetermined instructional objective.

Factors affecting the discussion method are:

1. group size
2. arrangement of the discussion area
3. student differences
4. discussion leader

An instructional question is a carefully structured series of words that direct the learner toward a correct response, as predetermined by the instructional objectives.

Several considerations that must be given to the instructional questioning method are:

1. use care in constructing questions
2. provide positive feedback
3. redirect questions aimed at the teacher
4. work with the nonresponder

REVIEW QUESTIONS

1. What is the relationship between the discussion and questioning methods of instruction?
2. What is the difference between formal and informal instructional discussions?
3. What is the best size for a discussion group?
4. Of what importance is room arrangement in facilitating an instructional discussion?
5. How can the teacher assist the discussion group leader?
6. What are some ways that instructional questions can support the learning process?

7. Why is positive feedback important to the success of the instructional questioning method?
8. How can you help the nonresponder in the instructional questioning method?

STUDENT ACTIVITIES

1. Organize a panel discussion. Select from the following topics:

   a. The Role of the Discussion Leader
   b. What Makes a Discussion Effective?
   c. Helping the Nonresponder in the Questioning Situation
   d. Improving Positive Teacher Feedback During the Classroom Discussion

2. Visit a local school's exploration- or preparation-level program during a discussion or questioning session. Observe both the instructor and students. Prepare a written analysis of the experience.
3. Discuss possible causes for the nonresponder. Identify alternative approaches to solving his or her problems.

CHAPTER

11

Simulations and Games

If all occupational teachers were to carefully review the commercial
world, they would find that packaging or presentation of products
and services is a large industry. In fact, it appears in some instances
that the package costs more than the product. Educators would do
well to analyze the motive behind the packaging industry, for motivation is the focus of their efforts. Similarly, packaging or method of
presentation is a critical part of the educational process. Packaging for
learning is a complex and involved process. It involves the selection
of instructional modes and strategies that are tailored to particular
objectives and goals. Simulation/games as an instructional method is
essentially a packaging method. That is, through such learning
strategies students become active, rather than passive, participants in
the educational process. This chapter will enable the reader to:

- **Outline the origin and history of serious games.**
- **Define an educational game.**
- **Define a simulation activity.**
- **Describe the steps of simulation/game design.**

A primary concern of occupational educators at all levels is the
motivation of their students. Because of the changing nature of our
society, schools cannot teach all the available knowledge. Students,
therefore, must develop the desire to learn if they are to be successful

both in school and when they enter the world of work. Each person must also develop the feelings of effectiveness and control over the situation in which they find themselves.

The use of educational games and simulation activities at the awareness, exploration, and preparation levels in occupational education can provide each student with a simplified slice of reality. The use of educational games will reflect real-world process, provide the learner an opportunity to test various work roles, to make decisions, to apply knowledge, and to make mistakes without suffering the serious consequences found in the real world. Furthermore, most educators agree that when students are active participants in the educational process, learning is more effective.

ORIGIN AND HISTORY OF EDUCATIONAL GAMES

The origin and history of games from a form of play to a serious undertaking can be traced to games like checkers or chess. Chess was developed, as a representation of war, more than two thousand years ago. Military war games have been used to analyze possible battle situations since the early eighteenth century. By the start of World War II, the military establishment was serious about the use of gaming to predict the possibilities which might occur on the battlefield.

The need to find quick and effective solutions to problems during World War II heightened the use of games and simulations. Techniques of dealing with complex problems of supplies, available troops, ships, and the myriad of war materials spawned at least five developments which have become a part of gaming: computers, operations-research, the mathematical theory of games, simulations, and the early business games.

Since World War II, the gaming technique has been applied to other enterprises. In the business community where mistakes can be disastrous, games provide businessmen with an opportunity to make decisions under a variety of circumstances which may confront their particular industry. The consequences of their decisions can be evaluated in a few hours rather than in several years, which might prove to be very costly. Serious games have been developed and used for management personnel, sales, investments, personnel development, and in other related areas such as collective bargaining and supervision. Games are now being used in a number of other areas of social concern such as domestic politics, ecology, economics, health care, and sociology.

The number of career fields in which simulation and games are being used is growing at a phenomenal rate. A review of a publishing company catalogue will reveal an increasing number of entries in all fields. Games and simulations do represent a viable method of teaching which needs to be investigated by the occupational education teacher. It is especially valuable at the exploratory level. Games represent a method or an approach to solving serious problems, as well as to bringing about an understanding of the world of work. A definition of both simulation and games would help to clarify their purpose.

Games

Mention the word "game" to a group of grade school youngsters and each one will probably think of some type of activity which is fun to do. There exists a fundamental difference between games which are played for entertainment and serious educational games. There are also some similarities. In both types of games there are players or adversaries. The actions of the players are constrained by an explicit set of rules which are peculiar to that specific game and the result of the behavior of the players is a certain outcome—win or lose the game. It should be noted that the term "player" need not be a single person but may be a team, a corporation, or a nation. Any group of individuals who have identical interests, with respect to the game, may be considered to be a single player.

Educational games are quite similar to contests engaged in for entertainment, but they have two distinguishing features. First, they are simulations of real-life situations. Second, educational games are not always pure competitive contests where there is clearly a winner and a loser. For, in many cases, the cooperative aspect of real-life situations is built into the game.

Simulation

Simulation, on the other hand, is the process of conducting an experiment or establishing a model of a physical or social system. Reality is replicated to the degree that the simulation designer is able to select the essential elements from the physical or social environment. For example, the job-simulation laboratory is established for most occupational areas; it simulates reality, i.e., the model office for business and office occupations, the store for distributive occupations, the hospital laboratory or hospital room for health occupations, and the shops and laboratories for trade and industrial occupations.

Simulations represent some real-life object or event. There may be direct experimentation with the system itself, or some problem associated with the system will be analyzed.

All educational games are simulations; however, not all simulations are games. The basic difference between games and simulations is that in a game there will be some method of scoring points and a winner is determined. In a simulation, a winner is not declared; the focus is upon analyzing how the system functions.

CURRENT USES OF GAMES

We live in a day when most youngsters are "information rich and experience poor." Through the use of simulation techniques and educational games, students are provided an opportunity to make application of knowledge they have gained.

Simulation and games have some major advantages over other teaching strategies. Most games offer immediate feedback; they provide low-cost experimentation, the opportunity to make mistakes, and they shorten the time span over which the results of decisions will come to fruition.

With the above mentioned advantages in mind, a closer examination of the educational advantages of simulation and games is in order. Educators and parents are keenly aware of the seriousness exhibited in the play activities of children. In fact, quite often the source of trouble, both in the neighborhood and at school, is the violation of known rules of play. If this same intensity and concentration could be focused upon the learning tasks to be accomplished in the classroom, both parents and teachers would be ecstatic. Educators are fully aware of the intense involvement in play; yet, they fail to capitalize on it. Play is not viewed to be a viable tool in the classroom; yet, it represents a powerful method of bringing about student involvement.

With the development of educational games and simulation activities, teachers can increase student participation in the educational process. Games increase student motivation. They aid in clarifying basic concepts and, in many cases, enable the student to view the total system and their role in the system. This type of learning activity is especially appropriate at the orientation and exploration levels where broad categories of occupations are being explored. Further, educational games help to socialize the student, and provide an excellent method of integrating students with diverse abilities and educational levels. It should be noted that educational games are not a learning activity which will replace all other teaching methods; but, they represent a method which is most suitable for certain learning objectives. Specific educational advantages are as follows:

Motivation is a key to all learning. Through various means and methods, every teacher attempts to motivate students. Educational games are intrinsically motivating. As participants in a game, most individuals have a competitive nature, in that they wish to win the contest. In these cases, learning becomes a by-product.

Games also require active *participation* on the part of the students. While students may have an understanding of a process or work role, when placed in a dynamic situation common to educational games, the experiences become very real for the individual. For example, simulation games which require negotiations with the other person or team take on new meaning when the participants face each other across the negotiating table.

The dynamics of the simulation game also allow the participants to cause events to happen that permit them to feel that they can control their environment. Because of the shortened time span, the players receive *feedback* about the correctness of their decisions. Feedback or confirmation is vital to the learning process. Unlike the normal classroom where confirmation of correct responses is slow to happen, in a game where students are struggling to gain an advantage, confirmation happens rather quickly. Confirmation becomes a natural part of the learning process and is not dependent upon the teacher.

Another important feature of serious games is the fact that they are *goal-directed* and they bring about *closure*. Winning is the objective of a game. This is the initial motivating force for many educational games. While competition between students is a motivation, some will lose interest when the outcome of the game is evident. However, the game must be completed and scored to determine the winner. The determination of a winner brings about closure on the learning activity and is an essential element in the learning process. Simply put, each person involved should learn to see the project or game through to completion, regardless of the unpleasantness of the outcome. A parallel could be drawn for students in occupational programs; they need to see all jobs through to completion. This may involve "winning," i.e., doing a good job; or it may involve failing to do an adequate job and perhaps a need to repeat the work.

A further aspect of an educational game is the fact that some games will be *open-ended*. That is, there will be no "correct" answer. For example, in matters dealing with ecology and the effects new industries have upon the environment, there would be no clear winner in this type of game. Students would deal with the complexities faced by adults in the real world. Also, role playing in health occupations has been found to be a very effective method of providing an opportunity to practice the human relations skills which are so vital to those occupations.

At the exploratory level, games are a vital tool for the occupational teacher. Through games, a greater degree of reality and relevance can be introduced into the classroom. As students focus upon real-world problems, each participant would act out a role of the various individuals who are working in a specific setting. For example, if a business enterprise is established, the various work roles would be carried out. This would range from the president and stockholders of a corporation through the assembly-line workers. It should also include sales personnel. In a competitive frame of reference, the objective would be to create more sales than a similar corporation. Such games or simulations reflect adult roles and have great appeal to young people.

A quite vital part of an educational game or simulation is the *interaction* which takes place between students. Educational games require interaction among players. Through interaction, the students learn from each other and, in some cases, learn more efficiently than if the teacher attempted to teach the same objective. In most learning situations where grades are norm referenced, this type of learning is not encouraged. If the competition is keen, students may not work together and this important learning method is not utilized.

While all games are competitive, an educational game which is played by groups or teams requires *cooperation* on the part of each participant. Cooperation is a strong element of any team game, whether it is a sports activity or an educational game. A properly selected educational game can also utilize all students, regardless of their level of educational achievement; and each team member can feel a sense of achievement.

Just as games can be selected or developed which will cause students to consider all aspects of a social system or business process, games can also be utilized as a vehicle for conveying information. Role playing, in the job interview process, is an important method of teaching students about mannerisms, habits, and general attitudes toward other individuals.

Simulations and games, when carefully selected, are activities which can be a method of teaching that is dynamic and interesting. This technique holds forth great promise because of the active participation of the learner in the teaching/learning process. However, educational games are not a panacea. Like any other teaching method or media, they must be used in the appropriate situations if they are to be used to full advantage. There are, however, some limitations which must be recognized and controlled by the teacher. It is important that the occupational teacher be aware of these limitations. From the teacher's point of view:

1. Games or simulations of a job situation or a production system require the cooperation of all students involved.
2. Games must be reviewed without the key ingredient, the students themselves; thus it is more difficult to select an appropriate game or simulation activity.
3. The teacher may have had a limited amount of training and experience in using games as an educational tool.

The teacher should also be aware of the following limitations which affect students:

1. At times, games may be too motivating and may produce anger or other emotional problems. The teacher must be aware of critical points in the game and be prepared to discuss problems with the students which will cause them to attempt to deal rationally with situations which may occur in the world of work.
2. It is difficult, if not impossible, to develop instructional materials which cover all aspects of the game. Unlike a textbook, the game designer must describe simultaneous events in sequential order. This aspect of the activity may cause problems for some learners.
3. Some activities may require behavior or knowledge which the student does not know or practice. That is, some degree of role playing is required. In such cases, role cards or information must be provided and students must act out behaviors which are not a part of their own personal behavioral patterns. Thus the reality of their part is slow to develop.

Games and simulation activities have several advantages and

limitations; but, they also represent a medium in which the student can practice decision making, negotiating, and other complex skills. These methods are especially valuable where an understanding of complex and interacting factors is important.

CRITERIA FOR USE

A review of the list of references cited at the end of this chapter will provide some indication of the number and variety of commercially prepared educational games and simulation activities that are available. With so many educational games and simulation activities available, selection of the proper activity becomes a problem for the learning manager. The following criteria are listed to provide guidelines for their selection:

1. The time required and the expected benefits must be compared with other media which are available to teach the objective.
2. The carryover of motivation must be carefully evaluated. In other words, can one expect the students to be involved in the subject matter when conventional materials are used later?
3. When a complex issue or process is involved, a simulation activity or an educational game may be appropriate.
4. If stated learning objectives call for problem solving and decision making, will the simulation game provide the learning activities which allow students to practice these skills?
5. Games should allow students to practice interpersonal relations.
6. Simulation and games should also provide for diversity of ability levels. That is, all levels of ability should be accommodated in the educational process.

THE ROLE OF THE TEACHER

Selection and use of educational games and simulation learning activities requires that the teacher assume an important part in the educational process. First of all, each teacher must realize that he or she will not be playing a leadership role once the activity gets underway. The value of the above mentioned activity is achieved when students assume positions of leadership within their own groups.

This does not mean that the teacher is not involved. The teacher may wish to assume the role of a regular player, an advisor, or an arbitrator if one is needed. Once the game or simulation activity is underway, the instructor may wish to be an observer and record the important events which could be used in the debriefing sessions.

The students should not feel threatened by the game or simulation. To accomplish this, the students should be involved in evaluating the objectives of the activity; and, as a learning manager, the instructor should guide the students, but not *test* for the accomplishment of the objectives. If the activity has been carefully selected and implemented, learning is expected to take place.

A post-game discussion is also an important aspect of any simulation/game. During this period the students should be encouraged to do some reflective thinking, and through discussion, reinforce the basic concepts learned. As a discussion leader, the teacher can then point out concepts which may have been overlooked.

It should also be noted that depending upon the type of simulation/game selected, the teacher can expect the noise level within the classroom to increase. Life itself is not docile, and neither is a good educational game. While the game may look like bedlam to the casual observer, the instructor will need to maintain a measure of control.

SIMULATION/GAME DEVELOPMENT

One problem which will become apparent to many occupational educators, especially at the preparation level, is the fact that specific simulation/games are not readily available. It may be necessary for the teacher either to modify existing games or to design and develop his or her own. This will require considerable time and effort, but the development of other media also requires a similar amount of time and effort. The following procedures should be considered when designing simulation/games:

1. Define the probable areas to be simulated. This may involve a social issue, an organizational structure, or a problem to be solved.
2. Determine the specific objectives and scope of the activity.
3. Identify the key elements or people and organizations involved.
   This may involve individuals, groups of individuals, or

organizations. The various roles which will be played by the participants will need to be defined. An ecology simulation may involve governmental agencies, business enterprises, and interested public preservation groups. Roles within each group will also be identified such as, chairman, consumers, voters. For example, a business enterprise would include management, labor, customers, sales personnel, and competitors.

4. Specify the participants' roles.

Role statements will specify the actors motives, desire for wealth, power, influence, and the general goals to be achieved.

5. Describe or determine the resources available.

This is important for simulation activities as well as games. Each enterprise, no matter how large, has some limit on resources. Resources should represent a plausable expectation for the simulation/game. Resources may include finances, ownership of goods and services, authority, and influence.

6. Specify the interactions to be simulated and the rules to be followed.

At this stage in the development of simulation/games, the designer must determine how the participants interact with people and, in simulation, how they interact with the simulated system itself. It is important that realistic rules be established and that they parallel rules and methods which are in existence in the real world. The designer should check these against the objectives specified earlier.

7. Establish the evaluative criteria to be used.

Depending upon the type of activity developed, i.e., simulation or a game, various methods can be devised to determine the outcome. In the case of an educational game, method of scoring and eventually declaring a winner must be specified. In a simulation activity, a variety of techniques may need to be employed, depending upon the enterprise or system to be simulated. If a product is involved, in a business enterprise for example, then sales, quality of the product, and profit may be the criteria to be used. In other instances the activity may require that the individuals evaluate their own progress.

8. Determine the format for the simulation/game presentation.

Depending upon the resources of the institution, simulation/games may be presented in a variety of ways. The designer may utilize a board-game format, role playing, paper and pencil exercise, or a computer simulation. In the job-simulation laboratory, the role-playing format may be used to simulate a manufacturing assembly line, a health occupations setting, or a model office.

Once these decisions have been made and all the essential materials have been developed or purchased, the designer is then ready to try out the simulation/game with the group of students for which it is designed. The implementation and modification period is essential, and the effect of the activity should be evaluated according to the specified objectives.

SUMMARY

Simulation and serious games have become a viable teaching/learning activity which is suitable for most educational levels. Serious games are basically a simplified slice of reality. They have a specific set of rules with "players" and a win criteria. Simulation, on the other hand, does not have a win criteria; but, it allows the participants an opportunity to establish, operate, and/or modify a system which is found in the real world.

As a learning activity, simulation/games cause the students to become active participants in the educational process. Each student will have an opportunity to view complex and difficult environments in a dynamic setting. Because of the shortened time span of most games and simulation activities, students will receive almost immediate feedback on their decisions. They will have an opportunity to make mistakes where the resultant decisions will not be costly or harmful.

While simulations and educational games have several advantages and limitations, their selection and use should be based upon a sound evaluation of educational objectives.

REVIEW QUESTIONS

1. How are educational games used in the business world?

2. What is the difference between a simulation activity and an educational game?
3. What advantages exist for the use of a simulation activity vs a field trip to a particular business?
4. What are the specific advantages of simulation/games over other educational learning activities?
5. Why is closure important, and how can simulation/games cause students to bring this about?
6. What are the advantages and disadvantages of educational games?
7. If the appropriate educational game or simulation activity is not available, what factors should be considered in devising or developing such an activity?

STUDENT ACTIVITIES

1. Review a catalogue of educational games and simulation activities. Select an appropriate activity for the orientation level, exploration level, and the preparation level.
2. Select a game used for business; revise it so that it can be used at the exploration level of instruction.
3. Prepare a bibliography of at least ten simulations and educational games which would be appropriate for the orientation, exploration, and preparation levels.
4. Visit a classroom or laboratory when the instructor is utilizing this teaching method.
5. Select an educational game and try out this teaching method with a group of your peers.
6. Prepare a list of publishers who distribute educational games and simulations.

REFERENCES

Abt, C.C. *Serious Games.* New York: Viking Press, 1970.

Abt Associates, Inc. *System Analysis and Educational Simulation of 20 Years of the Machinist Vocation.* Cambridge, Mass.: ABT, 1967.

Babb, E.M. and Eisgruber, L.M. *Management Games for Teaching and Research.* Chicago: Education Methods, 1966.

Glazier, R.E., Jr. *How to Design Educational Games.* Cambridge, Mass.: ABT Associates, 1970.

Gordon, A.K. *Games for Growth*. Palo Alto, Calif.: Science Research Associates, 1970.

Horn, R.E. and Zuckerman, D.W. "Getting into Simulations" *The Guide to Simulation/Games*. Lexington, Mass.: Information Resources, Inc., 1973.

Kahn, H. and Mann, I. *Game Theory*. Santa Monica, Calif.: Rond Corp., 1957.

Oen, U.T. *Simulation: A New Dimension in Vocational Education*. East Lansing: Research and Development Program in Vocational-Technical Education. Department of Secondary Education and Curriculum, Michigan State University, 1968.

Twelker, P.S. *A Manual for Conducting Planning Exercises*. Teaching Research, Oregon State System of Higher Education, Monmouth, Oregon.

Zuckerman, D.W. and Horn, R.E. *The Guide to Simulations /Games for Education & Training*. Lexington, Mass.: Information Resources, Inc., 1973.

CHAPTER

12

Media
for Improving Instruction

The use of instructional media to help facilitate the teaching/learning process is a skill that must be possessed by the occupational education teacher. This skill involves more than just the production of audiovisual aids. It demands that the successful teacher be able to identify specific learning problems that can be corrected through the use of various media; that the appropriate media can be selected or produced by the instructor; that the learning environment can be modified to assure that maximum benefit may be attained through use of the media; and finally, the effect that specific media have on the learning process must be evaluated so that a decision can be made relative to future utilization in similar circumstances.

Audiovisual media selection and production is a common core in nearly all teacher education programs. Therefore, this chapter will not deal with media production techniques, but will concentrate on the integration and utilization of media in the occupational education program. Emphasis will be placed on how the successful teacher makes effective and efficient use of instructional media in meeting the day-to-day learning needs of his or her students.

This chapter is designed to assist the reader in the accomplishment of the following objectives:

- **Define instructional media.**
- **Describe the advantages of utilizing various instructional media to facilitate the teaching/learning process.**

- **Differentiate between teacher-made and commercially produced media.**
- **Describe the various types of instructional media and general approaches to their utilization.**
- **Describe specific techniques that may be implemented when planning, utilizing, and evaluating various instructional media.**

A precise definition of instructional media is difficult to derive. Generally speaking, instructional media tend to maximize the use of several senses (audio, visual, etc.) by the learner in an effort to clarify specific concepts, procedures, techniques, etc. Most media experts will agree that the use of instructional aids serves as a vicarious activity that relates real-life experiences where such experiences would be impossible, or at best difficult, to recreate in the learning environment.

For example, the function of the human heart as a unit in a health occupations class would best be learned if students could actually see the heart and all its components operating in the human organism. Of course, this would be virtually impossible, but models do exist that recreate the functions of the human heart and could be used in lieu of the real-life situation. The model would serve as a vicarious experience, but students would be able to see its function and better understand the process. Consider the difficulty of explaining the human heart's function without the use of any instructional media.

In industrial education power mechanics programs, students are often required to describe the process that characterizes the operation of an internal combustion engine. Watching such an engine in operation gives little hint as to what is going on inside each cylinder. The relationship of spark, air, fuel, compression, and exhaust are difficult to determine through a cast iron block. Even if the engine were made of glass, the speed at which it operates prevents any kind of real visual analysis. However, movable overhead transparencies and models can be utilized that will illustrate the process in a slow-motion, yet realistic, manner. Instructional media may be utilized to illustrate many real-life situations that cannot be adequately analyzed in their natural state.

FUNCTIONS OF INSTRUCTIONAL MEDIA

The occupational education instructor often asks why he or she should utilize audiovisual techniques in the classroom or laboratory. After all, instructional materials are expensive when purchased commercially and quite time consuming when produced by the teacher or support personnel. To answer this question, the specific values of instructional media as related to occupational education must be described. Following are six primary answers to the question, "Why should I use instructional media in my occupational program?"

Simplify Procedural Concepts

Occupational education is representative of a rather unique learning process. Most of the learning that occurs in occupational education is related to systematic steps or activities that must be effectively combined into a procedural approach to problem solving. Whether it involves rewinding an electric motor, planting a tobacco seedbed, designing an accounting system, or preparing a patient's diet, specific procedures must be linked together to achieve the end result.

Instructional media can be employed to assist the learner in visualizing the specific procedures that are involved, and systematically linking those procedures in sequence to assure the correct approach necessary to meet the prescribed goals. Occupational education teachers must utilize media to present these often complex procedural approaches to problem solving. Various flow charts, graphs, and models will assist the learner to visualize these procedures.

Simplify Technological and Biological Systems

This was illustrated in an earlier example. The internal combustion engine is a unique and complex system. It consists of various subsystems and components that are effectively combined to assure that the engine is operative. In the event that a subsystem or component ceases to function, the entire system may stop or operate inefficiently. Therefore, the relationship of the various subsystems and components is an important concept for learners to understand.

Often, real-life systems are difficult to analyze in the instructional environment. Even our glass engine operated at a high rate of speed. An integrated electronic circuit may be the size of a pinhead. The human lungs are enclosed in a living organism. For these reasons, real-life analysis is virtually impossible. However, the various systems can be illustrated and animated through effective instructional media. Students can visualize the operation of the system through vicarious experiences such as models, schematic diagrams, and other audio and/or visual aids.

Condense Time Sequences

Occupational education, like all educational programs, is operated within certain time constraints. Many processes that are studied do not fit the time schedule that legislators and administrators have elected to utilize in the schools. As a result, procedures must be employed to bridge this barrier.

Learning theory suggests that most students, in order to derive maximum learning from various instructional activities, need immediate feedback. Often, this cannot be accomplished in real-life situations. In such instances, instructional media can be of great benefit to the occupational education teacher.

For example, an ornamental horticulture experiment may be based on the effect fertilizer has on certain types of grass or flowering plants. It may be impractical to conduct the experiment with every group of students over the years because of the time that elapses between treatment and effect. In such a situation, a 35mm slide/tape series illustrating the results of such an earlier experiment may be quite useful. Learners may discuss the treatment and view the results of such a treatment during the same class session. This is an example of how time can be condensed through the use of instructional media.

For another example, the growth rate of infants may be based on a particular type of diet. The results of experimentation with this diet over a period of several years can be graphically depicted through various visual media. Such information would be impossible to present using the real-life experiment.

Expand Time Sequences

Important time sequences often occur in real-life experiences in milliseconds. The effects of alternating electrical current on an electrical coil is a good example. There is no possible way that a student can see the process that takes place when alternating electrical impulses are boosted in a coil. Various charts and graphs can be utilized by the vocational electricity instructor to illustrate this rapid process. Animated films can be used to depict the process so that students can visualize what is happening.

Free The Instructor To Work Individually With Students

Instructors often complain that the development, use, and evaluation of instructional media consumes too much time, and they would rather devote this time to individual students. In most cases this is an erroneous assumption. While time is involved in the initial preparation of instructional materials, over the long term, their utilization will save considerable instructor time. In fact, their utilization may also reduce the number of instances where the teacher will have to spend time with individual students, because concepts were not presented clearly during the initial presentation.

From a practical standpoint, the instructor cannot expect to have prepared complete instructional media packages for all instructional units during the first or second year of teaching. This does take extra effort, but these materials can be developed and further refined as time goes on. Instructional media development is a continuous process because the technology of the occupational area changes, the nature of the learner constantly changes, and media technology itself is in a constant evolutionary mode. However, the use of media in a systematic fashion does ultimately reduce instructional time spent on basic or core concepts.

Consider how long it would take to verbally describe the process that takes place in the operation of our internal combustion engine. Also consider, because words are very abstract symbols, the amount of repetition that would be necessary to thoroughly explain the various aspects of the system. An audiovisual approach would surely reduce the required instructional time. This would free the instructor to work with students who are having individual difficulties.

The past decade has witnessed a tremendous growth in the amount of available commercially produced instructional media for all occupational service areas. The instructor does not have to individually develop much of the media that is now available in his or her specialization. Valuable time can be devoted to other instructional duties when commercially produced media are utilized.

Meet Individual Learning Styles and Patterns

All students possess individual learning styles and patterns. In Chapter 4, the special needs of disadvantaged, handicapped, and gifted learners were discussed. Instructional media can be utilized to meet these special needs.

Audio tapes can be developed for blind and hearing-impaired students. Overhead transparencies, slide series with written narratives, and printed job sheets can serve the deaf and hard-of-hearing student. Special instructional devices can be developed for the health-impaired and orthopedically handicapped learner. Many kinds of instructional media can be developed to meet the readily identifiable and not so readily identifiable individual learning needs of youth and adults enrolled in occupational education programs. Instructional media can maximize the use of all senses in the learning process.

INCORPORATING INSTRUCTIONAL MEDIA INTO THE DAILY INSTRUCTIONAL PROCESS

The following analysis of various instructional media is designed to assist the reader in making determinations relative to the incorporation of such media into the instructional program. Other sources should be consulted regarding the development and preparation of these media.

Chalkboard

Probably the most readily available visual aid, the chalkboard, is also no doubt the most abused medium in education. All too often, the chalkboard is used to convey illegible information or random thoughts of the instructor. Most teachers are not fully aware that with a little ingenuity and several pieces of colored chalk, the resourceful instructor can make the chalkboard come alive. The chalkboard has several features that make it an indispensable tool for the occupational education teacher. To assure that it is successfully utilized, these features must be recognized and their use maximized.

The chalkboard is generally a large surface designed for use with groups of students. Written materials, charts, diagrams, graphs, sketches, and illustrations should fill the entire surface of the chalkboard rather than being crowded into corners or into the very center. Colored chalk should be utilized to highlight features that are important to the learner. The instructor should practice neat and legible lettering. This practice should also include emphasis on techniques related to drawing sketches, diagrams, etc.

This instructional medium is extremely versatile and can be effectively utilized in nearly all specialization areas. For standard illustrations such as electrical symbols, flow charts, circle graphs, and various maps, templates can be constructed of heavy cardboard or particle board. The instructor can trace around these templates as information is presented.

The secret to effective utilization of this medium is practice and care. Good chalkboard presentations must be neat and simple. The surface should be cleaned daily so that illustrations and written material contrast with the background. Chalk trays should also be kept clean and free of dust. A large blotch of dust on the instructor's back will generally attract more student attention than any material presented on the board.

Overhead Transparencies

Overhead transparencies, sometimes called view graphs or projecturals, are often used in occupational education programs. These transparencies may be purchased commercially or developed by the instructional staff. They may be produced by several processes including thermo, diazo, lifting, or printing with transparent ink.

Special kinds of transparencies are available that illustrate movement (generally with polarized materials). Some overhead projectors can be equipped with devices that pump water over the table in a closed container so that by adding opaque particles, principles related to the venturi and airfoil effects can be illustrated.

The overhead projector with transparencies serves much the same visual function as does the chalkboard. However, there are several factors that add versatility to this medium. Transparencies can be developed in multiple colors and are easily stored in the instructor's notebook or in regular file cabinets. They may be reused many times without noticeable effect on quality. The overlay technique permits systematic presentation of new material that is not previously seen by the learners. They permit the use of very high-quality artwork that is difficult to develop on the chalkboard. The overhead projector can also be utilized in a fully lighted room.

Many instructors feel quite comfortable with this medium and use it almost exclusively in their classes. This can cause problems because learners quickly tire of the same medium. Overhead transparencies should be combined with other instructional media to assure that learners do not become bored with its use. The occupational education teacher must realize that the overhead projector is an aid to the teaching/learning process and not an end in itself. Overhead transparencies should be used when needed to clarify procedures and concepts that otherwise are difficult for students to learn. Remember, this medium is a visual device and represents only one of the senses through which learning occurs. The effective utilization of instructional media demands that all senses are involved in the learning process.

Audio Tapes

The magnetic tape recorder is a very useful instructional tool. It can be used alone or in conjunction with other instructional media. It is particularly useful for students suffering from reading deficiencies and visual handicaps. It can also be utilized by the instructor as a self-evaluation device.

Many disadvantaged and handicapped students enrolled in occupational education programs suffer severe reading problems. For these students, the textbook and job or information sheets commonly used in the instructional programs may be totally useless. For that matter, written tests and instructional modules may be difficult for students to understand. In such situations, the magnetic tape audio recorder can be very useful.

Written information and job sheets can be recorded on magnetic tape cassettes and neatly filed. Students suffering from reading difficulties can refer to the audio tapes as they read through the written material. Often, the occupational education instructor will discover a student who performs particularly well on performance and verbal activities, but does miserably on written examination . In many cases, this is caused by poor reading skills. The student simply cannot read the instructor's written examination. Record the examination questions on an audio tape and provide time between each item for the student to respond on an answer sheet. Quite often, student test scores will rise significantly through this approach.

One of the most enlightening experiences an instructor can have is to listen to one of his or her classroom presentations on an audio tape. Voice inflections, student interaction, and other factors can be thoroughly analyzed after the lesson. It is a good idea to ask a colleague to listen to the tape and give suggestions for improvement.

35mm Slide/Tape Presentations

Slide/tape presentations serve a very important function in the occupational education program. This approach is especially useful for presenting related information relative to various local business, industrial, agribusiness, and health-care agencies. Most occupational education preparation-level program completors will be seeking employment in the local area. The instructor can work with local agencies in the development of 35mm slide/tape presentations so that students (potential employees) can be made aware of the nature of local employment opportunities.

At the orientation and exploration levels, these same slide/tape presentations can be utilized to show people at work in various occupational settings. This approach is particularly useful at this level when field trip experiences are limited by financial constraints or local agency policy.

A problem that continually faces the preparation-level occupational education teacher who works with handicapped learners is that of student placement after achieving program goals. Quite often, employers are skeptical as to the ability of handicapped individuals in performing tasks required in their business. A slide/tape series can be a very effective selling tool in this situation. The presentation should include slides depicting handicapped students at work in similar situations and at typical kinds of machinery or equipment. It is important that the potential employer see the handicapped person performing tasks which are a normal part of their business or industrial operation.

Occupational education guidance and instructional personnel are often asked to make presentations about their programs to various community groups. In such situations, a well-done slide/tape series is an outstanding public relations medium. This presentation can show general aspects of the school program, as well as specific activities in which students are involved. These community groups generally listen to many presentations each year. A quality slide/tape presentation will linger in their minds much longer than will an oral presentation.

Single-Concept Films

The super 8mm film loop has evolved as a significant instructional medium during the past decade. These so-called single-concept films (because they are generally quite short and cover very limited material) are particularly useful for individualized and/or remedial instruction. Most of the more recent single-concept films are accompanied by a magnetic sound track, and the super 8mm film is suitable for projection in a classroom or laboratory.

While single-concept films can be teacher-made, most currently used single-concept films are commercially produced. As such, they are generally available in complete sets for use in specific areas. These film loops are generally kept at individual study stations or in separate learning laboratories. When available, the occupational education teacher should plan them into the curriculum. They should be made available to students on an individual basis, and time should be set aside each instructional session for individualized study and review.

Where motion or movement is an essential component of a learning activity, films of this nature are extremely valuable. In many cases, other audiovisual media are inappropriate for such instruction. These films are relatively expensive, so extreme care should be exercised in their selection.

Posters, Charts, and Bulletin Boards

Posters, charts, and bulletin boards, like the chalkboard, represent basic instructional media. As such, they are often overlooked by teachers as effective instructional devices. This is unfortunate because they do have a place in the teaching/learning process.

Posters, charts, and bulletin boards may best be utilized for reinforcement activities where various kinds of information need to be kept visible to students for long periods of time. For example, in many occupational areas, safety is an important part of the learning that takes place. The development of safe working attitudes requires constant reminders to the student. In such cases, safety posters and bulletin board displays are extremely effective (and often can be obtained from the various state workmen's compensation agencies).

Posters can be placed near work stations where specific information may be appropriate. Bulletin boards can be changed or updated on a periodic basis to reflect new instructional units that are being covered in class.

Like the chalkboard, posters, charts, and bulletin boards require that the instructor have some basic skills in lettering, layout, and sketching. These media are certainly more effective when presented in a neat and orderly format that is easy to read and understand.

Commercially produced charts and posters are available in many occupational areas. While often expensive, these media are quite useful when effectively combined with regular instructional units. Commercially produced materials can be combined to make bulletin board displays.

Models

The use of models gained greatest emphasis as an instructional aid during World War II. Enlarged and/or reduced models proved to be very effective instructional devices when real objects were too large, too small, or not readily available for instructional purposes.

While models can be made by the classroom teacher, the amount of time necessary for their production often makes this approach impractical. In many occupational areas, commercially produced models are available. The health occupations and power mechanics areas being two good examples of this.

Nearly all human organs are available in model form. These are generally easily assembled and disassembled affairs that permit students to see the various parts of the article with little difficulty. In addition to basic organs, teeth, skeletal structure, etc., are also available.

In the power mechanics area, internal and external combustion engines, fuel systems, suspension systems, and many other models are available and quite useful. They simplify the real objects, are generally much easier to store, and are less expensive. When planning and selecting media to support learning, models should not be overlooked by the occupational education teacher.

Television

In the secondary and post-secondary schools, educational television is being utilized as an instructional medium. Many new facilities include formal studios for television presentation production activities. While television is a very expensive and technical medium, it must be considered by the occupational education teacher when planning total media support activities.

When planning and preparing instructional television media, two primary concerns must be kept uppermost in the teacher's mind. The first involves the specific function of the television presentation. It must serve a particular purpose. If the same presentation can be made by the instructor in the classroom or laboratory, it probably does not need to be videotaped for television. Second, to hold the learners' attention, the instructional television presentation must be of equivalent quality to the commercial presentations that students view daily on their home television sets. A detailed analysis of each of these concerns is essential.

The function of the educational television presentation must be carefully analyzed. This should begin with the question, "Why use television?" All too often, the instructor will simply lecture or give a simple demonstration on a videotape. This approach, unless large groups of students are involved, would be more effective if done live in front of the group. Remember, television hinders reinforcement through feedback to student questions. However, if large groups are involved, or the presentation is designed for remedial learning purposes, the television presentation is in order.

Instructional television presentations compete with their commercial counterparts viewed by students in the evenings or on weekends. In short, learners are accustomed to viewing high-quality and high-cost programs almost daily. Therefore, the instructional television presentation must be of equivalent quality. This is a particularly difficult task because of the amount of available resources that can be devoted to the instructional television effort. However, by combining various media such as transparancies, charts, graphs, film loops, and others, the television presentation can be of high quality and interesting to the student. Closed-circuit television, without the videotape, can be used quite effectively when the teacher wishes to demonstrate a process to a group. Through this media, the process can be enlarged. Also, with one or two monitors, the students at the back of a group will be able to see as clearly as the student in front row center. Consult a local media specialist for assistance in planning the television lesson.

Duplication Procedures

Next to the chalkboard, instructional handouts in the form of job sheets, assignment sheets, information forms, and written examinations are the most common type of instructional medium. Because of their extensive utilization in the occupational education curriculum, the teacher must be proficient in their preparation and use. Because of general availability, three duplication procedures will be analyzed. These include ditto or spirit duplicating, mimeograph process, and offset printing.

Spirit duplicating procedures.   This process is better known as the ditto process. It involves transposing a carbon substance in reverse form onto a paper master, and through the use of an alcohol-base liquid, causing the carbon-base image to be transposed onto separate sheets of paper FIGURE 12-1.

The spirit duplicating process is probably the most commonly used procedure for handouts in the public schools and colleges. It is easily recognized by blue or purple lettering on white paper. Fresh copies tend to hold the odor of the spirit liquid used in the transfer process. Copies can be made by directly drawing, writing, or typing on the master after removing the thin tissue which separates the master and the carbon back-up sheet. Printed matter can be transferred to the master by use of a heat process, provided special masters are used and the original was printed with a carbon-base ink.

Many instructors are not aware that ditto masters are also available in multiple colors. Red, blue, purple, black, and green are the most common colors available. By changing the color of the back-up sheet, multiple-color handouts can be produced.

The ditto process is relatively fast. However, where more than 100 copies are needed, multiple masters must be prepared. Also, after

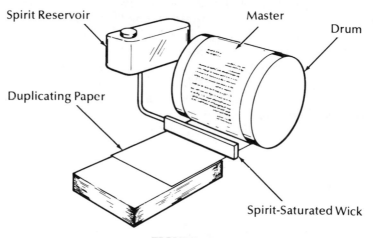

FIGURE 12-1

The Spirit Duplicating Process

**The spirit-saturated wick moistens the duplicating paper which,
upon contacting the master, removes a small amount of the image.
Multicolored masters can be prepared.**

time, ditto copies tend to fade and become difficult to read. For larger runs and more permanent copies, the mimeograph process may be a better selection.

Mimeograph process. This process is also commonly used in educational agencies. It is generally characterized by back images on white, porous paper. The mimeograph procedure utilizes a cut stencil through which thick ink is forced on the separate sheets of paper FIGURE 12-2.

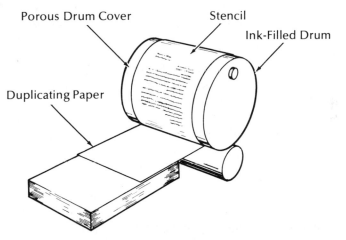

FIGURE 12-2

The Mimeograph Process

Ink passes through the drum and through images cut on the stencil onto the duplicating paper.

The mimeograph process utilizes a waxed or plastic stencil that is backed by a hard-surfaced paper. By removing the typewriter ribbon or utilizing special styluses, the wax is removed allowing ink to pass through the stencil in the form of the image that remains. The stencil is placed on a drum containing ink on the mimeograph machine. Thus, ink passes through the drum and through the stencil on the sheets of paper.

The mimeograph process provides a more permanent handout that does not fade with time. Many more copies can be duplicated from a single master than through the ditto process. Also, the mimeograph masters can be retained for future use. However, this process is somewhat messy, since a thick ink must be placed in the duplicating machine. This ink also makes the masters sticky, and they must be pressed between sheets of newsprint before storage. Like the ditto process, only line drawings can be utilized. For regular pictures and even greater numbers of copies from a single master, the offset process must be utilized.

Offset Process.   The offset printing process provides the greatest amount of flexibility with regard to color, illustrations, and number of copies. It is the procedure used in printing most textbooks, magazines, and newspapers. However, because of the relatively expensive equipment needed for this type of duplication, it is not commonly utilized by the classroom teacher for daily handouts.

This process may utilize either paper or metal masters. Images may be drawn or typed directly onto the paper masters, but pictures requiring shades and shadows are placed photographically on metal masters. Because of the complex nature of the offset printing equipment, a trained printer is usually required to operate the press. For those special handouts or for very large dissemination, the offset procedure will be the best.

Handouts must be carefully developed, free from errors, and easy to understand. They should always be punched along the left-hand margin so that students can keep them in a binder or notebook. Multiple colors in both the printing and paper should be used for clarification and a pleasing appearance. The quality of the instructional handouts directly reflects the concern for quality exhibited by the instructor.

EFFECTIVE UTILIZATION OF INSTRUCTIONAL MEDIA

There are several important techniques that should be employed by the occupational education teacher to assure that instructional media are effectively utilized. These techniques include:

1. previewing all media before use
2. inspecting media hardware
3. preparing the learners for the media presentation
4. reviewing the presentation
5. evaluating the effectiveness of the media

Previewing Media

Prior to utilization in the instructional setting, all media should be carefully previewed by the instructor. Not only must new or commercial media be previewed prior to its use, but teacher-made materials that have been previously utilized should also be checked for possible damage during storage or for other defects that may have occurred. Commercially produced transparencies, filmstrips, and films must be previewed to assure that they meet the instructional objectives of the program. In many commercial 16mm films, care should be taken to determine whether the commercial component of the film is overemphasized. Often a particular procedure utilized by one company is not indicative of the standard procedures utilized in the total industry.

During previewing, the instructor should make note of special aspects of the instructional media that he or she wants to emphasize to the class prior to or during the presentation. For example, if a particularly unsafe act is demonstrated on a film, the instructor may wish to point this out to the students.

Inspecting Media Hardware

Perhaps one of the most embarrassing things that can befall an instructor is to have a detailed media presentation ready for the students, only to find that the audio recorder does not function properly or the lamp in the projector is inoperative. If this is discovered during the lesson, it will seriously reduce the effectiveness of the presentation. Therefore, the occupational education instructor should thoroughly inspect all hardware associated with the media that are to be utilized. Not only must the various hardware be inspected, but the facility where the presentation is to be made should also be carefully analyzed. Power outlets, window shades, screens, chalkboard condition, etc., should be considered. This is particularly important when the classroom or learning laboratory is not commonly used by the teacher.

Preparing the Learner

Prior to the actual use of specific media in the classroom or laboratory, the instructor should describe the materials that he or she is about to use and call attention to any specific items that might be particularly interesting to the learners. This preparation component is particularly important where films, instructional television, and slide/tape presentations are utilized. Since feedback during these media approaches is somewhat limited, the good teacher may pose several questions prior to the presentation. Instructors can use these questions as interest stimulators or attention getters to draw students into the lesson and highlight specific parts of the presentation.

Reviewing the Presentation

Once the media lesson is presented, an immediate review may be advantageous. Student questions should be answered where such questions may be impossible during the presentation itself. Once again, media such as films, instructional television, and slide/tape series must be followed by a review. Many teachers prepare written outline reviews for these media and hand these out after the presentation. This review procedure is extremely important for reinforcement of various concepts and feedback to the instructor.

Evaluating Effectiveness of Media

As soon after the media presentation as possible, the teacher should take a few minutes to review the lesson. Did the students appear interested? Was the media of high quality? What was the student feedback? Should this approach be used again? What needs to be done to strengthen the presentation? Media is useful only if it provides a better way for the learners to meet the instructional objectives. If this has not happened, the media should be revised or discarded in favor of another approach.

Many instructors prepare a short check sheet that can be utilized in this brief evaluation process. The preceding questions can serve as the basis for such a form. The specific nature of the check sheet should rest with the instructor. This approach is quite valuable, because a written evaluation exists that can be consulted during the next term or the next school year. Mental notes regarding the strengths and weaknesses of a particular presentation are too easily forgotten.

SUMMARY

Instructional media are primary components of the instructional program. As such, media perform several functions supportive to the learning process. These include:

1. simplifying procedural concepts
2. simplifying technological and biological systems
3. condensing time sequences
4. expanding time sequences
5. freeing the instructor to work individually with students
6. meeting individual learning styles and patterns

Media must be carefully selected to meet the needs of learners. Specific media are more suited to various kinds of situations than others. Therefore, media must be matched to both the learners' and the instructional content and process.

There are five basic techniques that are essential to the effective utilization of instructional media. These include:

1. reviewing all media before use
2. inspecting media hardware
3. preparing the learner for the media presentation
4. reviewing the presentation
5. evaluating the effectiveness of the media

REVIEW QUESTIONS

1. Define the term "instructional media."
2. What are several functions of instructional media?
3. How can instructional media be used to simplify technological and biological systems?
4. How can instructional media be used to meet the individual learning styles and patterns of students?
5. How can the chalkboard be more effectively utilized by the occupational education instructor?
6. What special learning needs can best be met through the use of audio tapes?
7. What is a single-concept film?
8. List three types of duplication procedures that are generally available to public school and community college teachers. What are the advantages and disadvantages of each?

9. Why is it important to preview media?
10. How should the learner be prepared prior to the media presentation?
11. List the five techniques that will assure the effective utilization of instructional media.

STUDENT ACTIVITIES

1. Using stiff cardboard, particle board, or plywood, prepare three or four templates that will be useful for chalkboard work when teaching your specialization area.
2. Identify and develop a list of commercial producers of models, films, filmstrips, and overhead transparencies for your specialization area.
3. Design and develop a preview form, a hardware check sheet, and a media evaluation form. Use mimeograph, multicolor spirit, and offset processes to duplicate these forms for each member of the class.
4. Review various media using the forms developed in item number three above. Identify strengths and weaknesses of each of the media that you review. For example, why is a particular film good or bad? What are several significant points brought out in the medium? At which occupational education level should these media be utilized?

REFERENCES

Brown, J.W.; Wilson, R.B. and Harcleroad, F.F. *A V Instruction: Technology, Media, and Methods.* New York: McGraw-Hill, 1973.

Dale, E. *Audiovisual Methods in Teaching.* 3d ed. New York: Holt, Rinehart, and Winston, 1969.

Drier, H.N. *Career Development Resources.* Worthington, Ohio: Charles A. Jones, 1973.

Gerlach, V.S. and Ely, D.P. *Teaching and Media - A Systematic Approach.* Englewood Cliffs, N.J.: Prentice-Hall, 1971.

Goudket, M. *An Audiovisual Primer.* New York: New York Teachers College Press, 1974.

Smith, H.R. and Nagel, T.S. *Instructional Media in the Learning Process.* Columbus, Ohio: Merrill, 1972.

Tanzman, J. and Dunn, K.J. *Using Instructional Media Effectively.* New York: Parker Publishing, 1971.

13

Cooperative Education as an Instructional Method

Interest in vocational preparation and exploratory programs is at its highest, and the outlook for these programs is bright. Occupational teachers and administrators also recognize that each program being offered must reflect the job requirements of today's labor market. Further, there is a need to combine formal education with meaningful work experience. Through a cooperative arrangement with business and industry, students will be provided learning experiences which will enable them to develop attitudes and to refine previously developed knowledges and skills that are required for the occupations they wish to enter.

Cooperative vocational education is an instructional method which is most appropriate for occupational education, and each occupational teacher must have a sound knowledge of its purpose and function. Upon completion of this chapter you will be able to:

- Define cooperative vocational education and distinguish it from other cooperative programs.
- Describe the scope and duties of the cooperative vocational education teacher-coordinator.
- Identify alternative cooperative education activities.
- Develop adequate training stations.
- Develop a plan for student supervision.

- **Identify program components which would be used in assessing the effectiveness of a cooperative vocational program.**

Cooperative education is not a new concept. Many educational systems have been developed which combine in-school learning with learning gained in the world of work. For example, the early Hebrews, through their apprenticeship programs, effectively combined the educational and work roles of youth. In that day, Jewish boys went to school in the mornings and spent their afternoons learning a trade from their fathers. Similar examples of this system can be found in the various apprenticeship programs operating throughout the United States.

While the value of learning which takes place on the job has been recognized for centuries, the majority of today's secondary and post-secondary youth are excluded from these educational benefits. Such experience can provide a realistic environment in which the student is able to refine and develop realistic job skills.

Cooperative vocational education is a purposeful blending of vocational instruction and employment in order to assist each student in developing the competencies required for employment. In its proper educational context, cooperative training becomes an instructional strategy for meeting performance objectives and program goals. It is recognized as an integrated part of the instructional program and merits the same attention that is given to in-school learning experience.

Widespread acceptance of cooperative education, at any educational level, did not come about until the concern for "education which will ease the transition from school to work" became a high priority. A review of educational programs at all levels indicates that some type of cooperative arrangement is being used to transmit the desired competencies. Cooperative arrangements can be found to exist between professional engineering schools and business and industry. Similarly, such arrangements are a part of professional and managerial training programs, as well as for the numerous occupational education programs. The value of learning experience gained through the live work situation is also indicated by the numerous administrative internships which are included in programs for school superintendents and principals.

Cooperative vocational education has been an integral part of secondary and post-secondary distributive education programs, and until recent years, accounted for the bulk of secondary school cooperative education enrollments.

With the passage of the *Vocational Education Amendments* 1968, considerable emphasis was placed on cooperative vocational education. In these amendments, Congress recognized the importance of removing the artificial barriers which separate the world of work from the educational setting. Further, cooperative education will also bring about the interaction between business, industry, and education which makes it possible to revise curricula to reflect the current needs of each occupation.

While the move toward cooperative vocational education in all programs is commendable, all teachers of vocational subjects should keep in mind the educational or training objectives for their particular program. These objectives must become the focus of each and every cooperative educational program. Participation in cooperative programs should come about, because it has been determined that specific competencies are best developed through this type of experience.

Various types of cooperative programs have been developed and implemented through the efforts of labor, management, and education. As a result, a number of different "school/work" -oriented programs have emerged. The three basic types which have implication for vocational education are: *Cooperative Vocational Education, Cooperative Work Training,* and *Work-Study.* In order to clarify these terms, the following definitions are provided.

Cooperative Vocational Education is an instructional plan which combines learning experiences gained through vocationally oriented in-school instruction with regularly scheduled supervised employment in the community. Such a program requires that the individual be employed in a setting which will serve as a laboratory where the student will have an opportunity to apply the principles and practices learned in school. The changing world of work will, therefore, provide a dynamic environment for student interaction. Such a program requires a cooperative arrangement between the school and the employers; and it includes the academic courses and related vocational instruction taught during the regularly scheduled classes in school and the work objectives learned at a particular job site. Work periods and school attendance might include half days in each setting, full days, weeks, or other periods of time which fulfill the requirements of the cooperative vocational education programs.

Cooperative Work Training (CWT) is a program designed to provide students experiences which will enable them to develop into mature, responsible, and productive individuals. The part-time work need not be related to the occupational or career goals of the student. This program is designed to serve youth and adults who need the social, emotional, maturation, and, in some cases, the career exploration which is essential for future success. All elements of the cooperative plan are present in the operation of a cooperative work training program. The work station or employment may not be in the occupation which the learner hopes to enter and need not be related to any occupational courses taken in high school or post-secondary institutions.

Work-Study is a program designed to provide financial assistance, through part-time employment. The students must have been accepted for full-time enrollment in vocational training. The part-time employment is in nonprofit agencies and is not necessarily related to his or her career objective. The primary focus of this program is to provide financial assistance. Job-related instruction is not required of work-study students.

The above definitions comprise those work experience programs which have been recognized and which also are designed to establish a viable employer-employee relationship. It is possible, however, to utilize a community resource through a cooperative arrangement which is not in the mode of cooperative education. The concept of clinical experience, which is used primarily in the field of health occupations, is the most notable example. This type of experience does not involve an employer-employee relationship in the normal sense. Simply put, it means that the students are not paid for the services they provide. The students are, however, provided an environment whereby they can practice their skills and apply knowledge learned in the classrooms and laboratories. Such activities are carried out under the close supervision of the clinical supervisor. Clinical experiences offer an alternative to the cooperative vocational education mode of instruction and provide the link between the school and the work place.

Other types of work experience have been utilized in the schools, and each serves an educational purpose. Learning is not confined to the four walls of the classroom, and each work experience program may have some characteristics of cooperative vocational education. These types of work education may be grouped as (1) exploratory work experiences which are usually short in duration and a viable component within the framework of career education; and (2) general work experience which is not tied to a vocational instructional program.

Cooperative education has certain identifying features which help to clarify the functional aspect of this form of work education. First, there are identifiable on-the-job training activities which become visible through a documented training agreement. To be educational, the experiences in employment must be planned and structured to meet instructional objectives and student needs. Too often, unstructured learning takes place. While this may be contributing to the overall development of the learner, it does not promote educational efficiency even though the work performed has economic value to the employer. The teacher-coordinator, through the cooperation of the employers and unions, must provide the leadership necessary to develop training plans which meet the needs and desires of each individual student.

The second identifying feature is employment which is regularly scheduled as a part of the total educational plan. Such employment provides each student with a specialized laboratory. It creates and maintains motivation and permits the measurement of achievement.

A third major feature of cooperative vocational education is "pay for work performed." This is one of the features which clearly establishes the employer-employee relationship. For the student, it represents a tangible expression of the rewards of work, and at the same time, it protects the student from the possibility of exploitation. The pay-for-work-performed concept also protects all parties involved from possible liability from injury. The student is treated like any other part-time employee, which means the employers comply with all federal and state wage and hour laws, minimum wage provisions, and workmen's compensation laws.

The last important feature of cooperative vocational education is credit for proficiency learned through on-the-job assignments. The provision of school credit for employment underscores the instructional purposes inherent in the cooperative method. Students leave the school environment for their laboratory experiences; yet, at the same time, the school exercises approval and provides direction to that experience through coordination and supervision.

In summary, cooperative vocational education is a transition stage between the classroom and the world of work. At the conclusion of the cooperative program, the student should have both the theory and the practical ability to continue in the occupation of his choice at a level above that of graduates without exposure to business and industry.

BENEFITS OF COOPERATIVE VOCATIONAL EDUCATION

Cooperative vocational education provides substantial benefits to the students, the secondary or post-secondary local education agency (LEA), and the community.

Benefits to the Student

1. Learns to assume responsibility.
2. Acquires good work habits.
3. Gains knowledge and attitudes necessary for successful job performance.
4. Learns how to get along with fellow workers and employers.
5. Develops personality and poise.
6. Augments financial resources.
7. Develops an appreciation of the value of wages.
8. Develops an understanding of the relationship between formal education and job success.
9. Broadens understanding of the occupational world.
10. Provides job relevance for students who must work.
11. Improves job placement and advancement.

Benefits to the LEA

1. Helps to develop good school/community relationships.
2. Provides an opportunity for the school to relate training to job requirements.
3. Utilizes community facilities and resources not otherwise available to the LEA.
4. Provides assistance in occupational guidance.
5. Enables the teacher-coordinator to keep abreast of developments in the business and industrial world.
6. Acquaints employers with the work that people trained in the secondary and post-secondary vocational programs can perform.
7. Shows the community how the tax dollar is being used.

Benefits to the Employers

1. Provides trainees who have specific career objectives and may become permanent employees.
2. Trains prospective employees for small businesses or industries that cannot afford extensive training programs.
3. Reduces turnover because employees become adjusted to the job before they accept full-time employment.
4. Provides motivated employees.
5. Provides the employer input to the content of training programs offered by the LEA.

Benefits to the Community

1. Provides more well-trained workers who are more readily assimilated into jobs.
2. Increases cooperation between the LEA and the community.
3. Increases the possibility that students will remain in the community after graduation.
4. Provides assistance in solving business and social problems.

THE ROLE OF THE TEACHER-COORDINATOR

The teacher-coordinator in a cooperative vocational education program truly becomes a learning manager with responsibilities in school as well as to the community. Generally, the teacher-coordinator is only responsible for a single occupational area, and the size of the group to be served is contingent upon the geographical area to be served and learning rate of the students. The teacher's responsibilities include guidance and selection of students, placing students in training jobs, assisting students in adjusting to their work environment, improving training done on the job, correlating classroom instruction with on-the-job training, assisting students in making personal adjustments, directing vocational youth organizations, providing services to graduates and adults, administering activities, and maintaining good public relations.

It is not the intent of this chapter to discuss the full implications of each of the above responsibilities, since other references are devoted entirely to this topic. However, a brief review of each of the major areas of responsibilities will help to clarify the teacher-coordinator's role.

Guidance and Selection of Students

The teacher-coordinator for each occupational area provides information about the program when requested, and he or she counsels with students about to enter the program. Additionally, he or she must work with guidance personnel by providing occupational information, gathering information on students, and assisting students in formulating realistic career objectives.

Placing Students at Training Stations

Since each student has specific individual needs, this phase of cooperative education is quite important. Selecting training stations and the placement of students must be determined by the performance objectives established by the teacher and the student. This involves enlisting the participation of cooperating employers and selecting the training station best suited for each student. Students must also be prepared for job interviews. Orientation must be provided to training supervisors and co-workers regarding the aims and purposes of cooperative education and its effect upon their work.

Assisting Students in Adjusting to Work Environments

The teacher-coordinator's responsibilities do not end when the student is placed on the job. Further assistance may be required to help the learner deal with job problems. Planning personal development with training supervisors and evaluating job progress is also a responsibility of the teacher-coordinator.

Improving Training Done On the Job

An important, but often neglected, aspect of cooperative vocational education is the development of a training plan which establishes the student's responsibilities and outlines the objectives to be met through the experiences gained on the job. This involves consultation with employers and training supervisors.

Correlate Classroom Instruction With On-the-Job Training

As a coordinator, the teacher must determine what instruction is needed by the students. Appropriate instructional materials can then be prepared or assembled for individual use or for group instruction.

Further, individual projects may be utilized. Evaluation of learning outcomes must also be accomplished. The teacher-coordinator should keep the employer informed about related classroom instruction, to correlate this instruction with occupational duties to be performed.

Assisting Students in Making Personal Adjustments

Often, students will be working in a real work setting for the first time. The teacher-coordinator will aid students in correcting poor personal habits, and he or she may also counsel students with personal and socioeconomic problems. Further, the coordinator may need to resolve behavioral problems on the job and assist students with educational difficulties.

Directing Vocational Youth Organizations, if Applicable

This entails advising youth groups and guiding students in organization and participation in group activities.

Providing Services to Graduates and Adults

A natural outgrowth of many cooperative vocational education programs is that of providing guidance and placement services for graduates and adults. An active teacher-coordinator will have developed rapport with employers who, in turn, will solicit their help in locating new employees. The teacher-coordinator is in a position to be of service to both the employers and to youth and adults. Further, his or her knowledge of the employment market can be extremely valuable in program planning or operation of adult education programs.

Administrative Activities

The teacher-coordinator performs a number of administrative tasks which include development of curriculum, research, organizing and working with advisory committees, communicating school policy, and preparing budgets and reports.

Maintaining Good Public Relations

Continuation and improvement of cooperative vocational education programs is dependent upon a sound public relations program.

This involves the preparation of newsworthy articles and contacting the news media for coverage at the appropriate times. Good public relations is dependent upon communications with various segments of the community, employers, school administration, faculty, various labor unions, and the students themselves.

SELECTION OF THE TRAINING STATION

One of the major tasks of a teacher-coordinator is finding training stations which can provide the job experience needed by the student. Other students will have jobs when they enter the program and will request that they be allowed to keep their jobs and enroll for cooperative vocational credit. When such a request is made, it is the teacher-coordinator's responsibility to visit the student's place of employment and talk to his or her employer to determine whether the job is suitable for cooperative vocational education. For students who do not have a job, it is the teacher-coordinator's responsibility to help find suitable training stations. In choosing the appropriate training station for students, the teacher-coordinator may find it necessary to visit several employers before being able to make a suitable selection.

Criteria for Training Station Selection

The teacher-coordinator should consider the following in selecting the training station.

1. The employer understands the intent and purpose of cooperative vocational education.
2. The employer understands that the cooperative plan is a training program and not primarily a school employment agency.
3. There is a reasonable probability of continuous employment for the student.
4. The employer has adequate equipment, materials, and facilities to provide appropriate learning opportunities.
5. The student will be placed in the same employment status as that of other part-time employees in matters of wages, social security, insurance, vacations, and labor laws.
6. The employer will provide adequate supervision to insure a planned program of activities.
7. The job provides training in all phases of the occupation, rather than in routine activities only.

8. The training station is conveniently located with respect to the student and the instructor-coordinator.
9. The job provides training in an occupation in which a person would have a reasonable opportunity of finding full-time employment upon graduation.
10. Preplanned tasks to be performed on the job are within the range of the student's ability and difficult enough to provide a challenge.
11. The employer's relationship with labor, other employers, and customers is excellent and his business practices are ethical.
12. Hiring, promotion, and dismissal practices are consistent with program goals.

It is essential that employers of cooperative vocational students be strongly committed to cooperative education as training experience. Their attitude toward individual improvement is reflected in the manner in which they train their regular employees. A firm which has an employee training program and seeks to promote the maximum growth of each employee is potentially a suitable training station.

The Training Agreement

When the teacher-coordinator and the employer reach an agreement on the establishment of a training station, a written agreement is advisable. Before the agreement is signed, the teacher-coordinator should make certain that the employer understands and agrees with the objectives of the program, its advantages to him, to the student, to the Local Education Agency (LEA) and to the community.

The training agreement should include the purposes of the cooperative vocational education program and responsibilities of the student, the LEA, and the employer (FIGURE 13-1). The following points should be covered in a training agreement:

1. duties of the student
2. number of hours the student is to spend on the job
3. responsibilities of the student
4. responsibilities of the employer
5. responsibilities of the Local Education Agency

Legal Responsibilities

The teacher-coordinator of cooperative vocational education must also understand all local, state, and federal labor regulations which apply to students in their training stations. A teacher-coordinator should maintain a file of these laws and regulations and should also know where to find information on all applicable laws. The teacher-coordinator is not responsible for enforcing the law, but is morally responsible for, and is expected to, inform participating employers when they are unknowingly violating regulations. If the employer fails to comply with the law, the teacher-coordinator should cancel the agreement and place the student in another training station. Refer to the references at the end of this chapter for further information about the various federal and state laws which have direct implication for students enrolled in cooperative vocational education programs.

STUDENT SUPERVISION AT TRAINING STATIONS

Students once placed at their training stations require supervision by school personnel. This is one of the most important activities of the teacher-coordinator. The primary purpose of follow-up calls is to maintain and insure that each work station is a learning environment. In order to accomplish this objective, the teacher-coordinator must become an expert in human relations and salesmanship. Some changes will be necessary and are best brought about if a harmonious relationship is maintained.

To maintain good relations with students and employers, it is important that visits to the training station be scheduled at a time which is convenient to both the employer and employee. For example, food service institutions will be extremely busy between the hours of 11:00 A.M.-1:30 P.M.; however, around 2:30 P.M., there will be a slack period and sufficient time will be available for a conference. Similarly, each occupational specialty will have peak periods of activity which must be taken into account when scheduling visits.

One of the primary purposes of the follow-up call is to assess the effectiveness of each student's learning experience. The results of the assessment may require several approaches to bring about the desired learning. First, there may be a need for additional specialized related

SAMPLE TRAINING AGREEMENT

Student's Name _____ Birth Date _____ Age _____

Student's Address _____ Telephone _____

School _____ Telephone _____

Training Station _____ Telephone _____

Address of Training Station _____

Training Supervisor _____ Position _____

Dates of Training Period: From _____   To _____

Average Number of Hours of Employment: Per Day _____   Per Week _____

Student-Learner's Rate of Beginning Pay _____

Career Objective _____

Basic skills, attitudes, and knowledge needed in this occupation:

Major areas of experience and training to be provided at training station:

Major areas of related instruction to be provided in class:

RESPONSIBILITIES

The STUDENT-LEARNER considers his job experience as contributing to his career objectives and agrees:

1. To be regular in attendance, both in school and on the job

2. To perform his training station responsibilities and classroom responsibilities in an efficient manner

3. To show honesty, punctuality, courtesy, a cooperative attitude, proper health and grooming habits, appropriate dress, and a willingness to learn

4. To conform to the rules and regulations of the training station

5. To furnish the teacher-coordinator with necessary information about his training program and to complete promptly all necessary reports

6. To consult the teacher-coordinator about any difficulties arising at the training station or related to his training program

7. To participate in those co-curricular school activities that are required in connection with the COE program

The PARENTS of the student-learner, realizing the importance of the training program in the student-learner's attaining his career objectives, agrees:

1. To encourage the student-learner to carry out effectively his duties and responsibilities.

2. To share the responsibility for the conduct of the student-learner while training in the program.

3. To accept responsibility for the safety and conduct of the student-learner while he is traveling to and from the school, the training station, and his home.

From Virginia State Department of Education. *Vocational Education Sample Training Agreement*. Richmond, 1974. Reprinted by permission.

FIGURE 13-1

Sample Training Agreement

WORK EXPERIENCES TO BE PROVIDED	RECORD OF WORK	OUTLINE OF STUDY ASSIGNMENTS	RECORD OF STUDIES

The TRAINING-STATION, recognizing that a training plan is being followed and that close supervision of the student-learner will be needed, agrees:

1. To provide a variety of work experiences for the student-learner that will contribute to the attainment of his career objective.

2. To endeavor to employ the student-learner for at least the minimum listed number of hours each day and each week for the entire training period.

3. To adhere to all Federal and State regulations regarding employment, child labor laws, minimum wages, and other applicable regulations.

4. To assist in the evaluation of the student-learner.

5. To provide time for consultation with the teacher-coordinator concerning the student-learner and to discuss with the teacher-coordinator any difficulties the student-learner may be having.

6. To provide available instructional material and occupational guidance for the student-learner.

The TEACHER-COORDINATOR, representing the school, will coordinate the training program toward a satisfactory preparation of the student-learner for his occupational career objective and agrees:

1. To see that the necessary related classroom instruction is provided.

2. To make periodic visits to the training station to observe the student-learner, to consult with the employer and training supervisor, and to render any needed assistance with training problems of the student-learner.

3. To assist in the evaluation of the student-learner.

Additional Comments:

By _____   _____
                 Employer   Parent

_____   _____
              Job Supervisor   Student-learner

                                           DATE _____
_____
           Teacher-Coordinator

instruction. Second, the teacher-coordinator may need to assist the learner in making work adjustments, and third, the employer may need assistance in evaluating the student's performance. Often, a student evaluation instrument may be provided for the employer's use (FIGURE 13-2).

The results of each student evaluation should be thoroughly discussed with the student with the intention of improving learning. It is also important that the teacher-coordinator maintain a schedule of visits so that an assessment of each student's progress can be made at least once a month.

Cooperative vocational education, as in all other phases of education, is dependent upon the completeness and accuracy of records kept by the employer and teacher-coordinator. This is important not only from the grade assignment standpoint but also to insure that a systematic learning environment is maintained.

EVALUATING PROGRAM EFFECTIVENESS

The process of improving cooperative vocational education is a continual one. Evaluation facilitates the efforts of the teacher-coordinator and the Local Education Agency in meeting their goals and objectives for such programs. However, evaluation should include more than an assessment of the student's and teacher-coordinator's efforts. It must of necessity involve: (1) the administrative leadership, (2) program organization, (3) curriculum, (4) professional development of staff, (5) instructional materials and supplies, (6) placement and follow-up of graduates, (7) comprehensiveness of service to all needing vocational education, and (8) the adequacy of budgets.

It is not the intent and purpose of this chapter to deal with all the specifics of the above. However, the following data should be considered in measuring the results of cooperative programs.

1. Compare the number of students served by the program with manpower needs.
2. Document the occupations for which cooperative programs are available.
3. Follow up graduates to ascertain tenure, need for additional training, etc.

4. Survey the impact of the program in relation to reducing youth unemployment.
5. Survey the impact of the program in relation to reducing overall school dropouts.
6. Document facts regarding why students dropped out of the program or school.
7. Determine if the in-school training is providing the competencies necessary for satisfactory job performance.
8. Results of other research which has identified program needs and suggestions for improvement.

SUMMARY

Cooperative vocational education is a powerful learning strategy. It can bridge the gap between school and work. Further, such programs provide a dynamic learning laboratory for students to apply and refine skills and knowledges learned in their job-simulation laboratories. Cooperative programs also give youth an opportunity to assume adult responsibilities and monetary rewards which are provided only through a satisfactory job placement. As an instructional method, cooperative vocational education is in essence the "pay-off" for vocational education. Job placement and success are greatly enhanced.

REVIEW QUESTIONS

1. Explain why cooperative vocational education has received so much attention in recent years.
2. What are the three types of cooperative education, how are they the same, and how do they differ?
3. How would a health occupations clinical experience compare with a cooperative vocational program in terms of learning experiences?
4. What are the four major features of cooperative vocational education? Explain each.
5. How does cooperative vocational education benefit the student, LEA, and employer?
6. The teacher-coordinator play an important role in a cooperative vocational program. What are the major areas of responsibilities?

COOPERATIVE EDUCATION PROGRAM

EMPLOYER'S SUBJECTIVE EVALUATION

Student _____ Job Title _____

Employer _____ _____

Evaluator _____ Title _____

Evaluation Period　From _____ To _____ Date Prepared _____
　　　　　　　　　　　Month　　Date　　Month　　Date

INSTRUCTIONS: The student listed above is employed in your business as a Cooperative Education Trainee. Would you please rate him according to the criteria listed below, comparing him with other personnel assigned to the same or similarly classified jobs or with individual standards. The information supplied on this sheet will be used to help guide the student for self-improvement.

QUALITY OF WORK
Surpasses standards
Meets joint standards
Falls short on some standards
Very frequent errors

ABILITY TO LEARN
Learns very quickly
Learns rapidly
Average for his level
Rather slow to learn
Very slow to learn

QUANTITY OF WORK
Highly productive
Meets standard output
Production below standard
Excessively slow

JUDGMENT
Above average
Average for his level
Sometimes immature
Poor judgment

INITIATIVE
Willing worker, does more than expected
Works steady, does a good day's work
Must be prodded occasionally
Takes it easy, kills time

WORK ATTITUDE
Enthusiastic
Normal interest
Indifferent
Not interested

DEPENDABILITY
Completely dependable
Usually dependable
Sometimes careless
Unreliable

RESPONSIBILITY
Unusual pride in work
Understands importance of work
Lacks appreciation of job importance
Careless

PUNCTUALITY
Never late
Occasionally late
Often late
Usually late

APPEARANCE
Always acceptable
Sometimes questionable
Often questionable
Rarely acceptable

RELATIONS WITH OTHERS
Works well with others
Gets along satisfactorily
Has some difficulty
Doesn't get along

STUDENT'S COLLEGE PREPARATION
Well prepared
Acceptably prepared
Lacking in some areas
Not adequately prepared

From Bellevue Community College, *Student Kit Cooperative Education*, Bellevue, Washington 1974. Reprinted by permission.

FIGURE 13-2

Employer's Subjective Evaluation of Cooperative Education Program

OVERALL PERFORMANCE

☐ Outstanding   ☐ Very good   ☐ Average   ☐ Marginal   ☐ Unsatisfactory

Please list student's strong points:

Please list areas where improvements would greatly benefit student:

Would you recommend this student for future employment in your own or another firm?

Yes ☐   No ☐
Please comment

This report has been discussed with the student.   Yes ☐   No ☐
Signed: _____ Date: _____

WORKSHEET ONLY
COMMUNITY COLLEGE
COOPERATIVE EDUCATION PROGRAM

_____
DATE

_____   _____
EMPLOYER   SUPERVISOR

STATEMENT OF JOB PERFORMANCE OBJECTIVES

Each quarter that a student is enrolled in the Cooperative Education Program, it is necessary that the college help the student determine what new or expanded responsibilities or learning opportunities are possible on his job. These objectives enable us to determine the learning value of the student's work experience.

These objectives should be specific and measurable. They will be reviewed with the supervisor. At the end of the quarter, the student/employee and the supervisor will be asked to evaluate the level of attainment of each objective and relative value of each objective (in relation to the other objectives).

	*RATING		VAL. OF EA. OBJECTIVE (%)	
	STUDENT	SUPER.	STUDENT	SUPER.
1.				
2.				
3.				
4.				
5.				

1. _____

2. _____

3. _____

4. _____

5. _____

FIGURE 13-2 (Cont'd)

Worksheet for Supervisor's Evaluation of Student/Employee

If you were to issue this student/employee a letter grade for the level of attainment of these objectives, what would it be: _____

*RATING SCALE
1. Meets minimum performance requirements   (D — barely passing)
2. Normal or expected level of performance   (C — average)
3. Meets and frequently exceeds expected performance   (B — above average)
4. Unique performance   (A — excellent)

AGREEMENT

We, the undersigned, agree with the validity of the learning objectives listed above. The employer and the college agree to provide the necessary supervision and counseling to insure that the maximum educational benefit may be achieved for the student/employee's work experience.

There are three participants in the Cooperative Education venture. The student agrees to abide by the Cooperative Education guidelines. The supervisor will evaluate the student/employee's performance objectives at the end of the grading period. The college will award academic credit for work successfully accomplished.

_____   _____
STUDENT'S SIGNATURE   INSTURCTOR/COORDINATOR'S SIGNATURE

7. Selection of training stations is critical to the success of a cooperative program. What criteria should be used for this selection?

STUDENT ACTIVITIES

1. Develop a short presentation which will inform businessmen about the different cooperative education programs.
2. Survey ten employers to determine whether they utilize part time help.
3. Interview two teacher-coordinators to determine how they set up a public relations program.
4. Interview three vocational teachers and three related instructors, and have them define cooperative vocational education cooperative work training. Compare and contrast their definitions.
5. Arrange to accompany a teacher-coordinator as he or she visits training stations for two days.
6. Prepare a comprehensive job description for a teacher-coordinator in business and office occupations.

REFERENCES

Crawford, L. and Meyer, W.G. *Organization and Administration of Distributive Education.* Columbus: Merrill, 1972.

Mason, R.E. and Haines, P.G. *Cooperative Occupational Education.* Danville, Ill.: Interstate, 1972.

Meyer, W.G.; Crawford, L. and Klainens, M.K. *Coordination in Cooperative Education.* Columbus, Ohio: Merrill, 1975.

Mosbacken, W. "The Role of the Coordinator", *Journal of Cooperative Education,* May, 1969.

CHAPTER 14

Guest Presentors and Field Trips

Guest presentors and field trips are two closely related instructional methods which may be utilized in occupational education programs at all levels. Their relationship to one another stems from the fact that both involve the utilization of resources external to the regular program. Unlike cooperative education, which also utilizes external resources, these two methods are generally short-term measures that serve to support regular instructional activities rather than being primary and long-term approaches to instruction.

Upon completion of this chapter, you will be able to:

- **Define the role of guest presentors in the instructional process.**
- **Describe techniques for assuring effective utilization of guest presentors in occupational education programs.**
- **Define the role of field trips in the instructional process.**
- **Describe techniques and procedures which are utilized in planning, implementing, and evaluating field-trip experiences.**

The utilization of guest presentors and field trips demands careful and systematic prior planning. Both procedures not only impinge on the regular instructional time set aside for a particular program, but they also demand time on the part of the community resources that are to be utilized. Therefore, it is essential that both techniques be used at just the right time, preceded by adequate instructional orientation, and followed by appropriate follow-up activities.

GUEST PRESENTORS

Presentations by individuals from outside the regular instructional program serve several important instructional functions. First, outside speakers can bring to the instructional program extensive expertise in an area being studied. Second, student motivation can be increased by a new face in the teaching/learning setting. Finally, the guest speaker can increase the instructor's credibility with the students when a person from the community supports concepts initially presented by that instructor.

Expertise

Outside speakers are often invited to present materials to occupational education classes, because of special skills and knowledges they possess that are related to current instructional topics, At the orientation level, this might include individuals skilled in various occupations being studied. These guest presentors may describe their occupational area in terms of the training necessary for entry and the benefits they derive from their occupation. They may also conduct job interviews to add a greater amount of realism to that simulation activity. At the preparation level, these individuals may discuss specific techniques and procedures that they utilize in performing certain aspects of their occupation. For example, a skilled auto body repair person might describe the procedures that he or she utilizes when estimating cost on particularly difficult jobs. The personnel representative from a local industry may describe those attributes that are sought when hiring a new employee.

When seeking possible presentors to represent special areas of expertise, the occupational education instructor should discuss his or her needs with colleagues, local labor officials, and members of local business, industrial, or health-care associations. Careful consideration should be given to finding an individual who not only possesses the necessary expertise but also can present information in an effective manner.

Motivation

There are times when a guest speaker may be selected to present material that may be effectively taught via another method. In such cases, motivation may often be the prime factor that determines the utilization of this method of instruction. Especially at the preparation level where students spend considerable time with the faculty, a "new face" is often a good motivating factor.

When selecting guest speakers for motivational reasons, care should be exercised to assure that the guest can, in fact, motivate the learners. Emphasis should be placed on how dynamic and interesting the speaker actually is. If the speaker is dull, lacks animation, or tends to be uninterested in the presentation, the motivational aspect of this approach will be lost.

Credibility

Instructor credibility is an important aspect of occupational education programs. This is especially true at the post-secondary occupational preparation level. Adult learners must believe in the instructor and what he or she says. While many factors (such as age, knowledge of subject matter, etc.) enter into the credibility assessment of the instructor, guest speakers can have tremendous input into this attitude possessed by students. When a highly qualified individual, well known in the occupational area, presents information that corresponds to that which has been presented previously, instructor credibility climbs. Do not overlook the guest speaker as a means to this important end.

MANAGING THE GUEST PRESENTOR METHOD

Managing this instructional method consists of four primary activities. These include:

1. Selecting the guest speaker
2. Preparing the learners
3. Presentation follow-up
4. Evaluation

Selecting the Guest Speaker

When selecting a guest presentor, be certain that he or she is fully aware of what you expect. Describe the objectives of the program and those specific objectives that are to be accomplished by the presenter. Give the guest speaker a little background into those activities that have preceded his or her presentation and those follow-up procedures that will be utilized.

If the initial contact with the presentor was informal, prepare a formal letter requesting his or her services. Be sure that the school principal or director is aware that a guest speaker is being utilized and who the guest speaker is. Inform other faculty members teaching in related areas of the identity of the speaker, the time(s) when he or she will be in your class, and the topics that will be discussed. Your colleages may wish to involve their students in the presentation.

Preparing the Learners

The students must be prepared for the guest presentor. Related reading, laboratory, or discussion assignments should be made. A student may be selected to introduce the speaker. Key questions may be assigned to students as discussion items in the event that the speaker wants this kind of communication. A reminder, subtle or not, regarding manners and courtesy is always in order. If you are going to take the speaker to lunch or dinner, be sure that appropriate arrangements have been made.

The learners must be aware of why the speaker is there and what specific objectives are being accomplished through his or her visit. Therefore, prior to the arrival of the guest presentor, an information handout identifying the speaker, his or her specific qualifications, and the instructional objectives should be distributed.

Presentation Follow-up

Following the presentation and any resultant discussion, the instructor should be prepared to present a follow-up activity that will tie the guest speaker's presentation to the continuing instructional processes. This follow-up might be as simple as a discussion of the topic or as detailed as a complex laboratory experiment or work activity.

The nature of the follow-up assignment will be determined by the initial objectives established for the speaker and the nature of his or her presentation. Whatever the activity, this follow-up is extremely important in assuring the maximization of the utilization of the guest presentor.

Evaluation

Materials and information presented by guest speakers, provided they fit the overall instructional objectives, are worthy of evaluation. This includes both evaluation of learning and evaluation of the presentor. Therefore, information presented should be included in the ongoing system of evaluation of student performance. Test items, based on the guest presentor's topic, should be constructed and included in future examinations.

The instructor should assess the presentation in terms of its applicability to ongoing instructional objectives. Emphasis should also be placed on how well the presentation met the basic goals of expertise, motivation, and credibility. This evaluative information should be written and placed in the unit file for future reference. Such information will be extremely valuable in determining future guest presentors.

FIELD TRIPS

Field trips are extremely valuable instructional methods. At the preparation level, they can be used to supplement regular laboratory or classroom learning by relating these activities to real world of work processes and procedures. At the orientation and exploration levels, field trips can serve as primary instructional methods by permitting students to watch people at work in a variety of occupations in real work settings. Whatever the program level, several techniques and procedures must be followed to assure that the field trip will serve as a successful instructional method. These procedures include:

1. Identification of field-trip site
2. Coordination with business, industrial, or health-care managers
3. Scheduling
4. Coordination within the local education agency
5. Preparing the students

6. Conducting the field trip
7. Student follow-up
8. Follow-up to field-trip site

Identification of the Field-Trip Site

Determining just where to go on a field trip must be based on the objectives established for the activity, the amount of time available, and the nature of various business, industrial, or health-care enterprises in the local area. The field trip can be several days in duration or, if local facilities and sites are available, it might be accomplished during a regular instructional day. If local agencies are nearby and can meet the needs of the learners, the short field trip is in order. In many areas, however, the location of the local education agency will demand that overnight trips be taken.

A strong and active advisory committee is of great help in determining field-trip sites, since membership on the committee represents local business, industry, or health care. Most advisory committee members will be more than willing to assist the instructor in determining a suitable field-trip location. Other instructors may have several ideas. Often, students will have good suggestions as to specific enterprises that may serve as outstanding field-trip sites.

Coordination With Field-Trip Site Managers

Upon determination of the field-trip site, the instructor must contact the agency or business to request permission for the visitation, determine specific schedules, and discuss special considerations such as safety, group size, and particular areas of interest. This initial contact will, in most cases, be conducted with the public relations or personnel officer. This phase of field-trip planning is important, because it establishes the ground rules for the visitation. When possible, the instructor should meet with the contact person and, if possible, tour the facilities.

Be sure to inform the business representative of the objectives for the field trip, the nature of the group that is coming, and any prior experiences the students may have had that relate to this particular field trip. If the field-trip site is more than one day's distance from the school, determine where the group will be staying. Check with the business contact to see whether he or she would recommend a particular motel. Also, check on eating accommodations in the local area. Can students eat lunch at or near the field-trip site?

The "check list" in FIGURE 14-1 may be modified to suit local needs. It does represent a formal analysis technique that will assure the field-trip coordinator that all possible variables have been considered.

Scheduling

As most experienced teachers know, scheduling the field trip is a very difficult task. Often, other instructors will have to be informed of the field trip and of those students who are planning to go. Permission to excuse these students from other classes will have to be obtained. This task often requires some tact on the part of the field-trip coordinator. Other teachers generally do not mind students going on field trips, if they are not too frequent and if the trip coordinator contacts them in sufficient time that they can plan instructional alternatives. *Do not* ask teachers, one day prior to the trip, to excuse students. This approach lacks professional courtesy.

If school buses are to be utilized, be sure to schedule them well in advance. This also holds true if commercial transportation is to be used. Plan plenty of time for the trip. Just because the instructor can drive to the field-trip site in his or her car in two hours does not mean that a bus load of students can make it in that amount of time. Plan on enough time for two or three extra restroom stops.

In the event that secondary-age students are going on the field trip, parental permission will have to be obtained. These permission forms will be available in the school office. Be sure to allow plenty of time for these to be returned. *No permission slip must mean no field trip for that student.*

Once local schedules have been determined, check again with the field-trip contact person, the motel where you will be staying, and the transportation agency to be certain that everything is in order. Have a copy of the schedule printed and distributed to the students, parents, and school administration.

Coordination Within the Local Education Agency

Coordination with other faculty was discussed in the previous section. This section deals with two primary coordinative functions. First, all field trips must be cleared with appropriate administrative personnel. This must be done in writing and should precede most of the field-trip planning. Second, the field trip schedule, objectives, and other specifics must be coordinated with the participants. How

FIELD-TRIP CHECK SHEET

COURSE _____ SECTION _____

INSTRUCTOR _____

FIELD-TRIP SITE _____

_____

_____

CONTACT PERSON _____ TELEPHONE NO. _____

DATE _____ NO. OF STUDENTS _____

TRANSPORTATION _____

LODGING _____

_____

_____TELEPHONE NO. _____

DEPARTURE (from school) _ ARRIVAL (site) _____

DEPARTURE (site) _____ ARRIVAL (school) _____

ATTENDING FACULTY _____

_____

_____

EMERGENCY TELEPHONE NO. (school) _____

(principal) _____

(transportation) _____

FIGURE 14-1

Field Trip Check Sheet

much money will they need? When will they leave? Return? How are room assignments to be made? These questions must be resolved prior to the trip. These questions must also be answered to the satisfaction of parents. This is especially critical at the orientation and exploration levels.

Preparing the Students

Before the actual field trip, students should be provided several kinds of preparatory information. Details regarding the enterprise to be visited may be important. Consideration should be given to a discussion regarding the nature of its products and/or services. If the instructor has had the opportunity of a previous visit to the enterprise, he or she should provide learners with information relative to operations, procedures, and processes that they will be seeing. This might include drawing attention to specific activities that will be of special interest.

Instructors and students should discuss the "code of conduct" that will be followed. This must be understood by all. Disciplinary procedures that will result when the code is not followed should also be explained. Students must be made to realize that their school and community is being represented by them. They must act accordingly.

Refer to the previous section for other questions that might be discussed.

Conducting the Field Trip

The actual field trip will be greatly enhanced if the preparatory steps have been taken. Enforce the discipline code, react to special personal problems that might occur, and lead student discussions and activities.

A bus full of younger students will always be a bus full of younger students. The discipline responsibility rests with the instructor. Remember, this field trip is a special experience for the learners. Enforce the code, but be fair. A little laughing and talking is good. However, do not permit activities which will be unsafe while in transit, at the site, or at the place of lodging.

Student Follow-up

After the field trip, some time should be spent with students in follow-up activities. These might include discussions, student reports, or a review of photographs or slides taken while on the field trip. The follow-up activity will help tie the field trip to the ongoing instructional program at school.

Follow-up to Field-Trip Site

Upon returning from the trip, a brief letter of thanks to the contact person at the field-trip site should be prepared. The letter should point out areas that were of particular interest to students and were well-suited to meet the instructional objectives. This type of follow-up will help assure the future use of the field-trip site by other groups. The follow-up letter may be prepared and signed by the instructor or by both the students and the teacher.

SUMMARY

Guest presentors and field trips are two related instructional methods that utilize external resources. Both methods tend to support regular instructional activities.

Guest presentors can bring greater expertise, motivation, and credibility to the occupational program. In implementing the guest presentor method, the instructor must select the speaker, prepare students for the presentation, follow up the presentor with supportive activities, and evaluate the total presentation.

Field trips can be valuable instructional methods, provided they are managed correctly by the instructor. This management includes careful selection of the site, close coordination among all people concerned, preparation of the students for the activity, and careful follow-up of the field-trip experience.

REVIEW QUESTIONS

1. How are guest presentors and field trips like cooperative education?
2. How do these two methods differ from cooperative education?
3. How can an outside speaker add credibility to your occupational education program?

4. What factors should be considered when determining a field-trip site?
5. Why is scheduling so important in field-trip activities?
6. If young students are involved in a field trip, what kind of information must be provided to parents? Administrators? Students?

STUDENT ACTIVITIES

1. Develop a written procedure manual for use by instructors in your school when planning the use of guest presentors.
2. Prepare a sample letter inviting a guest speaker to your class. Prepare a letter of thanks.
3. Design a field-trip guide complete with sample letters for use by instructors in occupational education programs at all three levels.
4. Take a short field trip with the entire class. Carefully note all the considerations that went into planning and implementing it.

15

Grading and Record Keeping

Providing a quality educational environment is the prime function of all occupational educators. Educators must also implement an evaluation and record keeping system that continuously monitors student progress and assesses the effectiveness of each program. The modern teacher is a learning manager. The learning manager is responsible for learning that takes place or fails to take place within the assigned classroom or laboratory. An effort must also be made to ascertain achievement of institutional and program mission, administration, course objectives, course content, methods, and evaluation.

Upon completion of this chapter, the reader will be able to:

- **Define some of the more common types of tests used in present-day schools.**
- **Describe the purposes of evaluation.**
- **Present a method for planning and administering an evaluation instrument.**
- **Discuss instructional record keeping systems.**

Assessment of instruction may be defined as a systematic procedure for collecting and analyzing information for the purpose of decision making. Assessment is more than examining the achievement of program and course objectives. Where are we? Where are we going? and, How are we going to get there? These are questions that instructional assessment should address.

Evaluation systems may contain elements such as standardized tests and teacher-made tests. Inherent in these tests are methods of describing test results and assignment of grades. Learning managers are accountable for their actions and their product (the performance potential and capability of their students). Accountability implies justification of actions involved in the educational process. Students can be tested or observed to determine their levels of cognitive, affective, and psychomotor performance. The results of these tests enable teachers to quantify and qualify student performance. This process requires that a proper record keeping system be developed and maintained.

One of the most commonly used devices to ascertain student performance is the standardized test. Teachers should review standardized tests and procedures prior to administering, to insure the following criteria are met:

1. Appropriate for student age level
2. Appropriate for student reading level
3. Pertinent to overall goals and objectives
4. The results can be used to benefit the student and the program
5. Measures what you want to measure

The standardized tests are beneficial to the teacher in that valuable time can be saved as these tests are prepared and keyed for usage. Standardized tests have also been field tested and modified to assure reliability.

Teacher-made tests are as varied in their use as are the teacher's objectives and circumstances surrounding development and administration of them. Teachers should vary their tests and assessment procedures in order to afford students alternative avenues for response. All students do not respond equally well to all types of tests.

In the grading process, tests are administered for two primary reasons: (1) to ascertain the effectiveness of teaching, and (2) to ascertain levels of learning.

The basis for all evaluation within the classroom or laboratory setting is the specific behavioral objectives to be accomplished during the educational process. Evaluation is an important factor in the accomplishment of the performance objectives. Through performance objectives, teachers have a foundation for testing, and test questions and techniques can be developed which reflect the accomplishment of these objectives. Can the student do, know, and be, those things specified within the objectives? If they can, learning has taken place; if not, the opposite is true.

Evaluation and measurement cannot be accomplished strictly by pencil and paper tests. Comprehensive evaluation is also based on objective and subjective appraisals. Student attitude, initiative, ability to get along, and cooperation are affective domain characteristics the teacher subjectively observes. In order to achieve grade assignment in this difficult area, objectives must be written to serve as a basis for evaluation.

Student evaluation results in two benefits. Achievement level is specified according to performance objectives and learning deficiencies can be diagnosed. The most important aspect of evaluation is to determine whether the content was taught adequately and the performance objectives have been reached.

Testing and measurement must be employed in order to determine class and student achievement, establish standards and norms of performance, determine quality of instruction, evaluate the effectiveness of teaching materials and methods, motivate students, and to assist in guidance and placement of students. Tests are also utilized to meet administration requirements, improve instruction, as teaching devices, and a basis for awarding grades. An effective educational program cannot be carried out without frequent appraisal of the students and their development.

TESTING

Evaluation involves determining those objectives which are to be measured, and then developing the instrument or device which will best measure them. A test is any series of questions, exercises, or devices for measuring the skill, knowledge, intelligence, capabilities, or aptitudes of an individual or group. Values resulting from testing can be used to assign grades, inform parents of status, promote students, and enable teachers to distinguish individual and/or group characteristics and differences.

Planning and administering evaluation instruments should reflect the question, "What should be the nature of the product?" The teacher may perform an occupational analysis and job analysis to determine teachable content. The total body of content can then be broken into identifiable competencies. These competencies can then be described in terms of skills, knowledges, and attitudes. Educational evaluation is the continuous process of collecting all pertinent data regarding student performance and then interpreting these results for students, parents, and possible employers. This information is placed on a permanent record. This record is then made available for use by people concerned. One teacher's evaluation system is only a small portion of a total school-wide system. Teachers must ensure that their individual system complements the total system.

Two broad categories of educational evaluation measurement are criterion-referenced measurement and norm-referenced measurement. Criterion-referenced measurement utilizes a set standard. The results of the evaluation are measured against this standard to determine levels of performance. An example of this category is utilizing a set score. Students performing at or above the score or cutoff point are seen as having the potential for success in the program or course. Scores below the cutoff point might predict failure or extreme difficulty in pursuing the program or course. This example of criterion-referenced measurement is utilized to determine whether a student may or may not participate in an "honor" course or program.

Norm-referenced measurement is the orderly procedure of evaluating students in relationship to other students. Utilization of norm-referenced measures enables teachers to compare individuals and groups with other individuals or groups which have taken the same test. For example, a norm-referenced reading test and a math test may reveal that a student may be at the seventh grade reading level and at the ninth grade level in computation skills.

These norm-referenced measures allow for finite determination of individual difference and performance level. Establishment of a level of performance, as related to other students of a similar age and grade level, allows the teacher to design a program which will meet general student needs and abilities.

Teacher-made tests are the most common type of evaluation devices found in education. FIGURES 15-1 and 15-2 illustrate important steps that should be used to develop a good teacher-made test. FIGURE 15-3 delineates the important qualities of a well-constructed test. (See FIGURES 15-1 through 15-3.)

STEPS IN BUILDING A TEST

1. Decide what you wish to test.
2. Determine the most appropriate type of test to administer.
3. Construct the test items to match your objectives.
   a. Fit the question with the subject matter, not the subject matter to the question.
   b. Limit the types of items in a single test to 3 or 4 types.
4. Assemble the items for the test.
   a. Arrange by type.
   b. Put a few sample questions first to afford the student a feeling of success and accomplishment.
5. Review the assembled test.
   a. Does each item measure something?
   b. Are the directions clear?
   c. Does any question give away the answer to any other question?
   d. Is there space to respond?
6. Construct the answer key.
7. Seek constructive criticism from colleagues and, if possible, have them take the test.
8. Make necessary revisions.
9. After administering, analyze, revise, and improve.

FIGURE 15-1

Steps in Test Construction

TYPES OF TESTS

FIGURES 15-4 through 15-9 provide examples of some of the various types of tests currently in use. These generally fall into one of three areas: objective tests (FIGURES 15-4 through 15-7); short answer and essay tests, and; performance tests. (See FIGURES 15-4 through 15-9).

RECORDING STUDENT PROGRESS

The teacher should maintain a set of permanent records. Individual student records should take priority. Most teachers have access to, or utilize, a standard grade book or record. This book is beneficial to record test results and attendance (FIGURE 15-10).

MORE SPECIFIC POINTS TO OBSERVE
IN TEST CONSTRUCTION

1. Is it impossible to measure all outcomes with one type of test?
2. Develop a comprehensive test and omit insignificant and trivial items.
3. Stress application of material learned, rather than recall or recognition.
4. Insure that the type of test item used for measuring each objective is the most plausible.
5. Omit trick or catch questions.
6. Include a large number of test items. This increases reliability and affords students the greatest opportunity for success.
7. Omit "lifted" statements directly from books or resource materials. Students may know the correct response without understanding what the response really means.
8. Avoid items with only two choices from which the student selects one. Modification of these items with the insertion of "why" can improve validity.
9. Make sure each item is independent of the others. Do not develop items which require dependence on the correct solution of another item.
10. Avoid "keying" words such as: all, never, always, along, may, none, and should. These qualifying words key the answer for the student.
11. Develop items at the vocabulary level of the students.
12. State items clearly to avoid ambiguity.
13. Keep the method of recording responses as simple as possible.
14. If appropriate, arrange response blanks along one side of the page.
15. Avoid arranging items so that the responses form a particular pattern.
16. Develop items in such a manner that students will not have to refer to more than one page in answering.
17. Underline crucial words in order to avoid misinterpretation or misunderstanding.
18. Avoid unequal weighting of test items. If an objective is particularly important, stress the objective with related multiple items.
19. Prepare a proper heading, including a space for name, identification of test, and grade.

FIGURE 15-2

Aids in Test Construction

CHARACTERISTICS OF A GOOD EVALUATION
INSTRUMENT OR DEVICE

1. Validity — stability or consistency in measuring what it is supposed to measure.
2. Reliability — accuracy with which a test measures what it is supposed to measure.
3. Objectivity — each item permits one and only one interpretation. In scoring, the instrument should be construed so as to eliminate personal bias, prejudice, and opinion.
4. Discrimination — distinguishes between different levels of ability.
5. Comprehensive — measures achievement in the program or course up to the time of the test.
6. Ease of Administration — easy to score. Purpose of test should be known, clear directions should be given and a place provided for response.

FIGURE 15-3

Important Characteristics of a Well-Constructed Test

The class progress chart can be utilized by the teacher to monitor the progress of each student as well as that of the total class (FIGURE 15-11). This record can also serve as a motivator for students and direction indicator for classroom or laboratory instruction. This record can also be a deterrent to some individuals who see themselves behind and display "give-up-itis" or apathy. Care must be taken to insure that there is no discrimination against any student to the extent that it becomes a deterrent to learning.

Anecdotal records provide a history of classroom happenings on individual students. This records the everyday activities and enables the teacher to evaluate student character. Care must be taken to record information without bias and prejudice. These records must be open to inspection and review by parents, students, and administrators. The record can serve to identify students with pronounced behavior differences. Proper utilization of the anecdotal record entails a high degree of professionalism with the students' best interest as the basis.

This record is maintained much like a diary. Records kept on junior and senior students should contain a photograph of the student. Many of these students will request references when they apply for positions. It is impossible to remember all students, particularly those who have graduated several years ago. The record and the photograph will enable the teacher to accurately and honestly respond to requests for references.

OBJECTIVE TEST: MULTIPLE CHOICE

INSTRUCTIONS: Each question has only one correct answer. Encircle the letter of the word or phrase that you feel correctly completes the statement or answers the question.

1. The basic parts of an atom are:
   a. a neucleus and orbits
   b. electrons, neutrons and protons
   c. molecules and compounds
   d. protons, neutrons, and orbits

2. Which of the following statements is true?
   a. An electron has a negative charge.
   b. A proton has a negative electrical charge.
   c. An electron has a positive electrical charge.
   d. Electrons and protons have negative charges.

3. According to the law of electrical charges:
   a. like charges attract
   b. unlike charges attract
   c. unlike charges repel
   d. two electrons will attract each other

4. A material is a good conductor if it:
   a. has few free electrons
   b. has seven electrons in its outer shell
   c. is a semi-conductor
   d. has many free electrons

5. Which of the following statements is true?
   a. Gold is a better conductor than silver.
   b. Copper is the best conductor of all metals.
   c. Silver is a better conductor than copper.
   d. Semi-conductors have less free electrons than insulators.

6. A batter produces electricity from:
   a. light
   b. heat
   c. chemical action
   d. magnetism

7. Electric current in a wire travels:
   a. a few inches per second
   b. at the speed of light
   c. too fast to be measured
   d. at a speed determined by the voltage applied

8. Electromotive force (emf) is expressed in:
   a. coulombs
   b. electron charge
   c. volts
   d. joules

FIGURE 15-4

Objective Test: Multiple Choice

OBJECTIVE TEST: TRUE — FALSE

DIRECTIONS: The following statements are either true or false. If the statement is true, circle T to the left of the statement. If the statement is false, circle F.

T F 1.   The chief reason for taking a course in general metals is to make some metal projects.

T F 2.   You must be a safe worker to be a good craftsman. The best way to avoid accidents is to follow directions and never take chances.

T F 3.   Under certain conditions, 110-volt house current can kill a person.

T F 4.   Lead is a lightweight metal.

T F 5.   The spark test is a very accurate method of identifying metal.

T F 6.   Use a steel hammer to pound on machine tools.

T F 7.   When the pattern is equal on both sides, the design is symmetrical.

T F 8.   The United States Standard Gauge is used to measure non-ferrous metals.

FIGURE 15-5

Objective Test: True-False

Performance-based education presents the teacher with the opportunity to record student performance in each competency taught (FIGURE 15-12). A listing of competencies essential for a course, followed by whether the student has successfully mastered the competencies, presents one of the most accurate pictures of individual competence and potential.

ASSIGNING GRADES

Grade assignment takes many and varied forms. Some of the most common forms are:

1.   letter grade (A, B, C, D, F)

OBJECTIVE TEST: MATCHING

INSTRUCTIONS: Column A contains a list of electrical terms. Choose from Column B the definition which best fits each term in Column A and insert the identifying letter in the blank provided. Responses may *not* be used more than once.

Column A		Column B
_____ 1. ampere	**a.**	ohms
_____ 2. atom	**b.**	a device capable of storing an electrical charge
_____ 3. capacitance	**c.**	a protective device
_____ 4. capacitor	**d.**	voltage
_____ 5. cathode	**e.**	insulator
_____ 6. conductor	**f.**	the unit of measure for capacitance
_____ 7. resistance	**g.**	emits electrons
_____ 8. farad	**h.**	smallest part of a chemical element
_____ 9. fuse	**i.**	direction of current flow
_____ 10. dielectric	**j.**	current
_____ 11. polarity	**k.**	the property of a capacitor that enables it to store an electrical charge
	l.	a material through which electrons can pass easily

FIGURE 15-6

Objective Test: Matching

2.   satisfactory or unsatisfactory (S or U)
3.   numerical or percentile rank (100, 99, 98, etc.)
4.   rank order (1, 2, 3, 4, etc.)
5.   descriptive report (example-competency listing)

Each of these approaches represents efforts to present a record of

OBJECTIVE TEST: COMPLETION

INSTRUCTIONS: Complete the following statements by filling in the missing words or phrases.

1. List three ways a plane can project in orthographic projection.

1. ————————— 2. ————————— 3. —————————

2. List three ways a line can project in orthographic projection.

1. ————————— 2. ————————— 3. —————————

3. A line that appears as a ————————— in the front view will appear true length in the left side view.

4. The first row of dimensions should be placed a minimum of ————————— from the object.

5. The second row of dimensions should be placed ————————— from the object.

6. and 7. Two methods of placing numerals on an object are

————————— and —————————.

8. Arrowhead on dimension lines should be the same ————————— as the height of the numerals used.

FIGURE 15-7

Objective Test: Completion

a student's progress at a designated point of evaluation. Grades report the status of the student with regard to:

1. motivation level
2. advancement
3. teacher interpretation
4. transfer of credit
5. level of attainment or progress

Students should be kept abreast of their individual progress as

SHORT ANSWER AND ESSAY TEST

DIRECTIONS: Answer each question in your own terms.
1.   Briefly describe the job of the assembly man in the furniture industry.

2.   Describe the process of lumber manufacture after the log has reached the sawmill.

3.   Describe the manufacturing process a log undergoes in the production of plywood.

4.   Describe the occupational characteristics of patternmaking.

5.   Describe the use of the fillet in patternmaking.

6.   Describe the apprenticeship system in industry.

FIGURE 15-8

Short Answer and Essay Test

they pursue a course. Norm referencing of grades provides a record of student performance in relation to other students. Criterion referencing of grades is directed toward specific competencies and how the student compares to a standard. Utilization of each has merit and depends upon the overall objectives set by the teacher, administrator, or advisory committee.

Grade assignments are used by teachers and administrators to indicate promotion and failure. Grouping students may be used as an indicator of individual progress. Grades should not be used for discipline, nor should passage or failure of a course hinge on only one test grade. Remember, when a student records a failing grade, the teacher may have failed in one or more respects as well.

PERFORMANCE TEST

Construct a right triangle

Construct a circle

Bisect this angle

Divide this line into 12 equal parts

Bisect this line (perpendicular)

Draw a tangent to the circle

FIGURE 15-9

A Performance Test

Permanent records or transcripts should be kept for a minimum of five years in an active file and in an inactive file from then on.

SUMMARY

The learning manager is responsible for providing a high-quality learning environment for students. Evaluation of instruction provides information for course direction and modification. Tests and measurement devices ascertain student learning levels and denote behavioral changes. An effective educational program cannot be maintained without frequent appraisal of students and their development.

STUDENT TEST RESULTS AND ATTENDANCE

Subject _____ Instructor _____ Period Beginning _____ 19 _____ Ending _____ 19 _____

Month																					Daily Ave.	Test	Six Wks. Ave.			Ave.	Ex.	Sem.		
Date																							1	2	3			Gr.	Ave.	Rank
Name	M	T	W	T	F	M	T	W	T	F	M	T	W	T	F	M	T	W	T	F										
1																														
2																														
3																														
4																														
5																														
6																														
7																														
8																														
9																														
10																														
11																														
12																														
13																														
14																														
41																														
42																														

FIGURE 15-10

Record of Student Test Results and Attendance

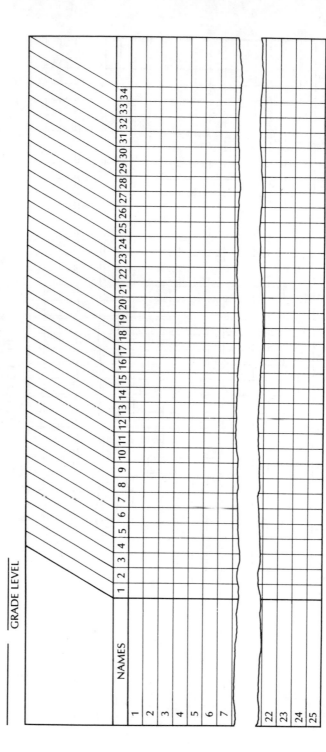

CLASS PROGRESS CHART

FIGURE 15-11

Class Progress Chart

STUDENT PERFORMANCE RECORD

Name ——————
Course ——————
Class ——————
Date ——————

GENERAL COMPETENCIES	DATE COMPLETED	TEACHING METHODS USED	TEACHING MATERIALS USED
Use mathematical principles in computations.			
Understand and use basic geometry principles.			
Understand and use basic trigonometry principles.			
Understand and use basic algebra principles.			
Understand and utilize descriptive geometric principles.			
Select and utilize appropriate instruments for a specified drawing.			

FIGURE 15-12

Student Performance Record

The types of test instruments used are dependent on the course objectives and types of responses desired by the teacher.

The age of accountability carries with it the need for careful student/program monitoring, record keeping, and reporting. Various forms and procedures assist the teacher in maintaining individual student progress records and course or program effectiveness information.

REVIEW QUESTIONS

1. Define educational evaluation.
2. What is the difference between measurement and evaluation?
3. What are the purposes of educational evaluation from the viewpoint of the teacher? Administrator? Public?
4. Should knowledge, manipulative skills, and personality traits be graded and reported as separate factors? Explain.
5. What is the relationship between course objectives and evaluation?
6. What are the characteristics of a good evaluation system?
7. What is the basic grade assigning system used in present day schools?
8. What advantages do standardized tests have over teacher-made tests? What advantages do teacher-made tests have over standardized tests?
9. What are some of the misuses of tests?

STUDENT ACTIVITIES

1. Develop a list of objectives for the specific occupational area you are going to teach.
2. Prepare a rating scale and progress chart for grading students.
3. Prepare a sample final examination in the area of your interest. Have at least four types of questions and their directions.
4. Prepare a paper giving criteria for the evaluation of tests.

REFERENCES

Anastasi, A. *Psychological Testing.* 3d ed. New York: Macmillan, 1968.

Bloom, B.S.; Hastings, J.T.; and Madaus, G.F. *Handbook on Formative and Summative Evaluation of Student Learning.* New York: McGraw-Hill, 1971.

Micheels, W.J. and Karnes, M.R. *Measuring Educational Achievement.* New York: McGraw-Hill, 1950.

Sax, G. *Empirical Foundations of Education Research.* Englewood Cliffs, N.J.: Prentice-Hall, 1968.

Thorndike, R.L. and Hagen, E. 3d ed. *Measurement and Evaluation in Psychology and Education.* New York: Wiley & Sons, 1969.

Wentling, T.L. and Lawson, T.E. *Evaluating Occupational Education and Training Programs.* Boston: Allyn and Bacon, 1975.

16

Laboratory Management
and Planning

Our technological society demands futuristic planning in both management and facilities in order to provide quality technical training in specialized occupations. Educational programs determine the facilities needed and basic management characteristics to be employed. Programs must be continuously evaluated to determine the effectiveness of management and the adequacy of laboratories housing each program.

Upon completion of this chapter, the reader will be able to:

- **Identify the special needs of specific occupational programs.**
- **Design an instrument to evaluate physical facilities.**
- **Describe a laboratory management system emulating conditions found in business, industry, and health care.**

The curriculum should determine the facility, however, this often is not the case. When a new facility is to be designed, the teacher should work closely with the architect prior to and during the design stage of facility planning. Without such coordination, school facilities may be designed and constructed which are not compatible with the type of instruction which is to take place. Most often, the teacher inherits existing facilities and has the responsibility for space utilization and maintenance. Facilities should safely accommodate prescribed learning activities and provide flexibility for future growth and development. The learning manager should be fully aware of the variables which affect space allocation for occupational programs. Space needs are determined by variables such as the following:

1. Curriculum: specialized or general content
2. Student enrollment: present and future
3. Work stations: student/teacher ratio must be considered
4. Equipment: cost, size, maintainability, and flexibility
5. Acoustic treatment: example; occupation with high noise levels may be located in separate (but close) building
6. Lighting treatment: 30 foot candles is minimum for laboratories; natural, artificial, or combination
7. Storage treatment: related to size and usage (example; student personal belongings, raw materials, projects under construction, consumable supplies, combustible supplies, and tools)
8. Number and lengths of periods
9. Space allocation per student
10. Size and space occupied by each piece of equipment
11. Washroom facilities: toilets and wash bowls
12. Teaching methods: conferences, seminars, lecturers, demonstrations, individualized instruction, job simulation

There are three basic kinds of laboratories found in occupational education. These are:

1. Curriculum cluster laboratory: only one general occupational cluster is taught at the orientation, exploration or preparation level (example; health occupations cluster)
2. Multi-cluster laboratory: education about industry and business at the orientation or exploration level characterized by diversified experiences in a compact space (example: business and office occupations)
3. Specialization: in-depth skills development and preparation in a single or specific occupation (example: vocational welding laboratory)

Facilities housing curriculum cluster laboratories and multicluster laboratories may allocate as much as 86 square feet of floor space per student. Specialization laboratories may vary from 30 square feet of floor space per student in drafting to 100 square feet of floor space per student in foundry. Space per student in each job-simulation laboratory will be allocated according to the activities involved. The floor space allocation for laboratory work should not be less than 55 square feet per student. When determining floor space needs, the teacher should check state and local guidelines, since space allocation recommended by state departments varies widely.

The size and arrangement of work stations in each laboratory is dependent on the number and type of programs offered within the facility. Single or multiple programs may be offered within one specific laboratory, and care must be taken to maximize facility utilization.

Orientation, exploration, and preparation programs require diverse facilities and management techniques. A school may have programs utilizing individualized and group instructional activities within the same laboratory or facility. Specialized groups, such as adults enrolled in a retraining program, may require facilities and management modification in order to meet their unique needs.

Many occupational programs, regardless of the level at which they are taught, require modification of facilities in order to maximize the use of available floor space. Floor space should be modifiable in the following ways:

1. adaptable: space can be used in more than one way (example; exploration activities taught in preparation laboratory)
2. flexible: space design can be changed without altering basic area or cubage (example; construction of large project within facilities)
3. expansible: additional space can be added to basic unit at a later time (example; occupational program technology requires new equipment)
4. contractible: space can be reduced in area and cubage (example; drastic reduction in number of students enrolled or program equipment becomes compact and old equipment outdated)

Many types and sizes of space can be provided, depending on the activities being performed and the number of students involved.

A laboratory plan should contain the following building components:

1. basic floor plan
2. outlets for air, gas, water, sanitary facilities
3. power outlets and switch panels
4. blackboards, display boards
5. stock racks and storage space
6. cabinets (tool crib optional)
7. machines (height, shape, and size)
8. benches
9. finishing room (specialized areas, such as dental or medical)
10. audiovisual support (computer, television, etc.)
11. safety needs (guards, zones, etc.)
12. color scheme

Teachers and administrators should be able to evaluate plans and specifications for new and existing laboratory facilities. An evaluation instrument should contain the following components:

1. laboratory space standards (ceiling height, space per student)
2. floor standards (materials)
3. door standards (height, width, hardware, etc.)
4. partition and wall standards
5. storage standards (waste, stock, project, equipment, etc.)
6. special area standards (students personal property, display area, assemble area, finishing room, instructor's area, visual aids area, open areas for traffic, wardrobe area, chalkboard area, planning center, etc.)
7. visual-comfort standard (window area and arrangement, artificial light sources, color scheme, light reflection values, illumination levels, etc.)
8. audio-comfort standards (sound absorption ceiling and wall)
9. plumbing standards (drinking facilities, washing facilities, work sinks, automatic sprinkler system, air compressor and gas outlets, etc.)
10. heating and ventilating standards (minimum quantity of air per student supplied by ventilating, fresh air induction, air velocity, ventilating system, relative humidity in lab and storage, temperature controls, location of radiators, exhaust system, etc.)

11. electrical circuit standards (power circuit system, branch-power circuit, space power circuits, overload protection, raceway system, power and light raceways, spare light circuits, convenience outlets, safety buttons, fire alarm systems, etc.)
12. miscellaneous standards (audiovisual capability, fire extinguisher agents, first aid cabinet, etc.)

This instrument should enable teachers and administrators in determining those areas that contribute to, or deter from, the effectiveness of the laboratory and, in turn, the program. This instrument should contain the latest building standards (state and local) and serve as a point of reference or departure when discussing construction or renovation with architects, school boards, and school administrative personnel (FIGURE 16-1).

Each laboratory should be served by an identified resource center; this center can serve many needs and functions. Some of the possibilities are:

1. large group assembly area
2. small group seminars
3. individual study areas
4. curriculum resource center for teachers
5. specialized library resource center for technical related information, general related information and guidance information
6. audiovisual media storage and retrieval

The primary reason for having a laboratory is to provide students actual experience with the materials, equipment, and processes relevant to the specific occupation taught. Each laboratory must contain a job-simulation zone for skill development.

The job-simulation zone should be shaped, subdivided, furnished, and equipped for the particular occupation(s) taught. Elements such as light, power, water, water disposal, and gas should be available. For some occupations, sound barriers should be constructed to buffer unwanted noise and provide an atmosphere conducive to optimum learning. Equipment should be movable and designated safety areas marked. Each job-simulation zone will require some unique and specialized equipment. Specialized areas for this equipment should be established to allow maximum use of all remaining areas for instruction in other occupations. Specialized areas should be set aside outside the main flow and remain relatively undisturbed until that specific skill is taught.

Equipment selection is determined by program and course objectives, type of work to be accomplished, type of student to be taught, size of class, and the amount of available resources. Frequently, money is the deciding factor and, as a result, a great deal of discrimination with regard to that which will be purchased is necessary. This, in turn, affects the course content or curriculum.

Equipment to be purchased should be given priority according to instructional objectives and proposed teaching methods. The teacher must consider the number of students enrolled and the number of work stations which can be provided. The teacher must also consider the number of skills a student can learn on a piece of equipment and how frequently each piece of equipment will be used. Buying a piece of equipment involves careful analysis of conditions for use and professional judgment by the responsible individual. Equipment should be purchased by the responsible teacher working cooperatively with the administrator and the advisory committee.

A list of priority items should be maintained to allow the teacher to quickly decide what to buy when money becomes available. This list should contain everything the teacher needs to create an ideal job-simulation laboratory.

The problem of requisitioning confronts every teacher when purchasing materials and equipment. Administrative policies differ from school to school with regard to how equipment is offered. However, the following basic guidelines are provided to assist the teacher in preparing specifications for ordering materials and equipment. Specifications should include:

1. item number—denotes this item from all others
2. quantity desired—do not leave to dealers discretion
3. name and description—catalog description should be quoted if possible
4. catalog—indicate the catalog number, date, and page from which the item is to be ordered
5. specify whether you will accept a substitute, and if so, what substitute

The vendor is likely to send that which he or she thinks or has interpreted you want. This interpretation may be influenced by what

SAMPLE FACILITIES EVALUATION INSTRUMENT

Recommendations for Improvement

1. The space allotted to instruction of (occupational area) is *_____ square feet per student. Your standards meet or exceed this.
   *Determined by state and local regulations.

   yes   no

2. The space allotted for floor materials in (occupational area) is ample. [wood, concrete, tile, resistant materials]

   yes   no

3. The space allotted for walls, ceilings, doors and windows are adequate and meet standards.

   yes   no

   a. Doors
   b. Walls and partitions
   c. Windows
   d. ceilings
   e. other

4. Project, supply, waste, stock, tool/instrument and equipment storage is ample.

   yes   no

   a. waste
   b. project
   c. supply
   d. stock
   e. equipment
   f. tool/instrument
   g. flammable storage area

5. The climate control system is adequate.

   yes   no

   a. heating system
   b. air conditioning system
   c. ventilation system
   d. dust collection system
   e. fume exhaust system
   f. heat exhaust system
   g. humidity control system

6. The laboratory is acoustically treated to promote good working conditions.

   yes   no

   a. general acoustics
   b. machine noise

7. The facility conforms to adequate visual-comfort standards.　　yes　no

    a. window area and arrangement
    b. light sources (illumination levels)
    c. color scheme

8. Utilities are present and adequate.　　yes　no

    a. water hot/cold (drinking and all purpose)
    b. compound air
    c. telephone-clock-intercom
    d. power circuit system
    e. branch power circuit
    f. convenience outlets
    g. overload protection
    h. main power control switch

9. Sanitary facilities are available for boys and girls and are adequate.　　yes　no

    a. toilets
    b. wash basins
    c. dressing rooms
    d. student lockers

10. Auxiliary rooms are provided and comfortably meet the needs.　　yes　no

    a. finish room
    b. office
    c. display area or case
    d. assembly area
    e. planning area
    f. audio visual capability and storage
    g. resource center

11. The machines and equipment are adequate and in good condition.　　yes　no

    a. machines
    b. tools or instruments
    c. safety lines present
    d. color coded
    e. safety guards on equipment
    f. work area or bench
    g. tool or instrument cabinets
    h. bookcases

FIGURE 16-1

is in stock or what will afford the greatest profit. Specifications must be clear and free from ambiguity in order to obtain exactly what is wanted. Quality equipment should be purchased whenever possible. The purchase of quality equipment saves the Local Education Agency money over a long period of time, because this equipment will last longer and generally requires less maintenance and repair. From the educational point of view, students must learn to use equipment which will be found in the world of work. Thus, the transition from school to work is more easily accomplished.

Storage of supplies and equipment is an integral component of any physical layout and program organization. Storage has implications for learning activities related to industrial utilization, safety, conservation, maintenance, and efficiency. The teacher must analyze the storage needs for each occupation and provide space for tools, instruments, supplies, materials, equipment, and projects.

There are several methods of storing and accounting for tools, instruments, and supplies. The closed storage system maintains all items within a locked area. This system allows the teacher or designated representative absolute control and supervision. The open storage system allows students free access of items during class sessions without permission or supervision. The open storage system saves teacher time, but results in some waste and loss. In programs where some items require close monitoring, because of expense or nature, a combination of these two systems may be appropriate. The teacher may keep valuable items under tight security while allowing students easy access to all other items.

A minimum of 5 to 15 percent of available laboratory space should be allocated for storage. The amount of space allotted for storage is dependent on such factors as:

1. activities to be taught
2. size of classes
3. type of personnel organization utilized
4. tool/instrument loss
5. use of facilities and tools by noninstructional staff (janitorial and maintenance personnel)
6. teacher philosophy and methodology

The teacher must determine the location of storage inside or outside the laboratory. Storage facilities should allow for movement of large and heavy items with minimum disruption. Storage areas for large items should also be accessible by delivery trucks. Efficient use of storage space allows for ease of access, checking, and display.

Each laboratory must rely on support facilities which contain such areas as dressing rooms, student lockers, and specialized materials storage. Delicate scientific equipment and furnishings, lavatories, and sanitary facilities must also be included in the support facilities. These areas accommodate the supportive functions for both the laboratory and the resource center. In many instances, particularly at the post-secondary level, a student lounge may also be provided.

The teacher assumes the responsibilities for the organization and management of occupational program job-simulation laboratories. To provide an authentic setting, the teacher should consider the following areas when organizing a laboratory:

1. student personnel organization
2. equipment and tool-instrument control
3. housekeeping and safety
4. record keeping
5. supplies and instructional materials

Organizing students within the laboratory affords the teacher more time for actual teaching. The students benefit through sharing and accepting responsibility, learning the significance of dependability, and developing leadership qualities. In laboratories where several learning activities are occurring at the same time, a student personnel organization is imperative if effective teaching is to take place. Students should be appointed to responsible positions as supervisors and serve on committees. A well-balanced student personnel plan may include the following specific duties:

1. laboratory superintendent
2. laboratory supervisor
3. tool/instrument and/or equipment supervisor
4. safety supervisor
5. cleanup supervisor
6. committee chairperson
7. committee member

These positions may be rotated in order to allow all students to participate at all echelons of responsibility. Assigned duties should be posted and responsibilities reviewed whenever positions are changed.

The success of any student organization is dependent upon clearly established objectives for the organizational scheme and the willingness of students to participate in the organization. It then becomes the instructor's job to carefully explain each role and the importance of each specific job to the overall effectiveness of the organization. Outside student organizations such as *Vocational Industrial Clubs of America (V.I.C.A.)*, *Distributive Education Clubs of America (D.E.C.A.)*, *Future Business Leaders of America (F.B.L.A.)*, *Future Homemakers of America (F.H.A.)*, and *Future Farmers of America (F.F.A.)*, serve full-time programs in trade, industrial, business, home economics, agriculture, and health occupations education. These national organizations offer opportunities for leadership development, personal development, and intercurricular activities that complement occupational skill development.

An equipment and tool or instrument control system is necessary to assure accountability and safety. Many alternative check systems have been successfully developed and utilized. The following are provided as examples:

1. stamped metal tags (open and closed storage)
2. unrestricted panels and cabinets
3. checkout through student supervisor

Each system allows for varying degrees of accountability. Students should be taught proper usage and maintenance procedures. Tools and instruments should be inventoried by the teacher or student supervisor at the close of each laboratory session. Tool and instrument inventory control enables the teacher to maintain an adequate supply and to know the exact condition at all times. An equipment control system has the same fundamental characteristics of tool and instrument control systems; therefore, stringent controls are sometimes necessary.

Laboratory housekeeping and safety means providing an environment conducive to effective learning. The physical condition of the laboratory affects the amount and quality of education. The teacher must be concerned with housekeeping and safety practices such as:

1. cleaning the laboratory
2. ventilating, heating, and lighting

3. tool, instrument, material, equipment, and project storage
4. locating and relocating equipment
5. safe environment and work habits
6. preventive maintenance

Students usually respond more readily and participate more enthusiastically in their work when the laboratory is clean. Respect for equipment and facilities are attitudinal attributes teachers want to instill in their students. Students who have responsibility for maintenance and safety in the classroom or job-simulation laboratory can contribute the preponderance of labor toward maintaining laboratory housekeeping and safety standards. A teacher should periodically make a complete detailed inspection of housekeeping and safety conditions.

No laboratory can function successfully without maintaining a set of records. Major records include student achievement and attendance. Teachers should also keep records of accidents, safety inspections, inventories (supply and equipment), finances, and student competence with regard to equipment operation. Many such records are required by law and aid the teacher in adequately supervising instruction and substantiating the performance of student and teacher responsibility. The teacher is accountable for all activity or inactivity within the educational laboratory and is not free from legal obligations. Records verify what the teacher has done in the required performance of his or her duties.

Care must be exercised by the teacher to be sure that the laboratory has adequate supplies and instructional materials to accomplish the program or course objectives. Supplies and materials should be ordered well in advance of intended use. Teachers should be constantly searching for supplies and materials to present the technological innovations of the society. Keeping abreast of changes in business, industry, and health care is extremely difficult. Teachers should subscribe to periodicals and progressional literature to maintain current knowledge of new processes.

The graduating students should leave the job-simulation laboratory with the necessary competencies to enter and successfully compete in their chosen occupation. The teacher should assume the responsibility for providing relevant materials, equipment, and methods to the departing students. Provided with such a base, the student has the necessary foundation and preparation from which to proceed to higher education or move on the career lattice.

SUMMARY

Instructional facilities do not happen overnight, nor do they manage themselves. The teacher becomes the primary agent for planning, developing, and implementing facility use. Care should be taken to maximize the utilization of laboratories, resource centers, and support facilities. Laboratory management should include a well-balanced student personnel plan and organization, as well as a record keeping, housekeeping, and safety program.

REVIEW QUESTIONS

1. What are the principal elements to consider when planning a new job-simulation laboratory?
2. What areas should be checked when evaluating a new laboratory facility?
3. What factors determine the type of storage method to be used in a laboratory?
4. List the suggested specification to be included when purchasing a piece of equipment.
5. List the various advantages of a student personnel organization.
6. List the records that should be maintained by the teacher operating a laboratory.

STUDENT ACTIVITIES

1. Develop the floor plan for a laboratory serving your particular occupational area.
2. Develop a list of equipment to be utilized in a laboratory serving your particular occupational area.
3. Develop a student personnel organization plan for presentation to your immediate supervisor.

REFERENCES

Boles, Harold W. *Step by Step to Better School Facilities*. New York: Holt, Rinehart and Winston, 1965.
Giachino, J.W. and Gallington, Ralph O. 3d ed. *Course Construction in Indus-*

trial Arts, Vocational and Technical Education. Chicago: American Technical Society, 1967.

The Oregon Board of Education, *Career Cluster Facilities Guide*. Salem: The Oregon Board of Education, 1973.

————, *Modern School Shop Planning*. Michigan: Prakken, 1962.

Stadt, R.W.; Bittle, R.E.; Kenneke, L.J.; and Nystrom, D.C. *Managing Career Education Programs*. Englewood Cliffs, N.J.: Prentice-Hall, 1973.

CHAPTER

17

Discipline

One of the major concerns of parents and educators regarding educational systems in the United States is that of discipline, or as is most often stated, the "lack of discipline." Each individual involved in the schooling process—student, parent, and teacher—probably has a different definition of discipline. The purpose of this chapter is to:

- **Identify components of classroom management which will enhance learning**
- **Describe management techniques which will help to minimize conflict**
- **Describe the importance of teaching discipline as a part of the teaching/learning process**

Perhaps no single aspect of education has changed as much in the minds of parents and teachers as discipline. In some quarters, it appears that there has been a dramatic shift from an authoritarian, teacher-centered learning environment to a learning environment in which the student has control. In the authoritarian era, the teacher's job was to "teach," and the learner was to absorb that which was taught. If the learner failed to learn, outside pressure could induce the student to apply himself. In such a system, those students who were affected by both internal and external pressure obtained the knowledge and skills deemed appropriate for that period. However, it appears that a large percentage of the student population was not affected, and they left the school system and went to work on the farms and in the factories.

In today's society, a greater percentage of the student population is remaining in school, and the autocratic method of classroom management is not effective. Furthermore, recent court decisions regarding the use of corporal punishment and the right of due process have caused educators to reevaluate the purpose of discipline and to analyze entire learning environments.

Discipline is a term that is often used and seldom has the same meaning for all people. The parent often views discipline as corporal punishment for children who have misbehaved, while the athlete and coach might view discipline as the dedication and effort directed toward training and performance. Most children and youngsters attending secondary and post-secondary schools probably would agree that "discipline" represents the constraints placed upon their actions by adults.

WHAT IS DISCIPLINE?

While the term will have many interpretations by various groups and individuals, for the purposes of classroom instruction, discipline shall be defined as the method whereby *two primary goals shall be accomplished*. First, the immediate instructional objectives which have been determined as valid for the occupational area to be studied; and second, the longer-term goals (which depend upon self-discipline) of personal development which extend beyond formal education.

The above definition means that students must be taught the self-discipline necessary for success in the occupational laboratory, and they must also be equipped to continue learning when they enter the world of work.

The primary purpose of discipline in the classroom and job-simulation laboratory is the efficient accomplishment of educational goals. Without discipline in the classroom, neither the immediate objectives nor long-range goals can be accomplished.

It is through the effective control and structuring of the classroom and job-simulation laboratory that each learner is able to achieve his or her personal objectives. Without discipline, both the individual and the class as a group will falter. Goals may be achieved without discipline, but seldom efficiently.

Discipline does not need to be a highly structured and rigid part of the learning environment. Many individuals are highly disciplined. Their behavior has been shaped by parents and the environment in such a manner that they were hardly aware of the process. For these individuals, their behavior is almost an automatic response. Similarly, some teachers maintain control of the classroom and job-simulation laboratory and are hardly aware of what they are doing to maintain the learning environment. They automatically deal with people and problems in a manner which causes little disturbance and seldom distracts from the attainment of the goals and objectives of the classroom.

Failure to achieve clearly-stated goals and objectives for a course is generally the result of poor discipline. Each individual must be taught to mobilize his or her resources in order to reach specific goals. By directing the resources of the learning environment and the students in a disciplined way toward the desired goals, the overall educational objectives can be met. Accomplishment of goals in the classroom involves a knowledge of the resources available, establishment of the goals and a method of evaluating progress toward the stated goals. A close relationship between achievement and discipline exists.

The purpose of discipline
is achievement of goals 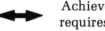 Achievement
requires goals

The concept of discipline for its own sake is not valid in the scheme described above; neither is the newer concept of *no* discipline. Discipline loses its value when separated from educational goals. Yet, when associated with achievement of one's own goals, it is a significant factor in the teaching/learning process.

THE TEACHER AS A FACTOR

One of the many fears of a beginning teacher is how to establish and maintain good discipline in the classroom or job-simulation laboratory. Good discipline does not just happen, it results from sound planning, proper execution, and follow-up.

Although it may seem desirable to allow each student to have as much freedom of choice as possible, certain natural tendencies must be controlled. Students at the orientation and exploration levels, for example, are inclined to be active. These youths need to be guided and their activity directed toward the educational goals for that particular level. Older students may have developed interests in subjects which require a lot of manipulative skills and, at the same time, have no desire to study subjects which require skills of the cognative and affective domain. It is not uncommon for occupational preparation teachers in the trade and industrial occupations to have students who enjoy working at manipulative tasks. Because of ineffective reading skills, these same individuals may not wish to study the related information which will enable them to perform effectively. Unless the teacher is willing to accept the spontaneously and haphazardly generated educational setting which youth and adults tend to develop without leadership, then he or she must control the classroom or job-simulation laboratory.

The teacher must exercise control by proper *planning* prior to the time students enter the classroom. This involves:

1. establishing educational goals and objectives which are clearly understood by each student
2. making clear and definite assignments
3. gearing assignments to the time allowed and to the ability of each individual student
4. establishing specific objectives for each period of time the student is in the classroom
5. having well-prepared lesson plans and proper organization for each period
6. providing successful experiences for each student
7. insuring that equipment works properly and that adequate supplies are on hand for the learning activities

While proper planning is an essential factor in maintaining good classroom discipline, it is also influenced by the *structure* of the classroom. Structure is the organizational pattern through which the classroom procedures are achieved. These include:

1. establishing a firm, but not rigid, classroom procedure or routine
2. recognizing the need for and scheduling work stations

3. establishing limits for student conduct
4. interpreting the reasons and purposes for rules and regulations

A third factor which the teacher controls and which contributes to effective discipline is *follow-up*. This involves:

1. recognizing student accomplishment and giving the appropriate rewards and praise
2. being friendly but firm
3. making an effort to reestablish rapport with students who have been dealt with harshly
4. being consistent in enforcement of rules, and enforcing rules without embarrassment, if possible
5. commending first, then criticizing in a constructive manner

The teacher is the key to establishment of a learning environment which is conducive to educational achievement and to social development. Discipline is important because no group of people can successfully work together without establishing standards of behavior, mutual respect, and a desirable system of values that leads each person in the group to develop self-control and self-direction.

Good discipline does not result if a rigid, inflexible, and punitive approach is utilized. Further, good discipline does not result if the teacher is too permissive and pretends that annoying behavior does not exist. The effectiveness of this aspect of classroom management is determined by an accurate assessment of the problem and a knowledge of needed stabilizing action. Teachers must maintain a pattern of equilibrium in the classroom in the face of disruptions, disturbances, and numerous changes in the school setting which are beyond his or her control, but which affect the work process.

The occupational laboratory is a system within a larger school organization. Rules, policies, and general student control practices can create problems within the job-simulation laboratory. Further, the actions of other teachers, administrators, or other school personnel can create problems which the occupational teacher cannot solve.

Inherent in much of the educational theory is that most individuals in the classroom will respond in an acceptable manner if teachers are able instructors, i.e., the lessons are well prepared and learning difficulties are diagnosed correctly. However, some discipline problems will come up in every learning environment. The sources of these are due primarily to outside influences. These, in turn, create problems within the classroom. Therefore, the student as a factor in discipline, should be considered.

THE STUDENT AS A FACTOR

While the teacher can control many factors within the job-simulation laboratory, there are many reasons why students misbehave. In most cases, these reasons are unique, personal, complex, and beyond the teacher's comprehension or control. To list or describe all of these would be a monumental task. However, there are some general causes of misbehavior which can be anticipated, and techniques have been developed which will enable the instructor to reduce these causes. Within almost any group, the occupational teacher will find some learners who have special needs and whose behavior presents a real challenge. Their behavior will manifest itself in a variety of ways.

Boredom. Many students are bored with the classwork, either because they do not understand what they are supposed to do or because the objectives are unclear.

Frustration and tension. Frustration and tension can result from a variety of factors: the home, school rules and regulations, the social setting, lack of basic skills in reading and mathematics, or a sudden change in the school system as a result of court decisions. When students are frustrated, tension builds and they often react with hostility.

Attention, recognition, and status. Some students react in a negative manner because they want attention; and some attention is better than none at all, even though it is negative.

The factors which are controlled by the teacher and students have been briefly discussed. It should be pointed out that good planning and an understanding of the general causes of student misbehavior will not necessarily guarantee success in the classroom. Discipline, like any other subject, is not learned in a day, a month, or a year. In fact, it may be a subject which few people master. However, as in any other subjects, discipline must be consistently and conscientiously included as a part of the learning process.

Since classroom control is so important to teacher effectiveness, the following suggestions are made to provide some guidelines for the beginning occupational education teacher.

Establish some class rules. A learning environment, like an athletic contest or game, must be structured in some manner. Much like the athletic contest, limits and rules have to be established. Further, all parties must know and understand each of the established rules. The occupational teacher, in an effort to create a good learning environment, must of necessity establish the limits or rules of conduct which are to be utilized in the classroom or job-simulation laboratory. The educational level of the students and their maturity will, in most cases, determine to some extent the number of rules which should be established. However, a general rule to follow is that of keeping the number to a minimum. Students should also have an opportunity to help establish rules in areas where they are capable. Once established, all rules should be thoroughly explained, with the reason and purpose for each one clearly established. They should also be consistently and fairly enforced. The instructor also has an obligation to set the example by following all rules. Established rules should be consistent with previously established school policy. Students should understand general school policy and how it effects the job-simulation laboratory.

All explanations should be introduced in a nonthreatening manner. Rules are established to bring about an orderly and efficient learning environment. Therefore, restrictions which are meaningful and reasonable are much more likely to be remembered and honored than ultimatums which are dictated by the teacher.

Develop personal qualities which will aid in the establishment of a healthy learning environment. The first few class meetings with a group of students are the most crucial as far as discipline is concerned. While few discipline problems surface during the first week of school, the students are assessing the strengths and weaknesses of the teacher. Self-confidence and a well-planned chain of events will ensure that a positive image of the new teacher is developed in the minds of the students. A teaching technique which should also be used on the first day or two of a class would be to provide activities which will introduce each student to the others in the class and also to the teacher. This could be accomplished through a variety of games designed for that purpose. The teacher could also ask each individual to fill out an information card about himself or herself.

It is important that the teacher learn each student's first name as soon as possible. This is an indication of the interest and liking that the teacher has for students, regardless of their age. Through the process of learning the names of each student, the teacher's confidence and stability will be exhibited. Regardless of what is done in the class the first few minutes or during the first week, it is important to give the impression that you know exactly what you are doing.

Develop a knowledge of biological, sociological, and psychological characteristics of adolescents and adult learners. Control problems frequently erupt unexpectedly, and they often demand solutions with an equal amount of spontaneity. Lacking experience in dealing with such problems, there is a tendency to "shoot-from-the-hip" with reactions which, in most cases, are ineffective. Ineffective controls tend to reinforce misbehavior, and the teacher may find himself or herself in an action/reaction cycle which is difficult to break. This type of situation can be avoided if several specific methods or techniques for dealing with student misbehavior are developed ahead of time. These methods should be consistent with biological, sociological, and psychological needs of the age groups which comprise the class. The teacher should be alert for possible causes of misbehavior; however, this does not mean one should always be looking for trouble.

The following techniques for control are provided to aid the teacher in developing methods for dealing with problems. Each student should be encouraged to develop self-control. This can only be accomplished when control techniques are designed to foster self-control.

Simple Control

In some cases, a subtle signal can put an end to a potential behavioral problem. This can be accomplished by a look at the offender, stopping what you are saying in midsentence, clearing your throat, or signifying your disapproval with a frown. This technique should not be used too often and is effective only in the early stages of misbehavior. Much of the success of this method of control rests upon the implied dissatisfaction of the teacher and the willingness of the student to comply to group needs rather than individual desires.

A more apparent control method is that of *proximity* or *standing* near the offending student, posing a question to a student, or movement of the teacher about the room to trouble centers. The use of humor, especially in tense situations, may be especially helpful.

Remember, however, humor should be gentle and good natured rather than derisive. *Interest* in the student's work can also be a controlling factor. Looking at their work, pointing out something good about it, and asking the student to explain what he is doing in an informational gathering rather than a threatening manner may also be helpful.

Situational Controls

Several techniques are used to eliminate behavioral problems. Some are directed toward anticipated student behavior and some toward prevention.

Remove barriers to learning. Make sure students understand what they are to do, and ascertain their ability to carry out an assignment. This will also require that work stations are available and that needed equipment and supplies are on hand and available for student use. A good many behavioral problems could be eliminated in occupational programs if supplies and equipment are ready when the students need the materials.

Establish routines. If a set pattern for getting started at the beginning of each day or period is established, it will remove some of the uncertainty. Trouble often develops when students do not know what the day's plans are or what they are expected to do during that particular period.

Nonpunitive exile. In some cases, it may be necessary to ask a student to leave the room because of his or her emotional state. Depending upon the maturity of the individual, some students will enter an occupational classroom or laboratory in a mental state which is not beneficial to themselves or others. In such cases, time-out from the class would be an appropriate action. The student would not be punished; he or she would simply be given time to control himself or herself before engaging in the learning activities. The time required may vary from five minutes to the entire class period.

Restraint. There may be times when a student will lose control to the point of endangering himself or herself or other members of the class. These students may have to be physically restrained. However, this restraint should be protective rather than punitive.

While the above techniques are directed toward anticipated student behavior, there remains the problem of dealing with misbehavior. Several approaches are outlined below. These approaches deal with a student's sense of fairness and are also designed to strengthen the ability to see the consequences of his or her own actions.

Direct appeals.   Individual conferences between the pupil and teacher resolve many behavioral problems. This will allow the teacher to explain in greater detail the consequences of the student's conduct. A private talk will also allow the student an opportunity to explain his or her position and to draw some conclusions. It is imperative that the teacher assist the student in determining the alternatives, but the student has the responsibility for the decision.

Criticism and encouragement.   Try to criticize students in private when such action is necessary. Public criticism often creates greater hostility, and may cause the class as a group to come to the aid of the student being criticized. In order to minimize the aftereffects, a word of encouragement or suggestions for improvement should be given.

Testing limits.   Even though rules have been thoroughly explained, students like to test the limits. This appears to be true at all levels of instruction and can occur in a variety of methods. Established rules should, therefore, be consistently enforced. Show the students that the rules are genuine and that there are limits.

The above mentioned techniques are directed toward prevention and teaching self-control. When efforts of this nature fail, punishment or retribution is necessary. That is, the guilty person must pay the penalty. This too is a part of the educational process. Punishment in itself is a negative process. Retribution should be as gentle as possible, and yet demonstrate to the student that he or she should not make the same mistake again. When there is no other choice but retribution, the following techniques should be considered.

Make the punishment fit the crime.   This is one of the most frequently stated rules for punishment. The basic concept is that of fairness in dealing with the student. Punishment should be strong enough to create an impression, and yet should be the punishment which has the least tendency to undermine the educational process. Punishment which might be used in today's schools is primarily that of *withholding a privilege.* This technique will be effective for some students. Others may not be affected by the same privilege. Therefore, it is important that the teacher know his or her students.

Detention. This is a time-honored technique, which if applied too frequently, loses its effectiveness. Ten minutes has about the same effect as one hour. It is believed, however, that a pupil/teacher conference could probably bring about the same results.

Punitive exile. It may be necessary to send a student to a quiet room, the principal's office, or some other appropriate "solitary confinement" area. This should be for a specified period of time so that the student may return to the class when he or she has paid the debt. Care should be exercised in the use of this technique for there are times when this is the treatment the student wants. In other words, if there is nothing exciting going on, the student may prefer to be in the hallway. This technique should be used after all other methods have failed, and it is essentially a last effort to bring about proper behavior.

Open defiance. When the behavior is open defiance and an appeal to the student to take one of the above mentioned routes for behavioral adjustment has not been effective, it is time to obtain the services of an outside authority. All other measures should be utilized before this route is taken. While most behavioral problems can be handled by other means, there may be cases when open defiance occurs. In such cases, it is far better to remove the student from the room so that all parties can have an opportunity to reflect upon the interaction which took place.

At this point in a student/teacher conflict, a teacher, student, school administrator, and parent conference is advisable. The primary purpose of such a conference is to bring the parents into the picture and, if at all possible, bring about a settlement of the dispute in a manner which is acceptable to all parties involved.

Build and maintain rapport. Establishing and maintaining rapport with students is an important aspect of discipline. The student/teacher relationship is often reflected in the peer relationship exhibited in the learning environment. It is important that the teacher be as courteous to students as he or she expects the students to be to the teacher. If one of the more drastic forms of retribution has been used with a student, make an effort to reestablish rapport with that student. An apology to a student who has been treated unjustly will cause the teacher to gain respect, rather than lose it, and will build rapport. Rapport can also be established by walking and talking among students and being available when the student needs assistance, rather than by appearing to be so busy that the student feels like an intruder.

At the secondary level, it is a good practice not to see and hear everything youth of this age say and do. Students of this age group often make remarks just for the benefit of the teacher and to observe their reaction.

Avoid threats which cannot be enforced. Perhaps one of the easiest traps for the beginning teacher to fall into is that of making threats which they cannot carry out. This often occurs in the form of ultimatums, an "either or else" statement. In many cases, depending upon the rapport established, students will rise to the challenge and take the "or else" alternative. If the teacher is unable to carry out the threat, some degree of control is lost. Often, threats, when carried out, represent punishment which does not fit the crime, and the teacher again is in an embarrassing position and the student has gained prestige because he or she has successfully provoked the teacher and gained the respect of peers.

There is also an occasional temptation to threaten an entire class with the loss of a privilege in order to punish a few. Not only is this unfair to the innocent, it hardly ever works and tends to unite those individuals who have been cooperative with the uncooperative students.

Correct student behavior promptly, consistently, and in a reasonable manner. Learning is most effective and efficient when the student has an opportunity to confirm the appropriateness of his or her actions at the time such behavior occurs. Behavioral control is also most effective, if the control method is applied as quickly as possible after the improper act has been committed. Do not postpone dealing with students, for by the time the act of retribution comes due, the students may have forgotten or rationalized the act as being rather minor, and as a result, will feel resentment toward any form of punishment. However, if the student is emotionally upset, retribution may be ineffective and compound the problem.

Consistently enforced rules are also an important factor in maintaining a learning environment which is efficient and effective. Strictness one day and leniency the next creates confusion. The students do not know what they can expect. As a result, they will often test the teacher to see what they can get away with. If it is a teacher's "good day," they will get away with it; if not, they will suffer the consequences. This game, however, detracts from the teaching/learning process and could be avoided with a set of rules which are consistently enforced.

When you have control, change the routine.   Establishment of a learning environment which is conducive to meeting the goals and objectives for a group of students will often require a strict enforcement of established rules. Being strict does not mean being dictatorial; it simply means that all persons in a classroom or job-simulation laboratory are expected to respect the rights of others. It is far easier to ease up once control is established, than to gain control after anarchy has become the rule.

Do not try to do the impossible.   In spite of the best efforts of the teacher, there will be a few cases which cannot be handled by the teacher. Students will enter the learning environment with emotional problems which only a highly trained person can solve. Each teacher should recognize his or her own capability, and if situations arise which appear to be beyond control, the students should be referred to a counselor or school psychologist.

SUMMARY

The primary purpose of discipline in the classroom and job-simulation laboratory is the efficient accomplishment of educational goals. Without discipline, both the individual and the class as a group will falter. Failure to meet objectives and goals is usually the result of poor discipline. The teacher is a key factor in establishing and maintaining discipline in the learning environment. The teacher must plan the educational program very carefully. He or she must structure the learning environment and follow up the activities of the students. A sound understanding of student needs will enable each teacher to deal more effectively with student problems at the early stage rather than at the crisis stage.

A sign of good classroom discipline is often the lack of evidence of student control, rather than the use of the many and varied methods of dealing with student misbehavior.

REVIEW QUESTIONS

1. Why is it a good policy to establish routine procedures to be followed every day?
2. Is a thorough knowledge of subject matter adequate for establishing discipline?
3. Why is discipline as important as the subject matter to be taught?
4. How can discipline be established before rules are violated?
5. What is the difference between friendliness and being a friend as relates to student control?
6. Does the statement, "Keep them interested and there will be no discipline problems," hold true for most students?
7. What effect does inconsistency have upon discipline?
8. What can teachers do to help students avoid misbehaving?
9. How would a knowledge of student activities for a school day assist the teacher in planning, thus avoiding discipline problems?
10. How would a "time-out" or nonpunitive disciplinary measure affect most students?

STUDENT ACTIVITIES

1. Research the "right of due process," and write a report on how this affects school discipline at all levels.
2. Discuss the advisability of bringing parents into the picture when retribution is to be administered.
3. How would you handle, (1) whispering and inactivity in a classroom setting, and (2) horseplay in the job-simulation laboratory.
4. Discuss how the setting of reasonable limits affects student behavior.
5. Discuss how proper planning and an established routine affects discipline.
6. Visit occupational classrooms at the exploration level, preparation level, and post-secondary level; list the student characteristics observed.
7. Describe how outside influences might affect the learning environment of an occupational program; i.e., court-ordered busing, community dress codes, etc.
8. Discuss the use of corporal punishment, pro/con in today's educational settings.

REFERENCES

Biehler, R.F. *Psychology Applied to Teaching*. Boston: Houghton Mifflin, 1974.

Brady, T.A. and Snoxell, L.F. *Student Discipline in Higher Education*. Washington, D.C.: American Personnel Guidance Association, 1964.

Cambier, D.W. "Good Discipline and the Beginning Business Education Teacher," *Journal of Business Education*. 40: 343-4, May 1965.

Chamberlin, L.J. "Group Behavior and Discipline," *Clearing House*. 41: 92-5, October 1966.

————. and Carnot, J.B. ed. *Improving School Discipline*. Springfield, Ill.: Charles C. Thomas, 1974.

Johnson, L.V. and Bany, M.A. *Classroom Management*. New York: Macmillan, 1970.

Kujoth, J.S. ed. *The Teacher and School Discipline*. Meuchen, N.J.: Scarecrow Press, 1970.

Prescott, A.J. "Classroom Control or Chaos," *Ohio Schools*. 41: 32-3, January 1963.

Wasel, D.N. "Discipline in the Classroom: A Positive Factor," *Volta Review*. 66: 514-7, September 1964.

Weiner, D.N. *Classroom Management and Discipline*. Itasca, Illinois: Peacock Publishers, 1972.

Index